5/05

Leaders Talk Leadership

"An impressive collection of insights in leadership . . ."
—Jay Fishman,
  CEO of St. Paul Cos.

"Whether you are leading a transformation of your business, identifying your next generation of leaders, or working to energize your organization's culture, this book provides valuable observations and advice from leadership's top echelon."
—Jonathan Ward,
  Chairman and Chief Executive Officer of The ServiceMaster Company

"It is so refreshing to read a book on leadership written in plain language by successful leaders. The easy to read style provides practical, proven and doable strategies that make a difference in company performance, shareholder value, and corporate responsibility. Those of us who lead and advise on corporate governance will find the collective wisdom of these leaders helpful in enhancing board leadership."
—Roger W. Raber,
  President and Chief Executive Officer,
  The National Association of Corporate Directors (NACD)

"A very refreshing look at leadership in action. The editor's probing questions get to the real guts of leadership because the authentic answers come from renowned practitioners of the art themselves. Leadership development is my passion. This book stands out as a must read because its lessons can be applied starting today."
—Deepak "Dick" Sethi,
  Vice President, Executive and Leadership Development,
  The Thomson Corporation

"Accomplished leaders sharing what works and why in today's globalized corporation is what makes this book unique. Finally, a book for leaders by leaders!"
—J. Douglas Holladay,
  Partner, ParkAvenueEquityPartners, LP and former United States Ambassador

Leaders Talk Leadership

Top executives speak their minds

Meredith D. Ashby and Stephen A. Miles
Heidrick and Struggles International, Inc.

OXFORD
UNIVERSITY PRESS

2002

OXFORD
UNIVERSITY PRESS

Oxford   New York
Auckland   Bangkok   Buenos Aires   Cape Town   Chennai
Dar es Salaam   Delhi   Hong Kong   Istanbul   Karachi   Kolkata
Kuala Lumpur   Madrid   Melbourne   Mexico City   Mumbai   Nairobi
São Paulo   Shanghai   Singapore   Taipei   Tokyo   Toronto

Copyright © 2002 by Oxford University Press, Inc.

Published by Oxford University Press, Inc.
198 Madison Avenue, New York, New York, 10016

www.oup.com

Oxford is a registered trademark of Oxford University Press

Library of Congress Cataloging-in-Publication Data
Leaders talk leadership : top executives speak their minds /
Meredith D. Ashby and Stephen A. Miles;
Heidrick and Struggles International, Inc.
    p. cm.
Includes index.
ISBN 0-19-515283-2
1. Leadership.   2. Executive ability.   3. Executives—Training of.
I. Ashby, Meredith D.   II. Heidrick and Struggles.   III. Title.
HD57.7 .M52 2002
658.4—dc21   2002005103

5-17-05

9 8 7 6 5 4 3

Printed in the United States of America
on acid free paper

Preface

Meredith D. Ashby and Stephen A. Miles

Business Analysts, Heidrick and Struggles International, Inc.

What gives companies competitive advantage? What are the burning issues for corporate leaders today? How do leaders lead in times of crisis or instability? How do companies identify, attract, develop, and retain the best and brightest people in the marketplace? These are some of the questions we sought to answer as we conducted interviews with hundreds of boards of directors, chief executive officers (CEOs), senior managers, financiers, academics, management and leadership experts, and many of our own executive search consultants to get cutting-edge perspectives on leadership today.

Throughout these interviews and written essays from some of the world's most respected leaders, one message emerged with unmistakable clarity: the best-led companies know and believe in the value of people.

On the heels of a global transformation from a physical asset–dominated economy to a service- and information-driven economy in which intangibles drive the marketplace, it is proven over and over again that the greatest single asset of any organization is its human capital. Accordingly, its greatest single challenge is the creation, nurturing, and optimization of that capital. Of utmost importance to corporate chiefs, therefore, is the construction of a model for managing people, a system that best serves the people who serve the organization.

From innovative and aggressive recruiting to progressive executive development programs to creating developmental opportunities for promising executives, and to the challenging task of retaining highly talented, motivated, and productive teams, chief executives today face the daunting task of creating an environment in which people want to, and can, perform at the highest levels of their potential.

Over the past decade, manufacturing, finance, and information technology have been the foci of corporate improvement programs. Today's more progressive organizations, however, have implemented action plans centering on people rather than on functional and transactional areas as the key to improving productivity.

The people component of a business model is intricately woven into the corporate fabric: in its infrastructure, its operations, its culture, its message to the market and indeed, its very significance in the market. Those CEOs who haven't questioned whether their companies are attracting, developing, and retaining good people simply aren't doing their company and their stakeholders justice. Companies whose leaders haven't translated the recognition that their people are a tremendous source of competitive advantage into action are highly unlikely to be enjoying a competitive advantage in the marketplace.

We found that some of the world's most respected, value-driven companies derive an increasing percentage of their valuations from the collective power of their intangible assets—that is, people, brands, suppliers, partners, and intellectual property. In terms of gaining and sustaining a competitive advantage, the strategic use of human capital is as critical as or even more critical than a sustainable and additive business model, technology, a global presence, a strong balance sheet, or physical assets. In boom times or busts, in calm or calamity, great leadership is the foundation of all great companies.

As we tapped into the collective wisdom of an unparalleled group of highly accomplished and experienced experts, men and women who have proven their credentials as leaders of thought and action in the global marketplace, we soon realized that we were in a unique position. We had the opportunity, and even the responsibility, to convey to a larger audience the essence of what these leaders told us about what they believe, what they have found to be of value, what lessons they have learned and put into practice—lessons that have proven their effectiveness through growth, profitability, and enhancement of shareholder value.

In offering this anthology of collective wisdom, we tried to preserve as much as possible the flavor and tone as well as the substance of what they told us. While it was necessary to create a consistency of style and format throughout all these interviews and written essays, we limited our changes to only those required to clarify the original intent of the sources.

That said, it is clear that the enduring value of this book is in the words of the people who are highlighted on the following pages, and we would like to express our deepest gratitude for their generosity of time and talent, their eloquence, and their openness. Their willingness to teach others by sharing—in many instances their failures—is unquestionably a characteristic of the true leader. The honesty of these leaders will no doubt resonate with the perceptions of other leaders who are facing the same kinds of challenges as they too grapple with the weighty issues of leadership and management in today's unsettling marketplace.

We also want to acknowledge the invaluable contributions of our colleagues and leaders at Heidrick & Struggles International for providing a framework and the resources that have enabled us to bring forth this human capital story. As the pioneer in executive search and, today, the premier firm in the recruiting industry, Heidrick & Struggles is a living testament to the value of the human equation in the world of business. By providing strategic counsel to corporate leaders on the matters of governance, leadership, and human capital, and often serving as intermediaries in the talent search, assessment, and negotiating process, our global partnership of executive search consultants has been helping clients build thriving, high-performance management teams worldwide for half a century. We continue to learn and our clients continue to benefit from the remarkable experience and knowledge of Heidrick & Struggles' consultants who lead the way in the ongoing evolution of talent supply and demand.

In particular, we would like to extend special acknowledgment to the consultants who provided introductions to many of the leaders featured in this book: Alice Au, Don Biskin, Peter Breen, Barry Bregman, Pepper de Callier, Lauren Doliva, Michael Flagg, Bob Hallagan, Lee Hanson, Ted Jadick, Randy Jayne, Dale Jones, Eric Joseph, Evan Lindsay, Jory Marino, Jürgen Mülder, Nancy Nichols, Madelaine Pfau, John de Regt, Gerry Roche, Jeff Sanders, John Thompson, Dora Vell, and Kyung Yoon.

We appreciate the foresight of John Strackhouse, who encouraged us to believe that this book would be a useful reference to many corporate leaders and MBA students, and to John Gardner, who not only shared that sentiment but also introduced us to the editors at Oxford University Press.

We thank our editor at Oxford University Press, Martha Cooley, her editorial team, and the team of academic reviewers for believing in this book and for guiding us through the entire process. For making this book make sense, we thank Billie Brown, who served as our outside counsel and sounding board to offer objective feedback as well as invaluable editing and proofreading services. We extend a special thanks to Jay Conger for framing our ideas as well as this book.

Finally, we are grateful for our firm's chief executives, who encourage us by giving their unwavering support and leadership guidance, in particular, Piers Marmion, chairman and CEO; David Anderson, president and COO; and John Gardner, vice chairman. It is largely their unceasing emphasis on partnership and quality as the cornerstones of Heidrick & Struggles' values that empowers us to embark on these initiatives.

To them and to all our colleagues around the globe, we offer our heartfelt thanks as we close with our firm's guiding principle:

"The Heidrick & Struggles partnership spirit creates an environment of mutual trust and respect in which all our employees are valued. We place the interests of our clients, the firm, and colleagues above our own."

Meredith D. Ashby and Stephen A. Miles

Contents

Chapter 2

Managing Human Capital

Chapter 3

Establishing Competitive Advantage in Today's Market Environment

About the Editors

In 1953, when a handshake sealed a business partnership between Gardner Heidrick and John Struggles in an office in Chicago, the two Americans unknowingly joined the advance guard of a new industry that we know today as executive search—an industry based on the management of human capital.

Fifty years later, Heidrick & Struggles International is the product of that agreement: a global network of professionals dedicated to the premise that human capital is unequivocally the greatest resource of the world economy. It has been the privilege of Heidrick & Struggles, in partnership with its clients around the world, to identify some of the most revered and respected leaders on the globe.

Heidrick & Struggles International, Inc. (Nasdaq: HSII) is the world's premier provider of executive search and leadership services consulting. Approximately 1,800 Heidrick & Struggles search professionals and employees operate from more than 70 locations primarily in North and South America, Europe, and Asia Pacific. For 50 years, its core business, Heidrick & Struggles Executive Search, has specialized in chief executive, board member, and senior-level management assignments for a broad spectrum of clients: multinational corporations, midcap and start-up companies, nonprofit entities, educational institutions, foundations, associations, and governmental units. The firm is expanding its range of complementary services to offer solutions to senior management teams for their leadership needs through its Management Search and Leadership Services practices. Heidrick & Struggles Management Search serves clients who seek midlevel managers and emerging leaders. The Heidrick & Struggles Leadership Services practice includes:

- Heidrick & Struggles Executive Assessment, which provides leadership and cultural effectiveness consulting, and management assessment services
- Heidrick & Struggles Professional Development, which provides executive coaching and related professional development services

- Heidrick & Struggles Interim Executives, which provides interim executive placement services for clients in need of transitional leadership

The firm's office of the chairmen (OOC) serves as the focal point for its board of director, chief executive officer, chief operating officer, and president assignments worldwide. The charter of the OOC is to provide the most qualified resources possible to affect outstanding results for search execution at the board of directors and chief executive level. The members of the OOC are John T. Gardner, managing partner and vice chairman, Board Services; Gerard R. Roche, senior chairman; and Vice Chairmen John T. Thompson, Jürgen Mülder, Joie A. Gregor, Theodore Jadick, Thomas J. Friel, and Kyung Yoon.

Meredith D. Ashby and Stephen A. Miles are business analysts at Heidrick & Struggles. They work with the firm's vice chairman of Board Services and the office of the chairmen to identify, create, and deliver cutting-edge thought leadership on topics such as governance and human capital to clients worldwide. In addition, Ashby is a business development specialist in the office of the chairmen and Miles is involved in the firm's Leadership Services practice.

For more insightful perspectives on the themes in this book and other interviews with senior-level leaders on today's business issues, please visit the Heidrick & Struggles website at www.heidrick.com.

Foreword

Leading in the New Century: Storm Clouds and Silver Linings on the Horizon

Jay A. Conger
Professor of Organizational Behavior, London Business School

This book comes at a critical moment. As we start off this new century, we are already witnessing a remarkable array of perils and opportunities for leaders. Their roots can be found in the closing decade of the twentieth century. On the one hand, it could be argued that the 1990s were an aberration, despite the fact that as they drew to a close, they were widely proclaimed as the starting gate to a "New Economy." The decade departed in a rush of technology-driven euphoria that is not likely to be seen again for a long time; 21-year-olds are not likely to have another opportunity to raise millions of dollars on the strength of simplistic business plans favored simply because they contained the word "Internet." In the frenzy, unproven but imaginative business models such as Amazon and Priceline and Yahoo and Webvan caused such a stir that their market capitalizations exceeded some of the world's most successful companies. These seedling firms were predicted to rapidly displace industry giants such as Barnes & Noble, American Express, AOL Time Warner, and United Kingdom's Tesco. Yet, as we now know, they did not. The end of the 1990s was also the era of Enron—a revolutionary company in an unrevolutionary industry: natural gas. As the icon for corporate transformation from the then-styled "Old Economy," Enron epitomized the sky's-the-limit thinking of the era. Its CEO, the wunderkind Jeff Skilling, claimed that companies no longer needed hard assets to be highly successful. According to this mindset, information—not hard assets such as pipelines and power plants—was the key to dominating, in this case, energy markets. Physical assets, so the thinking went, simply tied up cash. It was said to be the era of bits and bytes and brainpower. Brawn was out, imagination was in.

Euphoria aside, the true technological wonder of the late 1990s—the Internet—indeed continues to alter our lives in both mundane and profound ways. Unlike the dotcom mania of that time, it is not a short-term aberration. Internet retailing and net-based exchanges continue to grow. Several infants of the e-age, such as eBay, have proven their staying power: they are now more mature and more profitable. Email has become the primary means of communication within organizations. Mobile Internet-enabled technologies such as the cell phone and personal digital assistants are undergoing remarkable transformations in their capabilities. Although Enron underwent the most spectacular corporate collapse in the early days of the twenty-first century, other companies have become e-enabled revolutionaries—and at a rate faster than most critics would have guessed. For example, GE today has the largest business-to-business net-based exchange in the marketplace, and Tesco boasts one of the most successful net-based supermarket operations in the world.

The "War for Talent" so widely promulgated in the 1990s seems less intense today, as widespread layoffs thin the ranks of American business. The recession, while temporarily alleviating the intense competition for talent in general, ironically created a war for leadership talent. Nevertheless, the lesson remains: talent is the most precious of resources in this digital age. It now seems crystal clear that most of the true value-added work in this century will be performed by sophisticated knowledge workers; the upshot of this is that these people are ambitious, restless, and sophisticated and they can and will jump companies if necessary to keep their own value propositions strong and viable. Attracting and retaining these critical assets will remain one of the most important challenges and competitive advantages for any organization.

Other challenges for leaders will come from environmental concerns and important geopolitical trends that began in the 1990s. Growing concerns about global warming, water quality and supply, and the potential toxicity of components of today's industrial products are sleeping giants ready to create competitive pressures in the global marketplace. On the geopolitical front, China will continue her global ascendancy, having joined the World Trade Organization. While many Western companies see China as an immense market for their goods and as a place for inexpensive production, she will also become a fearsome competitor and is already moving into the arena of high-value-added products and services. Several Chinese hard goods companies have set up manufacturing operations in the United States. China and India now contain the world's largest populations of engineers. Soon both will contain a great number of software programmers. Those resources will give these nations immense competitive advantages in this century. Only politics, lax banking practices, and opaque financial systems will slow them down.

Leaders now face the added challenge of operating in a world where terrorism is not restricted to faraway lands or isolated incidents but, rather, is a possibility in one's backyard. Over the past decade, terrorism has undergone a clandestine process of global organization. Despite recent setbacks in Afghanistan and environs, the international network of terrorist cells established by Osama Bin Laden and the al Qaeda organization with the active backing and financial support of important Middle Eastern nations is far from dismantled. Some Middle Eastern and Near Eastern nations see this organization as absolutely vital to their interests, especially as a counterweight to the influence of the United States. As important, al Qaeda's mission has expanded from launching terrorist attacks on Western soil to a broader mandate of harming the economies of the West and disrupting global trade. At the very least, turmoil in the Middle and Near East and Africa will most likely worsen. We may be at a crossroads with implications that few of us truly understand.

In the world economy, leaders face a great deal of turbulence, like pilots navigating between mountains and storm clouds. The first part of the new century is already proving to be an economic challenge: Argentina's economy has crumbled. Turkey is in a precarious position. Germany is still struggling with employment problems, and Japan is like a mastodon trapped in quicksand. On the other hand, one of the grandest economic experiments of all time—the integration of western European countries into a common market—is entering a new phase with the conversion of national currencies to the euro. The success of this experiment will be determined within the first decade of this century. If it succeeds, western Europe could become the world's most dynamic market. National interests, however, could still derail the vision.

In hindsight, we may discover that many of the "well-led" companies of the 1990s were simply riding waves of a booming economy and an exuberant stock market. One barometer that lends weight to this idea is the rising number of ousted CEOs. Several of the glamour corporations of the last decade are already looking ragged. For example, Lucent Technologies and Nortel Networks have watched their valuations implode because of losses from poor investments in acquisitions and wrong choices in technologies. Several stars of the New Economy, for example, Cisco Systems, EMC Corporation, and Sun Microsystems, continue to struggle to regain the high ground they once held. The industry providing the pipelines for the digital age—telecommunications—is now facing massive losses from investments in both technology and licensing arrangements. Marconi's collapse was the first warning that the industry was in trouble. It was quickly followed by the high flyers—companies like Vodaphone and JDS Uniphase. The latter alone announced write-offs of $51 billion in 2001. Global Crossing, which spent five years and $15 billion to build a worldwide network of high-speed Internet and telephone lines, has gone into bankruptcy. These are instances in which the corporate vision was far ahead of the customer base.

In addition, the leaders of many of the remarkable mergers of the late 1990s will be tested hard during this first decade of the new century. Some of the most interesting arenas: the automobile industry—with the Daimler Benz–Chrysler and Renault–Nissan mergers—and financial services, with the Travelers–Citicorp merger and others. History would suggest that only a handful of these merged entities will live up to their promises of synergy. For example, the AOL side of the communications and entertainment gorilla AOL Time Warner has already announced potential write-offs of up to $60 billion, representing 30 percent of the company's assets. Tyco International, one of the world's largest conglomerates and long admired for its acquisition strategy, has talked about splitting itself into four independent companies because of market valuation issues. Are these harbingers of disillusionment to come?

Despite these storm clouds, silver linings still abound for leaders in the new century. Rapid advances in logistics and information technology, global financing, and shifting demographics all promise new marketplace opportunities. Advances in computer-assisted product prototyping and mass customization promise a dizzying array of ever-changing products for consumers. Thanks to fast-cycle logistics, which allow manufacturers to bring components together instantly without tying up lots of inventory, companies may invest only hours in working capital. Information technology and the virtual workplace will enable us to create organizations that were never before possible. For example, we can now "assemble" a company with employees around the globe. A venture capitalist friend of mine is putting together one such business. The technology is designed in Finland. The software programming is performed in India. The CEO and his executive team are based in Silicon Valley. The products are marketed by an entirely different group of companies who span the globe. The lesson of such an enterprise is that yesterday's management science fiction is today's reality.

The implications of these trends and others that we cannot yet foresee is that leadership will be the most important resource an organization can possess. After all, it will be leadership that determines whether organizations successfully harness the emerging opportunities and overcome the perils that await. It is no time for cowards; indeed, it is a time when leaders are being, and will continue to be, tested mightily. Not only that, but the stakes—financial and otherwise—have never been higher; the consequences of failure are devastating. In such circumstances, boards of directors are far quicker to oust poorly performing CEOs than ever before, and the news media are as quick to chronicle falling heroes as to point out rising stars.

Financial markets today punish poor performance with a vengeance. Cases in point are Enron and Lucent, one-time darlings of Wall Street, and the remarkable speed with which their market valuations imploded. Within weeks of serious performance problems being announced, tens of billions of dollars of market capitalization were lost. What took years to build in market valuation vanished in days.

It is in turbulent times such as these that we most need guides. That, in a nutshell, is the value of this book, which is an anthology of leadership tales and a traveler's guide to leading in the twenty-first century. Its teachers are leaders or keen observers of leadership. They have lessons for others along the way, and each one has its own value in terms of advice, experience, resources, and encouragement.

The book is organized around five themes: (1) leadership; (2) managing human capital; (3) competitive advantage; (4) strategic change and transformation; and (5) the stakeholder's view. A word about each.

Leadership

Constructive persuasion, talent assessment, leadership development, team building, and organizational design will become the critical capabilities for leaders. In short order, the old command model will become a rarity. One can already see this shift under way in the personal leadership styles of Jack Welch and his successor, Jeffrey Immelt, the current CEO of General Electric.

Of necessity, the capacity to lead change will become the most valued skill for leaders. They will need an acute and fine-tuned sense for when to cannibalize their strategies, their products, their channels, and their organizations and when to ensure continuity and stability. They must become adept at finding and developing talented missionaries to spread the new gospels and new visions. They must also learn how to protect and nurture the champions of change on their teams.

One of the hallmarks of effective leadership in this century will be the capacity to learn and adapt quickly. Years of experience will no longer be enough—and, in some cases, may prove a hindrance. The shelf life of knowledge today is simply too short. Instead, a winning characteristic of the new generation of leaders will be its commitment to personal learning and the ability to generate a "buzz" about learning throughout their organizations. The photographer Walker Evans's advice to novice photographers—"stare, pry, listen, eavesdrop"—will prove sound counsel for today's business leaders.

Senior executives are not the only leaders now charged with reinventing themselves. Powerful forces are redefining the roles and activities of corporate boards as well. Among these are the huge numbers of mergers and acquisitions that require due diligence, the new focus by institutional investors on the role of governance in underperforming companies, and the accelerating rate of turnover among CEOs. These forces are placing enormous pressures on boards to take a more active role in the day-to-day leadership and succession planning of the companies. These pressures, far from going away, are likely to increase.

As boards become more proactive, they must grapple with a conflict between the two main roles they are asked to play: Can a board be a strategic partner with top management in formulating the strategy and building the capabilities of the organization and still exercise independent oversight of management? Some are experimenting with nonexecutive chairs and lead directors as a counterbalance to the CEO's authority. In addition, important shifts have begun to occur, especially in the increasing responsibilities of board committees. Much remains to be done: Boards will need to transform themselves for leadership, for talent management, for globalization, for e-commerce, for greater accountability. Indeed, a great deal of reinvention lies ahead for leaders at all levels.

Managing Human Capital

If there is one profound note that this book rings loudest, it is that human capital is the most valuable of assets. While the demographics of the workplace will continue to ebb and flow with economic cycles, it will be talent—the ability to recruit and retain it—that distinguishes the truly great companies from the rest of the pack. Talent is the DNA of high performance. This precious form of capital will require senior executives to reprioritize their roles so that they are connoisseurs of talent—in effect, chief talent officers. The most successful organizations will be those that abandon the old mindsets about talent development—namely, that the fittest will survive and that the cream will always rise to the top. Such attitudes will prove both wasteful and detrimental. Instead, organizations must become more strategic about how they deploy their talent. They must reject the traditional view that jobs are rewards based solely on prior performance. Instead, promotions must be seen as arenas for development and enhanced performance. Organizations must align their operations in accordance with human capital strategies, not vice versa. In such an environment, how people are organized and supervised relates not only to current performance but also to future development. Coaching, mentoring, and timely feedback will be viewed as essential tools to maximize learning on the job. Great care and feeding of high potentials will become the rule. And, while tending the garden of talent is demanding of time and resources, its payoff is indisputable, as can be seen in the handful of companies that today are leading the global marketplace.

Establishing Competitive Advantage in Today's Market Environment

Leaders face a world of new and demanding customer expectations, of true two-way relationships in which customer feedback is instantaneous and can reshape a company's business with virtual immediacy. Customers will in essence be viewed as key components of a firm's human resources. Their goodwill and loyalty will constitute rich forms of investment for the high-performing companies in the digital age.

Competition will only intensify. The shelf life of market strategies is shortening. Technology and global players are driving products and services ever more rapidly through their life cycles. This morning's innovation becomes this afternoon's commodity. As a result, rapid-fire innovation will rank high on the list of strategic capabilities. All the successful firms in this century will possess a depth of entrepreneurial capability. This capability will be built around the investments that firms have made in resources, cultural values, and talent dedicated to strategic innovation and leadership. This capability will remain in high demand, thanks to empowered consumers and technologies that allow more rapid product prototyping and production. The dilemma for many managers is that management's time and attention tend to be dedicated to solving today's problems rather than addressing tomorrow's opportunities. Many organizations make the mistake of putting their best people in charge of only problems and not opportunities. Those who reverse the pattern will prevail in the marketplace.

A company's network of external relationships will also prove to be an absolutely critical competitive advantage. Business in this century will be network-centric, and partnerships and alliances will play pivotal roles in day-to-day operations. In contrast to the industrial age, in which companies sought strategic advantage by vertical integration, companies today seek strategic advantage horizontally. A critical trademark of high-performing firms, therefore, will be their ability to build powerful networks. These firms must be savvy about the partners that will help them acquire capabilities and knowledge and hence foster access and reach. Alliance management will take center stage among a company's strategic competencies. But all partnerships are formed around mutual benefits. Therefore, leaders must make their companies equally attractive dance partners or be left on the sidelines.

Strategic Change and Transformation

Just a few years ago, executives of the *Fortune* 1000 were looking over their shoulders wondering whether the twenty-something CEO of a Silicon Valley start-up was about to displace their corporation, thanks to some perceived e-enabled strategy. Much of this fear proved to be a mirage. It was the established competitors who turned out to be the real problem. After all, Toyota and Honda have done more to displace General Motors than Autobytel or Amazon and are likely to continue to do so. Yes, there will always be a few industries in the realm of technology in which start-ups can catapult themselves to the top overnight. But in most cases, the challenge is from other, more lasting forces—threats of acquisition, shifts in demographics, changing customer needs, savvier competition, changes in supplier capabilities, new and emerging channels, the appearance and disappearance of government regulations, economic ups and downs, and the inertia of our own organizations. The bad news is that this set of forces will never vanish. As a result, our world is in perpetual motion—a phenomenon with profound implications for organizational strategies; namely, the very strategies that provide performance advantages over the competition have remarkably short life spans. For example, research conducted by McKinsey & Company has determined that not a single company has continually outperformed the stock market over the long term. These studies have also shown that even survival can be challenging. Only 74 companies on the Standard & Poor's (S & P) 500 in 1957 made it to the same list in 1997. Of these, only one dozen outperformed the S & P over that time span. The implications are clear; leaders must constantly reconfigure their strategies and their organizations just to ensure survival.

The challenge for leaders is to build agile, perceptive organizations. One way to do that is to minimize bureaucracy. Another is to keep the organization exceedingly close to the customer in every possible manner. The third is to listen to voices on the front line in shaping corporate strategy; after all, they are usually the first to see emerging threats and shifts in consumers. The fourth is to protect the mavericks—the iconoclasts, those who often drive you crazy with out-of-the box ideas. The fifth is to promote people who support reinvention and innovation and back them up with rewards.

In addition, leaders must discipline themselves to continually reexamine their business models, engaging the entire organization to ask: Does our value proposition still make sense? What in our business model needs to be reinvented? Where are our noncustomers going and why? The biggest problem with such an undertaking is that the most powerful individuals stand to lose the most in an organizational transformation. Often, they will resist the changes necessary to move ahead in order to avoid losing power.

Finally, there is the issue of organizational culture. In any change effort, culture plays a vital role, either as a facilitator or a barrier. Leaders must learn to harness the positive dimensions of a culture in the change efforts. Culture is much like the water in an aquarium. While it is largely invisible, its chemistry and life-supporting qualities profoundly affect its inhabitants. An organization requiring transformation is like an aquarium polluted by too many algae and requires restoration of the right balance of elements in the environment. Leaders effecting an organizational transformation must understand the vital role the corporate culture plays in any change efforts.

The Stakeholder's View

The demise of Enron and the ensuing scandal will affect both individual and institutional investors, as well as corporate leaders, profoundly. Already financial reporting and auditing procedures are coming under far closer scrutiny. As the economist Paul Krugman has pointed out, the Enron story is not just about a corporate failure; it is about how one of the most admired companies in the United States proved to be fraudulent. Its books were not at all what they appeared to be, nor were its values—or lack thereof. In addition and as important, the credibility of one of the important pillars and guardians of the capitalist system—the accounting profession—has been deeply called into question. As a result, we are leaving an investment era of exuberance and laxity and entering one of vigilance and scrutiny. The days of accepting a company's books at face value and investing money based on corporate pronouncements are gone. Integrity, thus, assumes an even greater importance and value—for leaders, their organizations, and their accounting partners. The best companies have integrity built into their brands and their books.

This new century may also be a time of soul-searching for the investment community about the efficacy of its short-term orientation. As though afflicted with attention deficit disorder, the financial markets have difficulty looking beyond an operating quarter. This orientation creates undue financial pressures that encourage unethical behavior, such as pushing inventory into unreceptive channels in order to produce in the short term at the expense of the longer term. Despite the Enron wakeup call, it is difficult to predict whether the investment community will actually refocus its attention span to a more appropriate longer term. The most likely scenario is that the shift will be spearheaded by the institutional and individual investment communities as they adjust their expectations to a more realistic approach, rewarding firms that operate for the long term. Either way, leaders in this century will be increasingly called on to tell their "longer view" stories to accompany the quarterly financial results. The intensity of competition will also demand that these stories be supported by actual and substantial investments for the future.

Venture capital will continue to play an important role in facilitating the birth of new enterprises, but the glory days of the dotcom era are over for at least a decade. During the next few years, attention will be paid to protecting portfolios rather than growing them. There will be serious digestion problems from poor investments made in the late 1990s. This will result in shakedowns and consolidation in the venture capital industry. From the standpoint of investments, business models that have positive cash flow will regain their predotcom stature as the places to invest. Entrepreneurs will also be strongly tested. We are entering a far tougher and less forgiving environment for this breed of leaders. While vision will reign as the entrepreneur's trademark, execution and sound financials will be equally rewarded. As a result, entrepreneurial leaders can no longer rely simply on their charisma and storytelling abilities. They must become tough decision-makers, hounds for the best talent they can find, deeply persistent, and strategically and financially savvy—a tall order for this next generation of start-up leaders.

In conclusion, this book will take you on a tour of the most important challenges and opportunities that you will face as the new millennium unfolds. This new century will be characterized as both the best and worst of times. Like most of us, you may feel lost at times. Perhaps some advice from one of America's greatest explorers, Daniel Boone, will come in handy. Boone was once asked, "Have you ever been lost?" "No," he replied. "But I have been bewildered for a few months." In the end, he always found his destination as an explorer. These are words and an attitude worth remembering when you are leading in this new century.

Leaders Talk Leadership

Introduction

• Factors Affecting Leadership and Human Capital Management

Stephen A. Miles and Meredith D. Ashby
Business Analysts, Heidrick & Struggles International

At the threshold of a new millennium, corporations are faced with an unprecedented series of factors, both external and internal, that are accelerating the pace of change and disruption and ceaselessly reshaping the business landscape. Internally, the changing demographics and increasing diversity of the workforce are posing challenges to the traditional ways of structuring operations and of hiring, managing, and incenting employees. Externally, the relentless pace of technological advancement has given rise to a truly global marketplace, rife with opportunity as well as with danger—from previously undreamed-of access to new markets to the incomprehensible stresses of terrorism.

These internal and external factors are constantly meshing, forming a kaleidoscope of ever-shifting scenarios in which companies must produce, package, and market their goods and services—that is, provide value. In today's environment, "business as usual" clearly will not do. The need for leadership has remained throughout time. However, in today's fast-moving, volatile, and complex world, the need for inspired leadership, for substantive leadership, for distributed and meritocratic leadership, has never been more critical.

Following are some of the major forces that are reshaping today's corporation and are thus having an impact on leadership and the management of human capital.

Globalization

The force of internationalization has been creeping into our daily lives for decades, but it has become increasingly clear over just the past few years how economically interdependent the nations of the world have become. It is no longer sufficient for a corporation to compete locally or even nationally and ignore the rest of the world. Our world has become larger in one sense, smaller in another. We are all connected, but our expanded business universe is no longer homogeneous; it is pluralistic. The business of producing and marketing goods and services must now also take into account a wide spectrum of considerations, ranging from geographic and cultural differences to varying legal, political, and economic climates. Such pluralism renders leadership through a one-dimensional "command and control" style completely ineffectual, and possibly dangerous. Successful leadership in our interdependent world depends on the ability to strategically find, motivate, and deploy a diverse group of qualified people geographically—whether through specialized skill sets for specific functions, through a process of increasing responsibility for wide-ranging business operations, or both simultaneously—and lead through them.

The flattening of the organization and distributed leadership

Organizational structure has undergone a shift from a vertical orientation to one that is essentially horizontal. Corporations traditionally have been organized into departments according to function: sales, manufacturing, information technology, finance, and human resources, for example. These departmental "silos," when they interacted, did so primarily in a vertical way, by communicating upward or downward instead of to the side. Today, many companies are reengineering, refocusing on a core business, outsourcing noncore operations, and realizing enhanced productivity through technology. The consequence of these trends is that the middle ranks of organizations are disappearing; the pyramid structure is being replaced with a flatter, less hierarchical organizational architecture that is more flexible and able to adapt more efficiently to the current disruptive and pluralistic environment. Under the traditional concept of "command and control," orders emanated from an iconistic leader at the top and were carried out through a bureaucratic hierarchy. Today, we see chief executives articulating a vision and distributing authority across the organization to execute that vision into action.

The most successful businesses have been those able to free up their innovators from the traditional silos of corporate functional departments and throughout the organization and to allow them to strike out on new ventures, in new markets, and in new ways. Emerging business models demonstrate this reality through increased emphasis on the dissemination of decision-making throughout the organization and a sophisticated appraisal and definition of metrics and accountability at all levels.

In our interviews and discussions with hundreds of CEOs, we have observed some common traits among these highly successful leaders of complex organizations. Most defined their main responsibility as chief executive to be that of inspiring, influencing, setting the direction for, facilitating, coaching, mentoring, and developing their employees. The word "control" was rarely used; instead, they spoke emphatically about the importance of a strong team orientation. Their role was to identify and empower a team, not command it. Indeed, many of them characteristically used the term "we" rather than "I" in discussing success within the organization. Instead of thinking in terms of individual accomplishment, most tended to think in terms of what their management teams had achieved.

It is only through replication of leadership at all levels of the organization—distributive leadership—that a corporation can effectively compete and grow in the current global operating environment. Never has it been more vital to a company's success to be able to attract, develop, and retain the best people while continuously developing or managing out those who do not perform against the corporate objectives.

The age of intangible assets

If the twentieth century was the age of tangible assets, the twenty-first century is proving to be the age of intangibles. The movement is away from the managing of plant, property, and equipment and toward the leveraging of employees, customers, partners, and alliances. Historically, leadership models have been built on physical assets; in the new models, by contrast, success is a function of the ability to negotiate contracts, to build relationships with partners and even competitors, and, above all, to attract, develop, and retain today's most critical asset, people. There are, however, few if any metrics or systems for measuring these assets; the challenge is for leaders to use their own experience, training, skill sets, and personal style to drive the organization and its workforce forward in pursuit of a shared vision and goals. Generally, these goals are productivity, profitability, and sustainable competitive advantage in the marketplace.

Characteristics of leaders

Because of these unprecedented demands on today's business leaders, a new kind of leader is emerging. Leaders must possess all of the qualities that historically have resulted in change and progress and yet much more: not only vision, creativity, and skill at communication but also courage, empathy, and the flexibility to lead successfully through wholly uncharted and rapidly changing and often treacherous terrain.

Inherent in the notion of a global marketplace is the irony that leadership calls for skill at managing both consistency and diversity, since the world economy is "one village" and demands consistency, while at the same time its elements are made up of widely varying ethnic and cultural perspectives. Furthermore, unprecedented crisis, uncertainty, and volatility in world markets require pathbreaking models of leadership. Finally, because of the flattening of organizations, the span of control has in many instances expanded. Many senior managers are now leading hundreds or thousands of people—often, if not always, widely dispersed geographically—toward a common set of goals. Gone are the days of supervision by proximity and productivity to avoid penalty. Intangible assets—people and intellectual property—certainly require compassionate leadership.

The most successful managers use persuasion, persistence, passion, and empathy—a combination of qualities referred to by the psychologist and author Daniel Goleman as emotional intelligence and by others as emotional quotient, or EQ—to motivate a workforce, which in companies big or small can be widely distributed geographically and, as in many cases, also along product or service lines.

IQ is certainly required for leaders to lead; EQ is required for leaders to lead successfully. Active listening, an ability to understand and appreciate another's perspective, the ability to assess one's own as well as others' strengths and weaknesses, and the ability to represent and advocate the collective ethos of an organization all fall under EQ.

Achieving breakaway results in today's business environment also calls for leadership through persuasion, example and inspiration, mentoring and coaching, and other methods aimed at nurturing and optimizing human potential in the workplace.

At the same time, it is essential for today's leaders to be able to influence the organization in a boundaryless fashion, moving horizontally as well as vertically in order to convey and maintain the needed levels of motivation and mobilization against a shared vision and set of objectives. With these attributes, leaders have the opportunity to be wildly successful, achieving results on a scale that would have been inconceivable just decades ago. Without them, it is far more difficult to have an influence in today's and tomorrow's world.

Shareholder impatience

The tenure of CEOs has shrunk from an average of over 10 years in the latter part of the last century to about half that today. It is unusual for a CEO to last a full decade these days, and the norm is closer to fewer than three years at the helm. While 10 years might be too long, given the fast pace of global business, three years is barely long enough for even the most gifted leader of a complex organization to make his or her impact evident.

One of the main reasons for increased leadership turnover is the growing impatience of institutional investors for immediate results. In an era of instantaneous information, few institutional investors and boards of directors are willing to wait more than a few quarters for financial improvements, even though intellectually they may understand that substantive, strategic improvements that are designed to be sustainable over time cannot be achieved in a short time frame. That reality notwithstanding, CEOs today operate in a fishbowl of investor scrutiny in which risk-taking can be fatal and down cycles and false starts are simply not tolerated. Given these shorter windows of opportunity to make a noticeable, financial difference, and given that the chief executive's job has already become more complex, more stressful, and more accountable overall, leaders are churning at extraordinary rates. Further, a growing number of new CEOs come from outside the organization, and often outside the organization's industry, so additional delays in getting the company on course happen because of learning curve issues. Finally, the overall pool of seasoned leaders continues to diminish, exacerbating the difficulties of both recruiting and retaining good and great leaders.

Technology

The influence of technology in business and personal realms is virtually incalculable. It has toppled and re-created hundreds of business models, and has transformed the way companies interact with customers and vendors, how business people innovate, collaborate, and communicate, and the very way that goods and services are produced and sold. It is absolutely essential that today's leaders understand, advocate, invest in, and implement technology in every facet of their businesses.

Technology has given CEOs real-time access to their employees and customers around the globe—and vice versa. On the one hand, this is a great opportunity for enhanced communication; on the other, it is a challenge in the sense that it increases the pace as well as the nature of corporate accountability. Instantaneous communication facilitates the efficacy of the amorphous, flattened organization that, in large part, it is responsible for creating—but it also eliminates the boundaries that once made it possible for management to delay, if not avoid altogether, the consequences of poor performance and customer complaints, whether founded or unfounded.

Building companies to change

Sustainable competitive advantage is increasingly more elusive and fleeting. Companies must work harder to establish defensible positions in a rapidly maturing marketplace in which product quality has reached equality, new markets are quickly deluged with a barrage of barely distinguishable entrants, and the life span of technological advantage is calculated in months, not years.

In such a world, clearly, competitive advantage is gained most effectively and enduringly through a comprehensive, strategic approach to human capital management, one that fosters innovation and change. The ideal framework is one that recognizes and rewards people who are creating new and better ways of doing things and a change-ready culture that encourages innovation.

The most favorable architecture for such a system is a flattened, entrepreneurial-minded environment in which leaders have built a clear path for the realization of ideas.

Opening of new markets

Today, chief executives have unparalleled opportunities and threats in the global marketplace. Country after country has begun to deregulate various industries from financial services to telecommunications to energy. As these markets open up to competitive forces, it presents both opportunities and threats to multinational corporations. The most significant new market now is China as it becomes more involved in the World Trade Organization (WTO).

China will continue to grow as a formidable force in the global economy. While one concern has been that Chinese competition will continue to erode the market share of other Asian exporters to western Europe and the United States, in the long run, it is quite possible that very few emerging economies will be able to compete with China's highly skilled and low-cost workforce. Many U.S. and European companies will establish manufacturing and other operations in China, and we'll see an explosion of activity from China as a result. China will also become a customer of many corporations and economies. Corporate leaders take note: What is your strategy for China?

Demographic impact

In the United States, beginning over the next decade, there will be a huge gap in qualified talent available for companies. As roughly 77 million Baby Boomers reach retirement, they will be replaced by the far less populous Generation X, 44 million, in the senior ranks of the workplace. This is going to lead to a further flattening of organizational architecture as Generation X tries to learn very quickly how to fill the gap in experience and skills in the workplace. Smart companies are developing a leadership pipeline to bridge this gap. The next wave will be Generation Y, approximately 80 million strong, but they won't be ready to step into senior roles for several decades, so the need for companies to institutionalize developmental programs is mission critical.

Furthermore, Generation Y undoubtedly will crave the opportunity to make meaningful contributions and have significant impact; they won't accept being just another cog in the wheel. This unique group will be the first fully technology-literate generation to hit the workplace. This generation started multitasking and computing as toddlers, which implies that their tolerance for the mundane will be near zero and therefore their expectations of employers and jobs will be vastly different from those of previous generations. Job flexibility, the desire to be uniquely recognized and rewarded, and blurred work/life lines are what Gen Yers will expect. Workers with these traits are most productive in the new-style, flatter organization with a system based on motivation and inspiration rather than intimidation.

What are the implications for leadership?

Given the uncertainties inherent in today's economy and the outlook for tomorrow, the best course for leaders is a continued emphasis on the human equation. In a sense, CEOs need to function as chief relationship officers within their organizations, promoting distributed leadership and forging strong bonds with employees, customers, partners, and suppliers—bonds that expand their spheres of resources and influence. They need to remain immersed in the new business universe, in which success often depends not on a lone organization or a solitary leader but on creating and rewarding high-performance teams of motivated and empowered employees. Leaders must continue to harness the human imagination through the interconnectedness of alliances and networks, providing vision and direction in pursuit of the delivery of value in the world marketplace. They must be catalysts for the continuing optimization of human capital by finding, developing, retaining, and partnering effectively with the best and brightest talent available.

Chapter 1

• Leadership

The intangible qualities of leaders

John T. Thompson
Heidrick & Struggles International
Vice Chairman

I'm often asked about the "War for Talent" and what the landscape for talent looks like. I believe that there is a huge shortage of highly talented people having domain experience in relevant industry segments or with relevant business models but, in particular, there is a dearth of leadership skills. By leadership skills, I refer to the attributes needed to succeed in today's environment, such as the ability to energize a group of people to take on an objective and achieve it. In turnaround situations, it is the ability to take a company forward in terms of scale and scope. With all the mergers and acquisitions we've seen lately—which all look great in the short term but are being tested now in a tougher economic climate—leadership is the ability to come into a company and make cultures fit and work. Leadership is a rare asset that, on a statistical basis, only a handful of people have. To really energize a company in turnarounds, to mend broken cultures, to create long-term success out of mergers and acquisitions, to lead companies that are in the tank financially or are in a real growth mode but don't have the management skills or the team to scale the company through the next couple of revolutions of its life cycle—these are all leadership skills that are all too often missing from the talent pool. And, of course, there are many companies today in need of an injection of new leadership.

My colleague and fellow search consultant, and one of our firm's and industry's founding fathers, Gerry Roche, proclaims in this chapter his belief on what makes a great leader today: "Human understanding and sensitivity are absolutely critical for success. Only the fool finds total comfort in technical or specialized knowledge without developing his or her human and interpersonal skills." I agree. As I evaluate candidates, I absolutely look for the soft skills. Both IQ and EQ (emotional quotient) are partly innate and partly learned. Some of us are blessed to work for great companies where we are mentored by great bosses, and that kind of experience optimizes one's innate capabilities. EQ is hard to describe, but it is the granularity and richness of a complex set of behaviors and feelings you get about a person when you talk with him or her that lets you know whether he or she possesses the right set of soft skills. You know it when you see it. Finding people with both IQ and EQ is difficult, and pulling them away from something they are already passionate about is even more difficult. The people who possess EQ and the capacity for soft skills have a huge advantage.

Part of the soft skill set for leaders today is agility. Decisions need to made quickly, and teams have to be pulled together quickly. This requires extreme agility, and not many people are blessed with it. In fact, the reason that many CEOs and division presidents fail is that they cannot respond quickly enough to changing market conditions.

In addition to decisiveness and agility, there are basically three skills that are predictors for success. First, there is capacity. Capacity comes in many forms: innately, it is your knowledge and basic intellect. No amount of training or experience will help a person who lacks the intellectual capacity or who doesn't have a certain amount of innate ability in a given arena. Capacity also encompasses the experiences, both positive and negative, that teach and train you how to manage and how to handle the circumstances you encounter as a senior executive. There is also capacity in the form of physical and emotional tolerance for ambiguity and change. Some people thrive on ambiguity and some are averse to it. Uprooting your family to take a job across the country, for example, can be very difficult physically and emotionally for some people, while others find it challenging. However, those who thrive on ambiguity are likely to be far superior at leading a corporation in today's current environment. In this chapter, American Express CEO Ken Chenault describes himself as "an intellectually curious person who likes to take on a variety of challenges." His capacity to handle the ambiguity of a crisis was evident during the terrorist attacks of September 11, 2001, when he moved his company's Manhattan headquarters—approximately three thousand people—from Ground Zero to New Jersey. It's little wonder, then, that when he prioritizes leadership traits, he ranks courage, creativity, and integrity before smarts.

The second key soft skill that successful leaders possess is motivation. They have a passion for building teams and organizations. Motivation is something you can help people with by giving incentives, but it is not a definitive skill that can be acquired through training. Unlike capacity, you either have motivation or you don't. Steele Alphin of Bank of America most eloquently phrases it in his interview: "Influence many, control few."

Finally, there is the skill we probably look for most of all in leaders: authenticity. Everyone talks about charisma, but the fact is that an infinitesimally small percentage of the population are universally acknowledged to possess that quality. Among senior executives, real charisma stems from authenticity: who that person is when you talk with him/her versus when he/she is in the boardroom or in front of customers. An authentic, charismatic business leader is someone who is consistent and not a sort of chameleon, changing colors for certain groups. You get strong credibility if you establish yourself as the genuine article. People will follow a leader who is authentic and passionate, as management gurus Jim Collins and John Kotter attest in their interviews in this chapter.

While the general attributes of the new-style leader are consistent across industries and organizations, the sizes and developmental stages of various organizations may call for different combinations of competencies. Skills that delineate to early-stage companies, for example, include extraordinary amounts of energy and intensity, the ability to multitask, an unusually high tolerance for ambiguity, and the aforementioned agility. Typically, a company in this phase has only a few products or services or is building a broader service offering to one or two product lines, so every step counts and there is little room for a misstep. Orbitz's CEO, Jeffrey Katz, had the formidable task of launching a start-up dotcom company after the dotcom crash in 2000. He acknowledges that, faced with these pressures, "it is essential to be a good strategist and planner: to set goals, to build clarity and consensus around them, and to connect the short-term goals with long-term results through excellent execution. Meeting a series of short-term goals helps to bring about positive and lasting changes." In my experience, the most successful executives are also those who can morph to the market conditions, be they changing capital requirements or capital supply. Being the CEO of any company is difficult, but being the CEO of a start-up is like throwing yourself in front of a train every day.

At the midcap level, there is a change in the required mix, moving from absolute personal leadership toward the competencies involved in empowering the team, or teams. It is an issue of scope and scale for a rapidly growing company. You have to delegate very effectively and empower business units as the organization grows. Also, leaders here have to continue to be passionate about key objectives, meticulously examine the business, and put a focus on change management. Executives with these abilities are likely to have fun in this environment and to succeed in creating breakthrough organizations. Given today's burgeoning new technologies, a company's best practices can be copied very quickly. Competitors can emulate what another company accomplishes within weeks or months. They may not be as good at it, but in the process, your company may have lost its ability to differentiate its products and services in the marketplace; that is why the ability to stay ahead of the change curve is so critically important in midcap companies.

The executives leading a multinational company are more in the league of senior diplomats than CEOs; the demands are transcendent of traditional leadership skill sets and call for the ability to synthesize experience as much as to analyze it. Theirs is the realm of strategic alliances, industry exchanges, and information portals. Their stature is such, their EQ is at a level, that it is impossible to articulate, let alone emulate, how they do what they do. At this level, the ability to step beyond the personal and see the world and one's role in it with objectivity, compassion, and resolve is critical. These types of leaders are genuine and confident of their abilities. They have a statesmanlike approach to representing a company, and it is a learning approach in which they acknowledge and examine mistakes and opportunities not taken but still celebrate success. Michael Jordan claims that one of the ways he became such a great basketball player is by missing over nine thousand shots in his professional career. That says it all.

For companies of all sizes, the implications of the new demands and stresses on their leaders seem crystal clear: in the realm of human capital management, the time has come to translate lip service into action. The leaders featured in this chapter, Linda Sanford at IBM, Hank McKinnell at Pfizer, Fred Smith at FedEx, and David Pottruck at Charles Schwab, were among the first to turn talk into action by empowerment, by strategic recruiting, by investing heavily in management development, and in a myriad other ways that are evident without being easy to define.

Also inherently important for a company of any stage or size is the capacity for change management and corporate transformation on an almost daily basis. Greg Owens at Manugistics Group developed a people strategy concurrently with a turnaround strategy. He notes: "This series of strategies is ongoing, because to maintain success, an organization must constantly work at recruiting, developing, and nurturing its intangible assets." This emphasis on people has made the difference between success and failure, Owens believes.

Recruiting is tougher all the time, as the supply of high-potential managers continues to dwindle, and even landing the best of the lot is not adequate unless you can hang onto them in a very competitive marketplace for talent. The interviews that follow have a lot of excellent guidance on "best practices" in recruiting and retaining talent. And, interestingly, not all of them have to do with financial incentives. Look at WWF International, for example. Thanks to its mission and culture, notes director general, Claude Martin, the conservation organization rarely has to recruit. Candidates flock to the organization, wanting to serve, and, once hired, rarely leave.

It's something you can just feel, walking into a company where human capital is highly valued. It is palpable in the interviews in the following pages. A handful of others, such as Dell Computer and Cisco Systems, have figured it out, too. Changing the rules and making them stick in the marketplace—investing time, money, and talent into human development even though it will take years to see the results—takes courage and commitment. So when you see a company do it, it is very impressive. The companies that don't do it will soon wish they had.

Leadership by courage, creativity, and integrity

Kenneth Chenault
American Express Company
Chairman and Chief Executive Officer

- **What are some of the defining moments in your career that have shaped your leadership style?**

I describe myself as an intellectually curious person who likes to take on a variety of challenges. I'm very interested in taking what I learn about different areas and applying those lessons to the things I am involved in to make an impact. The first defining moment for me was the decision to work at Bain & Company. While my stay there was just shy of three years, it had a major influence on me by exposing me to a range of industries. It also gave me an appreciation for how to identify and focus on the key issues that drive a business. I also learned the importance of challenging conventional wisdom. As I moved into the corporate world, leaving Bain for American Express, I learned that leadership comes in different forms, in different opportunities. One of my first assignments was in strategic planning, where I had to evaluate a direct-response fulfillment house that serviced our credit card business. At the time, quite frankly, I thought it was a very unglamorous and potentially boring assignment. But one of the things it taught me is that when you study what appears to be a narrow subject, you've got to broaden the context. That assignment in direct response and direct marketing really gave me an incredible understanding of the power of the direct marketing distribution channel and the importance of customer segmentation. Taking what I learned there, I was able to put together a broader piece of work involving a range of businesses within the company. Suddenly, I was working with people for whom I had no direct management responsibility and figuring out how to get them aligned with a common set of objectives. That was a very important piece of work, both for me and for the company. From a leadership standpoint, it demonstrated to me not just the power of ideas, but also that you do not need formal hierarchical authority to get people to move forward with you alongside common objectives.

- **What a great lesson to learn, especially with organizations continuing to flatten. So you are saying that leadership is as much about influencing as it is about anything else?**

That is absolutely right. I was an early beneficiary of understanding that the old "command and control" structure was going to be difficult to operate going forward. My next move at American Express was to the merchandise services division, which at the time was an unprofitable unit that sold a variety of consumer products—televisions, luggage, jewelry—through the mail to cardmembers. It was not clear how the unit's strategy related to the objectives of the core businesses—in particular, the card business. It was, however, a unit very dependent on the direct marketing channel and on understanding customer segmentation. Many people in the company advised me that it would be a serious career mistake to go into that business. But I believed it was important for the company to make an informed decision whether to remain in that business or not; and, on a personal level, I felt that it would be a way for me to gain a wide range of experiences, especially in the marketing and merchandising area. My view was that if the company penalized me for taking a risk, then I probably didn't belong with the company. It turned out to be a terrific opportunity, and I learned a lot of the skills that help me to this day—skills such as team building, consensus management, and marketing. Most important, I learned how to take a dispirited organization and galvanize its people to create a turnaround.

- **These skills that you picked up along your career certainly helped you lead during and after the terrorist attacks. What are the leadership skills required in crisis situations?**

What is most important is to show compassion and listen very actively while continuing to be a strong and decisive leader. During a crisis, people want direction, but they also need to know that you empathize with them and that you can understand different reactions and different perspectives. The trust factor is absolutely essential. People can see right through insincerity, and in times of crisis, if you do not engender a level of trust and empathy, there is no way that you can lead your organization through adversity. Particularly in times of crisis, the job of a leader is to redefine reality by defining the new reality. We've got to give our organizations hope, and the hope has to be both factual and inspirational. The other point

I would make is that there is no rulebook for leading through a crisis; the way you lead is to follow your values and your beliefs.

- Leaders certainly need to master managing the intangibles as opposed to leveraging tangible assets. What are the "must have" skills for today's CEO, and how have these changed from 5 or 10 years ago?

Let me name some skills that I believe are constant and then some attributes in which the emphasis may have changed. First and foremost, leaders need courage: courage to make the tough decisions and courage to stick with a strategy that others think will not work. You can assume a certain level of intelligence exists if someone is in the CEO position, but it doesn't always follow that the person possesses courage. Sometimes that doesn't become clear until it's too late. Second, a good leader today needs to be a creative thinker, not just thinking in a step or linear process from a logic standpoint, but thinking in leaps and bounds. Not just connecting the dots but drawing new lines on the page. Third, he or she must have a very high level of integrity. Integrity has always been important, but it is critically important now because we are dealing in an ever-changing environment and a highly uncertain environment. And, increasingly, you're asking an organization's workforce to follow you when you are not providing a hundred percent of the answers. So, they have to believe in you on the basis of your courage, your logic, and the power of your arguments, in combination with trust and faith in your integrity. Now, moving to today's leadership challenges, it is essential to know how to use technology to move a business forward. It's not something that you can ignore any longer. Technology is now so integral to the various business issues and opportunities that we all face, that you have to have a strong understanding of and appreciation for it in order to be fully effective as a leader. It is also critical that you have a global perspective, because resources—both human and financial resources as well as raw materials and value-added services—are distributed across a wide spectrum, not only geographically but also culturally and ethnically around the world. Without a global perspective, it's going to be difficult to take advantage of the diversity of opportunities in the moderate to long term.

- What is your advice to executives who may be thinking about developing their leadership skills and pursuing a career as a high-level leader?

What I often tell our young executives is to focus on the job at hand. While most people have ambitions, most in fact do not follow up 100 percent on their current commitments. By following up on your commitments I mean execute on the assignment at hand, and place yourself in the shoes of your boss and your peers and your subordinates so that you understand how you need to execute at your current level in order to make those people successful. When you make those people successful, you're going to make the business successful. The second thing I tell up-and-coming executives is that after you have executed on the basic requirements of a job or project, step back and think about what more you can do to add both incremental value and breakthrough value. If people are focused on generating results, adding value, and making the business successful, they can then network off their performance. The third point I try to make is to listen actively to the customer and to ideas being expressed in the organization. You'll get far more insights and information by paying close attention than if you listen in a distracted way.

- **What does American Express do in the way of leadership development?**

We look for the key attributes I've mentioned, and we realize that you just don't evaluate those attributes in the annual performance review. You've got to evaluate on a daily basis. A good way to do that is in going through business reviews; ask why a particular result was accomplished or what the actions and behaviors were that led to that result. We look at the quality of thinking and the quality of the execution of each person. We have an environment that encourages people to take risks. You want to create an environment where people have a willingness to stretch and to take some chances, because that's how you really achieve breakthrough results.

- **Have you identified positions inside American Express that serve as testing grounds for leadership potential, or do you develop an executive in an existing position that the executive currently holds?**

We have a range of positions that are developmental positions, but we also look at the readiness of the individual. In some cases, we move a person into a job that he or she is fully prepared for in every conceivable way; in other cases, we promote the individual into a job that is a completely new challenge because this is a developmental experience that we want them to go through. So, sometimes we make nontraditional moves because we strongly believe that a particular person will excel in a role despite not being well trained for it. We know that person can handle a broader set of responsibilities, so we create the opportunity within a supportive environment. Our view is that in assessing what moves need to be made, you need to look at the leadership attributes required, the needs of the person, and the needs of the company. We don't have a rigidly structured system that says only these jobs are jobs for developing people. Rather, we are more inclined to match people to the jobs and to the objectives as they change and grow.

- Do you see the future of human capital management in firms as moving toward a 360-degree view of people?

The so-called war for talent is one of the most important battlefields in business. It is critical that a company create the kind of environment in which people really believe they can learn, grow, and prosper. The focus has to be on developing people.

- American Express has been innovative with its card services. For example, you were the first with the Gold Card, first with the Platinum Card, and now you have the Centurion Card. How have you been able to foster a culture that's built on innovation and built to change, which are important aspects of competitive advantage today?

What I try to do and what our other leaders try to do is to create both formal and informal forums and a spirit of openness in the company, so that people really feel they have both the opportunity and the obligation to come up with ideas and to innovate. Critical to this is our vision to be the world's most-respected service brand. We therefore have a responsibility and an obligation to constantly increase the value of our products and services to be a superior value provider, which means we can't be a "me too" company; we *have* to innovate and create. Another way we encourage innovation is to set very lofty objectives, not just in terms of finance but qualitatively as well. The search for qualitative aspirations, frankly, is a journey that we will always be on.

Level five leaders

Jim Collins
Author and Leadership Expert

- You recently completed a large-scale five-year study to identify and examine companies that have gone from good to great. Can you give us an overview of the study?

The study grew out of two simple questions: Can a good company or good organization ever become a great one? And, if so, how? When my colleague Jerry Porras and I wrote *Built to Last*, we left unanswered a gigantic question: If a company doesn't get the right parenting from early on—if it doesn't have a David Packard or a George Merck or a Walt Disney to get it off the ground—is it basically doomed to mediocrity? General Electric had Charles Coffin right off the bat, so it was always a great company; all its later successes have been based on that early foundation. So, in the latest study, we conducted a systematic research effort to find companies that had made a viable leap from good to great. We began with 1,435 companies that appeared on the *Fortune* 500 list from 1965 to 1995. We looked for companies that showed a sustained performance level no better than market performance—in other words, companies whose long-term performance, as compared with the yield on mutual funds, would have grown less than the mutual funds. We looked for companies meeting this criterion; and then we looked at those companies that went through some sort of a leap or a change and afterward, over the next 15 years, enjoyed growth at least threefold greater than mutual funds or the general market. Our findings showed that investments in these companies averaged sevenfold growth. To put this in perspective, GE, over the last 15 years, beat the market 2.8 to 1. We were looking for companies that went from good to doing better than GE at its best, on a dollar-for-dollar-invested basis. The companies we narrowed to, in fact, averaged twice the rate of returns of GE. Using GE as the benchmark of a great company, we found 11 companies that went from good to great, meaning they had better results than GE.

- What is "Level Five" leadership?

Some view leadership as a kind of religion; we didn't want to find a leadership answer to our study in that sense. I used to be a leadership atheist; now I'm a leadership agnostic. It's not that I don't think leadership is important, but in this kind of research, it's not a particularly helpful concept in the sense that it's easy to attribute everything we don't understand or comprehend to leadership. With greater scientific understanding, however, you can begin to understand many more variables at work. So, I really am very, very skeptical of leadership answers. I don't like them. I'm bothered by them. I think we put too much emphasis on them. In fact, the evidence suggests that most leaders who are viewed as successful leaders do not produce great companies. Now, that being said, I was very surprised with our findings. The data convinced me that we had a leadership answer. However, we found that it's not leadership itself that takes companies from good to great, because the comparison companies, the companies that tried but failed to make a sustained leap from good to great, had leaders like Lee Iacocca and Stanley Gault and Jack Eckerd. There's no question that these people were real leaders. Even Al Dunlap, some would say, was a leader. But yet, Chrysler, Rubbermaid, Eckerd, and Scott Paper didn't qualify as good-to-great companies. So, because the comparison companies also had leadership, we concluded that the answer to making companies great was not leadership itself. The real distinction was that there is a special form of leadership that takes companies from good to great. What you have in the great companies is Level Five leadership. The comparison companies had Level Four leadership. Here's the difference: Level Five leaders are ambitious first and foremost for the company and its long-term greatness, not for themselves as individuals. As a result, they tend to be personally modest, humble, and reserved, but enormously willful on behalf of the organization. They tend not to become celebrities. They don't have their egos wrapped up in making themselves well known. We identified the only 11 companies in the history of the *Fortune* 500 starting in 1965 that went from good to great using the top benchmarks and standards. In every single one of those cases, the CEOs were largely unknown. They were people like Darwin Smith, Lyle Everingham, David Maxwell, Cork Walgreen, George Cain, and Ken Iverson. These are not your household name leaders, and yet they absolutely blew away the well-known leaders in terms of actual results. We found that there is an inverse relationship between high-profile, charismatic, egocentric leadership—the Level Four leaders—and the journey of a company from good to great.

- ### Are Level Five leaders born or made?

Some are born, but most are made. That gives the Level Four leaders hope, although it is hard work getting to a Level Five. Personal growth of any kind is challenging. I believe in the capacity of humans to develop and evolve. That's even one of the great cornerstones of Christianity, the belief that humans can evolve and grow into better people. I believe the same thing with a progression toward Level Five. Most people have the capacity to evolve to Level Five.

- ### What would be some of the characteristics a person would want to develop to be a Level Five?

Think of it in three layers; the first layer is behavior. Level Five behaviors include things like using "we" instead of "I." Level Five leaders tend to use "we" and Level Fours tend to use "I." Another element of Level Five behavior is what we call "the window and the mirror." Level Fives stand at the window and look for someone or something to attribute success to, even if that success came about through good luck. We asked CEO Alan Wurtzel, "What were the main factors that allowed your company to create this extraordinary result?" He said, "Well, that's easy. The wind was at our backs." We then showed him the good-to-great stock chart which shows companies' results going along and then his company's results exploding upward. I wrote under his company "You" and under the others "Comparison Companies." At the bottom of the whole page I wrote "Same wind." After a long pause he said, "My goodness, we must have been very lucky." His remark is typical of the way Level Fives are always looking out the window to attribute success to something other than their personal performance. But during difficult times of setbacks, they stand in front of a mirror and say, "It is my responsibility." By contrast, the Level Four mentality tends to be more one of taking credit during good times and looking outward to assign blame during down times. Another Level Five attribute is the dual quality of being absolutely relentless in pursuit of company goals and yet possessing extreme personal humility. Level Fives will do whatever it takes to make a company great, including—and this applies to the deepest layer of Level Fives—at each decision point, choosing what is best and most ambitious for the organization instead of what is best for your ego, your career, or your reputation. Level Five leaders constitute the bricks and mortar of the corporate community. They are doing real work and getting things done. There's a huge difference between promoting yourself and delivering results—and the critical way in which Level Five leaders are different from the rest is that they deliver results, and, very often, extraordinary results.

• **What about the role of charisma?**

Charisma can be a leadership asset, but it can also be a liability. Sam Walton is an example of a charismatic Level Five leader. But, most of the time, because it leads to you-centric thinking and behavior, charisma is a leadership liability. Another reason it can be dangerous for leaders to be charismatic is that charismatic leaders are expected to be right all the time, and very few human beings are right all the time. People will blindly follow charisma, right into failure. The good news is that charisma is a liability you can overcome. I think of charisma as being like a stutter or a lisp. It just makes your job harder and ultimately, it makes it harder for you to create greatness—but you can overcome it. When I built my research team, I surrounded myself with people who are fundamentally irreverent so that my strong personality would not lead us down the wrong path. Since it is a liability, I need people around me who aren't too influenced by it. I also try to dramatically increase my questions-to-statements ratio. If you have charisma and you strongly assert something, it is likely you will be convincing—whereas, if you ask a question, you are more likely to get better answers. All the good-to-great leaders are superb at asking questions. Many have law degrees, and their legal backgrounds help appreciate a perspective of asking questions. Most are shy, introverted, reserved people who are uncomfortable talking about themselves. It is like pulling teeth to get them to open up, and, often, their answers are questions.

- **Does gender play a role in Level Five leadership?**

I don't believe there is a gender difference. One absolute archetype of a Level Five woman is the late Katharine Graham, who was publisher of the *Washington Post* during the Watergate era. I was rereading her autobiography the other day, and the part about Watergate is very fascinating and revealing. Everybody talked about how she had great courage, and her response was, "Well, actually, courage is only there if you have a choice. I never really felt that we had a choice." She wouldn't even take credit for her own courage. Also, when she's summing up the whole Watergate incident, she says, "You have to understand that, basically, we were lucky." Every sentence after that for almost 20 sentences in a row, she is attributing her success to luck. This is a perfect illustration of the archetype of the window and the mirror.

- **How can companies make a major transformation and go from good to great?**

Level Five leadership is a necessary condition for going from good to great, but it's not sufficient. You can have a Level Five and still have a company not be able to make the transformation, because there are other critical factors as well. One is a "flywheel for change." Think of taking a company from good to great as a leveraging process in which there is a very large metal disc that weighs 400 tons. It's on an axle 30 feet high, and it is large enough to fill a huge conference room. In effect, it is a giant flywheel that you have to push. You push really, really hard in one direction for awhile and, finally, it turns once. Then, after more hard work, it turns twice. You keep pushing it in that intelligent, consistent direction and eventually you get four turns and then six and then eight and then 16 and then 32, 64, and so on until the thing begins to build momentum and starts to make its own turns, turn after turn after turn after turn. At some point, you can feel all that momentum tick in your favor and you can feel the flywheel accelerate forward at increasing speed. Whoosh! That's the way a good-to-great transformation feels. It's pushing a flywheel rather than a single-stroke action. Push after push, turn after turn, until the momentum takes off. The pushes aren't necessarily small. Darwin Smith at Kimberly-Clark sold all the company's paper mills and the paper side of the business, which was the majority of the business. They had been in the paper business for 70 years. He put all the money into the consumer business with products like Kleenex and Huggies and went head to head with other major consumer companies and beat them. That represented both a huge push and many small pushes on the flywheel, and it made his company great. All of our research has led us to one conclusion: It is not any harder to create something great than it is to perpetuate something only good.

Leadership by knowing, developing, and empowering your people

Frederick W. Smith
FedEx Corporation
Founder, Chairman and Chief Executive Officer

- What is your approach to leadership?

All the best kind of leadership efforts are designed to maximize the individual efforts of a diverse group toward achieving an organization's goals. Compared to its
importance in sports or the military, many businesses historically have put a lower
value on leadership. In the military, for example, the reason that leadership has been
so important for centuries is that you are asking individuals to subordinate their
personal interests—even perhaps to die or be seriously injured—in order to achieve
organizational objectives. In the business world over the last 10 to 20 years, leadership has become widely acknowledged as being critical to corporate success as our
economy has moved more and more to a service-based model, even on the manufacturing side, which has a very large value-added component to the service element
of the business. As is true in so many areas, it is not the concept that is difficult so
much as the execution. The principles of leadership, as applied to the global marketplace, are now pretty well universally recognized; the problem is getting people
to follow these principles because they are, by definition, very hard to execute. It
takes a lot of time, energy, and effort to keep your workforce informed, to set an
example, to look out for the developmental needs of your people, to communicate
what is expected of them, to empower and reward them when they perform at a
high level. Practicing leadership principles on a day-to-day basis is difficult. At FedEx,
we insist that our managers practice good leadership in addition to good management. We have a very tough selection process for first- and second-level managers
before we put them in positions of authority. This process is largely based on a quantitative analysis of their leadership skills and their potential for being effective leaders. Our Leadership Institute emphasizes quality leadership and how to recognize
and nurture it in the selection and training of people on the front line.

- On the subject of empowerment, who gets empowered,
  just the potential front-line leaders, or everyone?

Everyone, absolutely. Empowering is one of the most important principles of leadership, and if you don't try to develop _all_ your people and give them the opportunity to perform at a high level, your people will, at worst, become resentful and
exert a negative influence on the team effort, and at best, become marginal employees, doing only what is necessary to get by.

- How formal is the executive development curriculum of your Leadership Institute?

Starting with our first-level manager positions, we have a program that assesses the leadership potential of both internal and external candidates. Internal applicants are encouraged to participate in our ASPIRE program, which is an acronym for Assessment of Skills, Performance, and Interests Required for Entry into management. This is an assessment module that quantifies an individual's potential for being an effective leader by evaluation against a very standard, specific set of attributes. Those who meet the standards are invited to participate in the Leadership Institute. For this special fast-track curriculum, we screen for those who demonstrate the basic attributes that have been determined to be most conducive to effective leadership. Companywide, we have five levels of management: [first level] manager, senior manager, managing director, vice president, and senior executive. At each of these levels, we have a developmental program geared to those we determine have high potential for going to the next level. We use a variety of instruments, including assessments by the reporting senior, by peers, and by subordinates—through a very thorough survey system that we've had for 25 years; it calculates individual capabilities for handling leadership issues at progressively higher levels in the organization.

- Having institutionalized leadership development, you must have a very well-developed human resources department. Is your top HR executive a part of the operating committee?

Absolutely. That has always been the case at FedEx. The senior HR executive has always had a seat at the very top management level. The input of human resources issues into all of the management decisions is as ingrained here as breathing.

- FedEx's business is packages, but your competitive advantage is your intangible assets, your people move packages speedily, reliably and at reasonable prices. Would you agree?

It's been interesting to watch the collision of our changing social imperative toward political correctness and the belated recognition on the part of business that it is potentially worth a lot of cold, hard cash to exercise good leadership. At the end of the day, what differentiates a high-performance organization—whether it's a football team, a military organization, FedEx, or a competitor—is the way people are treated and how well they are motivated to perform. When you are talking about the contributions of hundreds or thousands of individuals, what you're really looking at is a very broad spectrum that goes from the bare minimum that an employee will do to avoid getting fired to the very best job that a person is capable of. The difference in productivity between those two polar extremes is astronomical.

- **Is it important to identify who your "A" players are as a way of determining whom to put in leadership positions?**

Top-grading is absolutely important, but keep in mind that there are lots of people in the top 20 percent who should never be put in a leadership position. The key is for the organization and that individual both to understand and be satisfied with that position. It is counterproductive to have a "C" performer who is unwilling to recognize that he or she will not make an effective leader. Many organizations get in trouble in this regard, because the only avenue they have for financially rewarding top performers is to move them into management positions. You have to have rewarding, alternate career paths for outstanding specialists—engineers, for example, or R & D people—who can continue to make major contributions to the organization without going into management.

- **What is your personal style of leadership during times of crisis or a major disruption in the business?**

In a broad sense, we are all more sophisticated about crisis management these days. Few people respond well to the old-style directive type of leadership; they perform much better when they are well informed and given appropriate authority. Whether it is a major incident or a real-world crisis, one of the most important and fundamental traits of good leadership is good and timely communication. We have an enormous systemwide internal television network called FXTV and a very sophisticated internal information-sharing system that includes email. These tools allow me to get in front of everyone on a regular basis.

- **What skills and experiences does a young person need to develop today in order to be a successful leader tomorrow?**

My recommendation doesn't have anything to do with which business school to attend or what consultancy to join. Unequivocally, if you aspire to run an organization consisting of a lot of regular folks, the so-called blue-collar workforce, at some point—preferably sooner rather than later—you're going to have to make an effort to get to know all your people and understand how they think and feel about things. The employees in the trenches tend to have a more hands-on, practical knowledge of the business and are clearheaded about the reality of how things work, not the theoretical. Most senior executives today don't have enough contact at this level, and they are missing out on connecting with their constituencies and of being better leaders because of it.

Leading an Internet start-up in today's dotcom environment

Jeffrey Katz
Orbitz
Chairman, President, and Chief Executive Officer

- **What leadership challenges have you overcome in launching Orbitz following the dotcom crash?**

I had the unique professional experience of leading an Internet e-commerce site that was launched after the dotcom crash. That posed a series of leadership challenges, not the least being how to recruit talent, and what kind? Given that the information superhighway was littered with the carcasses of failed Internet companies, how would we convince executives and up-and-coming stars that we would be one of the survivors? These were among the considerations that I weighed in determining whether I would even accept the challenge of joining Orbitz. But it turned out that recruiting high-quality talent was easier than I had expected. The market for online travel was already huge—$15 billion sold in the year before our June 2001 launch—and there was a general perception that, with 80 percent of the airline industry as investors, if any company had a chance, it would be Orbitz. So I had the luxury of hiring from a quality pool of people who had a combination of travel and nontravel backgrounds. Ultimately, they shared my philosophy about leading our company and possessed the skills necessary to provide Orbitz with the strategic technology, finance, communications, and marketing skills that were vital to laying the foundation for a successful enterprise.

- **What is your leadership philosophy?**

Any discussion about leadership must begin with the acknowledgement that people want to be led. It is much more evident in times of crisis; look at George W. Bush's approval ratings after the September 11 terrorist attacks, when the American public looked to the president as a moral compass, and found comfort and inspiration in his leadership. But even on a day-to-day basis, people need and seek out guidance from strong leaders. Leaders mobilize people—whether in a multinational corporation, a civic or charitable enterprise, a family business, or a high school football team—around a vision and a direction in pursuit of shared objectives. A true leader helps people understand and buy in to the goals and objectives, take satisfaction in a job well done, and be motivated to perform at the top of their abilities. Compare this scenario to one in which there is no such mobilization, and in which many feel resentful, confused, and ambivalent about a task or goal that may have been superimposed on them rather than embraced by them. It's the difference between an exhilarating trek across the frontier with Lewis and Clark and a herd of cattle plodding westward to an unknown destination.

- **What attributes must a leader possess to be effective?**

Leaders may not always be the most popular people in the organization, for they may be forced to make the tough decisions and point out what others may prefer to ignore. But leaders know that applying their decisions in a consistent and rational manner eventually creates consensus as others begin to share more fully in the vision and direction. It is from that point of view that I have identified the leaders I have respected, followed, and learned from, and how I have tried to conduct myself so that others see me as a leader. I prefer to be viewed as a leader who happens to be the CEO, not as one whose position is mandated by the title. The foremost attribute of a successful leader is the overarching one of being able to use all the tools and resources available to optimize the team's performance. To do that, it is essential to be a good strategist and planner: to set goals, to build clarity and consensus around them, and to connect the short-term goals with long-term results through excellent execution. Meeting a series of short-term goals on diversity in recruiting, for example, helps to bring about positive and lasting changes. Meeting sales and revenue targets each quarter isn't just about short-term financial objectives and profit-sharing payouts; rather, it's about building cash flow and profitability in order to make new investments and acquisitions, expand and grow the business for the long term, and enhance shareholder value. Another vital attribute is articulating your vision in order to get buy-in and commitment from the team and also from key stakeholders, internally and externally. Much has been written about the interconnectedness of the interests of employees, customers, and investors, and I am convinced that vision and strategy and shareholder value are absolutely intertwined. Successful business leaders generate consistent returns for shareholders, and doing that requires a long path that is dependent on good strategy and planning as well as execution. A leader has to know how to find the path and keep it moving forward. In today's turbulent and fast-paced business environment, that can be a challenge that is far larger than the capacity of any one person, no matter how gifted or capable. So the next critical attribute is the ability to recruit and retain other talented and capable leaders, and let them lead down into the organization. The ability to recruit a strong team with a combination of skills and experience that enhance the organizational chemistry and culture so that the goals can be established and achieved is perhaps the strongest evidence and outcome of leadership. It is also the biggest challenge and at the same time the most energizing part of being a leader, because it opens the door to sustainable competitive advantage. As a business leader, I have the responsibility to ensure that my organization has staying power and the stamina to perform successfully— both to attract investors and to attract and retain the best and the brightest staff who invest their energy and ability in the organization over the long term.

- **What is the secret of sustaining excellent team performance?**

Once a team has been assembled it takes a lot of work to make a team grow. At Orbitz, we emphasize the concept of practicing being a team. It may sound unusual, but we find that it definitely has a favorable impact on results and makes the team and organizational leadership stronger and more effective. I've learned over the years that it is worthwhile to invest time in role-clarifying, strategy development with the team, and teamwork development.

- **How does one recognize what makes a strong team and what skills must be practiced to keep it dynamic?**

Seeing a lot of strong teams at work is the best way. I have been fortunate to work at companies with great leadership and lots of it. At American Airlines, where I spent the bulk of my career, the bench was very deep, and everyone benefited from the amazing depth of talent.

- **What is the outlook for Orbitz?**

It is too early to say whether Orbitz will be a long-term success, but our short-term victories have clearly been achieved with that goal in mind. Before launch, we faced enormous market skepticism and an orchestrated lobbying campaign by our competitors seeking to prevent us from even going into business. Then just four months after our very successful launch in June 2001, our industry travel faced the one-two punch of the September 11 terrorist attacks and an economic recession, threatening the future of our initial airline investors airlines as well as our other partners and suppliers of the travel industry. But we have stuck to our basics of easy-to-use technology, low costs for our suppliers and low prices for our consumers, and outstanding customer service. So far, the formula is working. We continue to exceed our forecasts and hope to be profitable by mid-2002, nearly three quarters ahead of plan. But each day calls for a new commitment and a new assessment of the ever-changing, ever-challenging environment, as we press on toward our long-term objectives.

Leadership at a nonprofit organization requires conviction in the business and the brand

Claude Martin
WWF International
Director General

• Your organization has done a masterful job of branding the WWF without the level of financial support that many _Fortune_ 500 companies have. Virtually everyone recognizes the panda logo. What is the secret of that success?

Our brand was conceived 40 years ago by Sir Peter Scott, son of the Antarctic explorer and a committed conservationist, who played a key role in our organization. Sir Peter, who was also a talented painter, decided on the panda as the symbol for WWF because it was already an endangered species at the time, but also because it is black and white. Then—and still to some degree today—a black-and-white motif enjoys a big advantage in graphic design and printing. Over the years, we have had extremely high-quality support in branding, brand protection, and trademark protection through our association with David Ogilvy, cofounder of Ogilvy & Mather Advertising and a long-time WWF board member. We have also been able to reinforce our brand recognition through effective and highly visible conservation work worldwide. However, a global brand is something that has to be constantly worked at and that has to be defended, as our recent litigation against the World Wrestling Federation over the three-letter acronym WWF dramatically demonstrates. A well-known brand like ours has to have constant, ongoing protection, and, like many corporate entities, we are willing to invest in defending and strengthening it.

• Have you found it difficult to attract, develop, and retain a high caliber of people?

Because people are emotionally attached to what we are doing, it has been relatively easy for us to attract and retain highly competent employees. We attribute our low turnover in staff primarily to the strong commitment our people have to our cause, even though it may force them to make a trade-off financially or hierarchically as compared to their potential in the for-profit marketplace. While there are differences in a corporate environment, companies can learn a lesson from this phenomenon in designing human resource strategies that capitalize on the natural desire to play on a winning team doing meaningful work.

- ### What are the specific leadership challenges for organizations such as WWF?

There are a number of distinctions from the corporate environment. Our product is, in a sense, an ideology, an ethic. This has a number of implications. First of all, the product is difficult to identify; it is not so tangible. It is a service, but not a service to a single client. It is a service to humanity at large, or to specific groups or communities. This influences how we behave, how we lead, and what kind of people we attract as staff. Typically, people working in nongovernmental organizations (NGOs) are highly motivated people, who at times can be rather opinionated. People like that, if they develop a negative attitude, can become loose cannons in this kind of organization, starting their own campaigns or agendas. So we look for positive people with the professional skills and experiences we need. If you want to lead a NGO or nonprofit organization successfully, you have to be able to draw on a highly creative, entrepreneurially oriented talent base in order to create and sustain a coherent and cohesive dialogue with your constituencies.

- ### What is your leadership philosophy?

I believe in three principles that are essential for me to lead successfully. The first is to know what the nature of the business is. There has always been a debate as to whether NGO leaders should be professional managers—professional in the for-profit business sense—but I believe the most important single criterion for our organization is a deep understanding of conservation, regardless of the professional skill set. Business acumen and a knowledge of conservation don't have to be mutually exclusive qualities, of course. But leading a business in which you really know what you're talking about is essential to building credibility. Credibility is essential to successful leadership, and you can gain a lot of ground by setting an example and by being modest and realistic about what your role is. Another aspect of the way I personally lead, my second key principle, is that I surround myself with good leaders. Appointing competent, imaginative, dedicated people and not interfering too much in the way they run their jobs is critical. If I were a micromanager, I would not only wear myself out, I would wear out everybody around me. My third guiding principle is to look ahead—always to look to the horizon. If you cannot anticipate what the general trends are—in our business, this relates to global resource development and the attendant pressures on nature—then your back is against the wall and you've become a very reactive manager. Your people need to see you point to a place on the horizon to know where to take the business. This translates to any business. Our product is different from most, but the leadership principles are the same.

- **What prior experiences have helped develop your leadership style?**

I started as a field biologist in the jungles of central India. That background has helped me gain a truly global perspective, and I believe it is critically important nowadays to have a multicultural understanding of the world, both individually and organizationally. Cultural diversity is a value that must be developed in an organization's workforce, because the human tendency in the workplace is to value what is most familiar. Leaders have a responsibility to actively promote diversity in their organizations. My background in biology made me a strong believer in its power to effect change. Through my studies in biodiversity, I have seen that diversity tends to operate as a stabilizing force in organizations as well as in ecosystems. Furthermore, cultural diversity in an organization is a huge asset in terms of pluralism and a rich variety of opinions and perspectives; it's a tremendous help in dealing externally with a highly pluralistic world. Later on in my career, within WWF, I saw a powerful demonstration of this fact when I managed a staff operation in Africa and witnessed the way the African culture exerted its influence over an administrative system that had been developed under colonial rule. It is easy to criticize bureaucracy, but dealing with the intricacies has taught me a number of valuable lessons about leadership.

- **What fundamental skills make leaders effective in today's nonprofit organizations?**

In the nonprofit, nongovernment sector, it is very important to be an effective communicator and good at convincing people. Unlike the structured hierarchy of the typical business model, our structure is much leaner and more decentralized, more democratic. You need to be able to convince people about the right way go, and since just ordering them around and commanding is not a way forward in our environment, your communication style becomes even more important. Of course, this also means being able to communicate well to the outside world, the ability to articulate a vision based on a down-to-earth agenda. Another important skill is flexibility. The world changes much more quickly now, so you have to have an inner preparedness to adapt to new situations, new opportunities, and new priorities. Compared to other NGOs, WWF is a big organization. Therefore, reaching major decisions and making changes within a short time frame presents a real challenge. That is why being able to anticipate change and adjust swiftly is a fundamental component of being successful in this environment.

- You have to have a business that is built to change.

Absolutely, and if you have an intimidated or inhibited workforce around you, it is even more of a challenge. That sort of culture will be very reluctant to change; insecurity in a workforce is toxic for change. Job insecurity, whether about one's current position or future career options, stunts change. So, you want to foster flexibility, yet at the same time give your staff a sense of security by placing trust in them.

- WWF works in over 90 countries around the world. How do you stay connected to your various parts?

We were among the very first NGOs to invest in email, and today, we are entirely connected throughout the world using this technology as well as an efficient intranet. Staying in touch with employees and program partners is not as challenging to us as staying in touch with the public and the customer, the people who support conservation action. How do you do that in China, for example?

- Good question. How *do* you do that in China?

In China, WWF is in a fortunate situation, as we are the oldest NGO there. Throughout our 20 years of presence in China, we have become personally known to and accepted by the Chinese leaders. We have a relationship of trust with them, and, having a seat on the China Council for Sustainable Development can exert some influence. We are involved in programs, for example, with the minister of education to help develop school curricula for environmental education. This gives us an outreach to all Chinese schools. We reach 300 million homes with television programs produced in partnership with the United Nations Environment Program (UNEP). In fact, our panda logo might be better known in China today than it is known in the United States.

- Many CEOs around the world are thinking about China as a potential market and as a potential competitor. Given your intimate knowledge of China, are there guiding principles you can share for establishing business relationships there?

The guiding principle is trust. You cannot do anything in China unless you are in a situation of trust, and this is often a very time-consuming proposition. You can't build trust overnight. The culture is a highly collaborative one, and Chinese leaders very much depend on your ability to function as a reliable partner. That has often stopped businesses that try to move in tomorrow and out again the next day; this kind of unreliability is remembered. You have to build good institutional relationships in China over time, as WWF has done. A network of good business relationships is important anywhere, but it is essential in China.

Leading through teams

Hank McKinnell
Pfizer
Chairman and Chief Executive Officer

- What is your leadership or management philosophy?

I'm a big believer in teamwork. In running a big, complicated organization, you need lots of information and different points of view. You can best lead a complicated organization through a team approach, in part to obtain more information, in part to obtain different points of view and, maybe equally important, to get the buy-in and support that is necessary to execute. The strongest part of the culture of our organization is teamwork, and we've found that the more diverse our teams, the more productive they can be. You get a creative rub by having views that are slightly dissimilar. But to make that work, you've got to encourage open discussion and debate. There is a natural reluctance for people to speak up, particularly when they don't agree. It's even kind of threatening to some executives. So, therefore, your culture must allow and encourage open discussion and debate. Only then do you get the best results. My leadership style is geared toward promoting teams and getting results through teams.

- How do you identify your top performers in a team-centric environment?

We have moved from something of a Darwinian system of human capital development, in which the best naturally rose to the top without much coaching or planning, to a much more formal process of identification, evaluation, and development. The stars often identify themselves. In my own career, for example, I never spent any time at all worrying about my next job; I simply concentrated on doing my current one to the best of my ability. The best way to become identified as a high performer is through performance—by doing the job you are in as well as you can. And if you're identified as a star as a result of that, that's the way it should work.

- Does Pfizer provide a framework for developing people's abilities?

We have two executive development programs, "Just in Time Training" and the "Leading Edge Program," designed primarily for first-time supervisors. We make the point that, up to the present, the employee has been evaluated based on personal contribution, but now, as a team leader or supervisor, he or she will also be evaluated on the performance of the team. New leaders need to build a different skill set, and that's the point at which we begin training. Then, we have an advanced leadership program called "Sharpening the Edge" and another, even higher-level "Leading Change" program that we run at Harvard.

- What are the skills CEOs must have to be effective today?

What comes to mind immediately is the way that, just in the past few years, we recognize the opportunities to do things we never thought were possible. The old model had us thinking about how to do everything better, faster, cheaper. With the new model, we are thinking of things that we weren't previously able to do at all. It's a matter of asking "What if?" and "Why not?" more and more, and actually getting answers. For example, I had a laptop with a 56K modem, but couldn't get it to run beyond about eight thousand bytes per second (BPS), and even dialing into different servers, I was only able to get it to about 28K operating speed. Frustrated, I called our technical support staff and asked, "What if we augmented our phone lines with added capacity, like cable, fiber optic, ISDN, DSL, satellites, or something else? What if we stretched the limit?" And the specialist said, "Well, television operates at about 450K, and our satellite operates at about four million BPS." Here I was trying to get from 8K to 56K when the potential was four million. Going from 8K to 56K means my email synchronizes faster; going to four million causes me to say, "Well, what could I do with that?" It raises some really interesting possibilities in improving the training of our professional representatives, for example. Currently, we take people out of their territories to train them, and that represents lost time spent with customers. With these technical capabilities, it may be that we can offer interactive video and a lot of other new technologies in the field. And all because we asked the right question: "What if we stretched the limit?"

- What is most important when leading during disruptive times or times of crisis?

There are two things that I believe, just from my own background and experience. One is that people need information. During a crisis, there are all sorts of rumors and speculation. People need current, valid information. The other is that they need visible leaders. For example, during the terrorist attacks of September 11, 2001, I went down to our Manhattan headquarters lobby and got on our public address system. I explained the situation as I understood it, asked people to move away from windows that faced the United Nations building, since that building was reported as a possible target. I assured them that we were keeping their safety foremost in our mind and that we'd keep communicating to them. On September 11 alone, I made four long and detailed announcements over our PA system. You can't overcommunicate at a time like that. Then, for a very long time afterward, I sent emails out on a daily basis, reinforcing and adding to what we knew and how we were going to handle the situation. We used our email system 400 percent more during that period than on a typical day. Amid chaos and disruption, people have a real need for information and they have a real need for visible, credible leaders. And they will respond with leadership of their own. During the terrorist crisis, Pfizer did not miss one shipment of vital medicine despite the fact that the air-freight system was grounded. Our people found a way to lead.

- **What are the issues facing your industry and challenging
  your leadership abilities over the next few years?**

A major issue is that we tend to run our businesses quarter-to-quarter or year-to-year, but we haven't given enough thought to running businesses generation-to-generation. I'm becoming more aware that the next generation of future leaders—the people now joining major corporations—have a different set of expectations. They are very comfortable with technology; they're comfortable working in teams. They want to know how information is shared, what technology is available to them, and how can they contribute and become productive very fast. They want a real sense of significance. CEOs need to accept and adopt some unconventional practices in order to successfully attract the next generation of leaders to their companies.

- **Do what extent does innovation influence your competitive advantage?**

Innovation is one of the eight key values we have identified as shaping our competitive advantage, or our ability to lead in the marketplace. The others are integrity, teamwork, respect for people, customer focus, performance, community, and role-modeling leadership behavior within the organization. The way we got to these values is that we set a goal several years ago, when we were the sixth largest firm in the industry, to become the industry leader. We weren't sure we could do that, but we knew to get there we would have to hire a lot more people who possessed the skills and qualities we needed. We recognized that, ultimately, our competitive advantage was our culture and that we really needed to be able to explain and demonstrate to new employees what it took to be successful here. So, we took our collective experience and years of institutional knowledge and identified the values that characterized the kind of company that could reach the top. We began evaluating people on the basis of how well they demonstrate those values. And we in senior leadership talked with colleagues about these values, and made certain everyone recognized that one important dimension of everyone's performance appraisal, including mine, is active demonstration of Pfizer's values. We're working very hard to reinforce this successful culture and, most important, ensure its sustainability in the winds of constant change.

- What advice do you have for young executives aspiring to leadership positions?

Focus on what you do best and be passionate about the job at hand. A lot of people spend all their energy focused on their next job, but they really should be in a job that they love to do and enjoy doing, because that is a job where excellence comes naturally. Performance will be recognized, and that's what will get you to the next level. Doing something you feel is significant and doing it with all your heart really is the best way to ensure your success.

Attributes of successful leaders and trusted advisors

Gerard R. Roche
Heidrick & Struggles International
Senior Chairman

- What are the skills and characteristics of the twenty-first-century CEO?

Today's CEO must possess all the traditional attributes that have been critical throughout the history of business: integrity, values, vision, energy, judgment, decisiveness, people skills, and communication skills. Team building and retaining talent are still critical. The current environment does not render these traits obsolete; indeed, they constitute the bedrock of other attributes that leaders need to function most effectively. To these enduring and essential qualities, add entrepreneurial skills, risk-taking and speed, the ability to "connect the dots" and cast an eye to the future, and the ability to avoid being hidebound by tradition. In this age, the effective chief executive must have a comprehensive grasp of information technology, a keen sense of the industries, markets, and customers served by the organization, a savvy competency in geopolitics, and a respect for diversity—

of perspectives and interests, of strengths, of skill sets, and of cultures. He or she must be action oriented, even in the face of incomplete information, and accountable for results, and must be able to deal with the changing dynamics of "distance and dialogue," both of which are amplified by today's speed of information and the disintermediation of traditional supply chain levels. Human understanding and sensitivity are absolutely critical for success in any field. Only the fool finds total comfort in technical or specialized knowledge without developing his or her human and interpersonal skills. Leadership means sensitivity for humans. Like it or not, communicators rule the world. The great ideas, causes, and hopes will sit stagnant until somebody can communicate them. The movers and shakers of the world, for good or evil, are great communicators.

- **What are the ideal governance and organizational structures for a market-leading company?**

Under the leadership of the optimal CEO, the ideal structure of the management team would be no structure at all. Instead of the traditional pyramid, a flat or perhaps a circular structure would be ideal. Whatever the organizational structure, though, it should stem from the mission of the organization and the ways it connects with its customers and other stakeholders. The board of directors should be small and independent and have a chairman, formally or otherwise. The board should be balanced functionally, geographically, by industry, and in personality. It should be empowered to challenge, while maintaining synergy and compatibility with the management team. In the twenty-first century, corporate leaders are challenged as never before to keep pace with the warp speed at which business is conducted, to compete in a diffused but powerful marketplace, to foster innovation and creativity in the face of unprecedented dependence on technology, and, above all, to resist the pressures of short-term expediency in keeping long-range, enduring accomplishments and human values in focus.

- **What is the role of the trusted advisor?**

The number one criterion of being a valued advisor is anonymity. When he was CEO, Jack Welch used Ram Charan as an advisor, but Ram Charan would never publish a lot of articles saying "as counselor to Jack Welch" or "and as I said to him the last time I was with him." CEOs want a "kitchen cabinet," a back-door counsel; they don't want somebody who's going to make a PR statement using them as a credential. Number two is informality. By and large, CEOs aren't crazy about a squad of consultants coming in and interviewing their whole organization, then preparing a four-inch-thick tome that they'll charge a million dollars for. Not that cost is a debilitating factor when trying to do great things for your company, it's just that many CEOs prefer informal counsel versus an academic or theoretical approach. They are really seeking a sounding board off which they can bounce problems and ideas and get objective feedback. These leaders, strange as it may sound, and as capable as they are, and sometimes being the stars that they are, would prefer to not have to reveal their vulnerability or their levels of relative ignorance to their boards or senior managers. They don't want to go into a board meeting and say, "Hey, I'm running up against something pretty big and I'm not sure that I know how to handle it, so why don't you 15 people sitting around this table give me your thoughts?" Now, to some degree, this can be a healthy exercise with boards, but boards much prefer and greatly respect a CEO who can walk into the room and say, "Here is the biggest challenge this company has and it has kept me up at night but I have three possible solutions and here's the one I'm picking and why." A board's fundamental responsibility is to put the right people in place and to review and ratify the decisions of the CEO and the senior management. They are not there to participate in strategic planning or in market decisions or the like. When they do that, it may be because the CEO is weak. Good CEOs are not eager to reveal any indecisiveness or insecurities to their boards of directors. The same is true of senior management, for whom the best model is a CEO who already knows the direction the company must take. CEOs need trusted advisors whose judgments they respect, people who have a good understanding of the industry. Mac Stewart at McKinsey & Company is such an advisor; most folks have never heard of him, but some major global organizations wouldn't make a move without his counsel. We act as trusted advisors to our clients, in particular, to issues regarding human capital and governance. Not only young, inexperienced chiefs need this kind of counsel; many graybearded ones do, too. Former President Franklin Roosevelt, for example, depended more on informal, nonappointed counselors than he did on his cabinet, and that kind of private guidance was invaluable to him. Trusted advisors—to be really effective—tend to operate on a subterranean level of anonymity so that everybody involved is comfortable with the kind of strategic brainstorming and decision analysis that underpins all good leadership decisions.

- **What advice do you have for up-and-coming executives in terms of career development?**

I will skip the usual answers here and give you what I truly believe in my heart. Whatever your life's call, concentrate on excellence and service first. Go the extra step, make the extra effort, run the extra test, pat the extra back, and put your heart and soul into everything you do. You'll have more fun that way, and the enrichment will follow naturally. Realize that when you invest in someone else's future, your own is guaranteed. Don't just accept change, initiate change. Change is healthy and necessary for life's progress, so be a vital part of change. Accept no unchallenged status quo. Challenge assumptions, then make your own, being as creative as you can. Relate the unrelatable, find new paths, and using your own ideas and actions, push back the veils of ignorance that others hide behind.

Differentiation by intangible assets

Gregory J. Owens
Manugistics Group
Chairman and Chief Executive Officer

- How can an organization successfully differentiate itself from the competition, and sustain this competitive advantage over time?

The intangible assets of a company—its people and their collective domain expertise—are really the differentiators of a company. Human talent is the one resource that can never be commoditized. You can always come up with a different idea or a different perspective or different way to execute, but it's the people who drive a business. When I came to Manugistics, we had to do a turnaround before we could even embark upon a high-growth strategy. We were able to do that by bringing on and promoting up the right people to drive the program. The intangible assets give an organization a longer and clearer level of differentiation than any other kind. Given that fact, the key for CEOs and senior managers is to properly motivate and build the type of environment that allows their people to continue to grow and develop to the maximum of their potential.

- What are the most critical skills for CEOs today?

If you're running a public company, you've got to have particularly effective communications skills, not only for motivating your own team but also to work successfully with all the external partners and other constituencies. In our case, our partners could include other software companies or systems integration partners. In order to instill confidence with these partners, and your own team, you must be able to clearly communicate your vision and strategy. Another important constituency for a public company is obviously the financial community; it is critical that you are able to articulate to the financial community that you have the right strategy in the marketplace and demonstrate that you are able to execute to that strategy. In addition to communication, strategic deployment of resources and capabilities is essential. It is important to understand how to deploy human assets for maximum effectiveness, putting "strategy people" in the strategic roles and "execution people" in the execution roles.

- How much time should a CEO allocate to intangible assets management? What other areas should CEOs spend time on?

My time is spent identifying people for specific roles, motivating people, structuring and executing deals with partners or clients, talking with the investment community, and trying to outthink the competition creatively, because in most cases you're not going to be able to capture the market by being first; you'll have to capture it by being best. It's going to be your ability to execute in the marketplace that makes the difference between success and failure. A CEO has to have a very well-balanced perspective because there are so many different aspects to an organization; bringing those perspectives into focus toward execution of a common business objective demands balance. Some CEOs focus too much on one aspect of the company's business; and that can be the downfall of a company. For example, a CEO can be too focused on sales and not on execution, or product development, or communicating to the investment community about how a product will add value. All these elements must work together; it is not effective to emphasize one to the exclusion of the others. Another critical skill for CEOs is decisiveness. In today's environment, you've got to make decisions quickly. You've got to be able to read people very quickly and evaluate whether they are telling you exactly what you need to know or if you need to dig deeper in order to make a good, informed decision. Not making a decision is usually worse than making a wrong decision, because if you make a wrong decision, at least you are headed in a direction—and you can always alter your path accordingly. You can't just tread water; sooner or later you have to swim, or you'll drown.

- What career experiences helped to prepare you for the CEO role?

I was global managing partner for supply chain at Accenture, my former employer. In this operational role, I was responsible for building and setting the strategic direction for Accenture's global supply chain management practice—a $9 billion organization worldwide. As we worked to build this practice within Accenture's partnership structure, I had to get a lot of different people to be on the same page and working together in the same direction. Then, we had to ensure that we were putting the right people in the right places—worldwide—and get them focused very quickly on the organizational strategy. We ended up building the largest supply chain practice group worldwide, and for that I am very proud. I believe having confidence in your knowledge of your market, knowing who the players are, and what kinds of strategies work in that space are key skills to develop. These kinds of skills will always be useful, in any environment. Being in a professional services environment also taught me to be very detail oriented. Some people have the misconception that once you rise to the CEO position, you can step back and not be involved in details. The reality is that if you are CEO, chances are you know your business better than anyone else and as domain expert, you are best qualified to set the direction of the company and to make the right strategic moves that will drive results.

- How is your leadership philosophy disseminated throughout
  the organization?

Everybody belongs to a leadership group within the company. I have two within my direct sphere. One is an executive committee, which is the strategic body of this company and consists of the organization's top executives. The second one is our operating committee, and that is made up of several additional executives who, along with the executive committee, are responsible for day-to-day operations. Thus, I interact with our top managers on a daily basis. Each one of these executives, in turn, has his or her own leadership teams and is responsible for mentoring and developing the leadership skills of those team members, as well as determining how best to manage and execute within their respective area of the company.

- Can you walk us through the transformation you led at Manugistics?

Within the first 30 days, we wrote a strategic plan for the company. We embarked on a program to formalize how we would go to market in all aspects of the business so that the strategy was clearly understood throughout the company. The main element of the strategic plan was heavy investment in our products and solutions so that we could generate substantial results in the marketplace. Once the investments had been made, we could start to take the lead in market share and then differentiate our organization. Investments were focused, shifting from a "product" emphasis to a "solutions" emphasis. We weren't selling software modules, we were selling solutions for getting greater inventory returns or for taking working capital out of your business, or for having higher customer service and customer fill rates. Also, we realized that the Internet allows us to make real-time, informed decisions, and it facilitates cross-enterprise optimization. Our focus going forward was going to entail a change from an applications-only company to a business-to-business e-commerce company. We developed software that gave us the edge in the B2B marketplace, as well as optimization solutions software. Finally, we had to change our orientation from a technically driven one to one driven by sales and marketing. So, after developing good software, we had to get it into the marketplace and we had to build the image and the brand awareness in the marketplace.

• **Did you have a people strategy as well?**

We had a number of people strategies. I brought in a new human resources director at the very beginning, somebody I believed would be in touch with what our people needed and could guide the growth of the organization accordingly. We needed to communicate where we were going with the company, in order to start building confidence among our people that the company was under the right leadership and that they were going to be able to make the changes necessary to grow the company. So we brought in a number of experts in specific areas of organizational development, people who also possessed the communications skills, style, integrity, mentoring ability, and other leadership qualities that were important to us. We opened up Manugistics University. We put all of our people through functionally specialized training courses. By demonstrating that we were making investments in our people as well as our technology, we created an atmosphere that had a positive influence on the way we executed our strategy. This series of strategies is ongoing, because to maintain success, an organization must constantly work at recruiting, developing, and nurturing its intangible assets.

Leadership by influencing many, controlling few

Steele Alphin
Bank of America Corporation
Principal Personnel Executive

• **How do you define leadership?**

We view leadership as a responsibility. The very best leaders are good listeners with a strong sense of caring about people and winning. We look for and develop leaders here who have the courage and ability to be catalysts of change. Just being in the right place at the right time doesn't define or guarantee any type of success. During times of great change, there should be less pressure on leaders to create this wonderful straight-line vision that gets everybody to the rainbow. Your responsibility is to observe, listen, change course, secure better resources, prepare yourself and others to lower the risk of losing, and be forthright about your position. You can't go through a time where you conveniently lead and then conveniently disappear. Leading is a full-time responsibility. It's a great motivator if you care deeply about your company, your associates, your shareholders, and yourself. Success comes about as a result of leading in our company, industry, and community. Leaders have to be very tactical and very flexible. You can't lead and not manage. Outstanding management skills are necessary. The leader must also bring forth the right type of celebration when the group wins to create positive reinforcement. Leaders must have a tolerance for different leadership styles. We're becoming more diverse in our leadership styles, not necessarily in our value proposition. Our values won't change, but the application of those values will change because people are different. Leaders have a very introspective view of themselves, and they often ask themselves such questions as "What do I need to make this better? I'm not giving up anything. I'm adding." It's always additive. Additive, additive. Finally, leadership is influencing, not controlling. A good approach is to try to influence many, control a few. It's an interesting mix of skills, and it's knowing when to apply those skills that makes great leaders.

- **Your company has recruited outside of the financial services industry for expertise and leadership. What are the motivations to do this?**

Let me give you the bottom line: If you are an introspective leader, and you truly understand what you're trying to accomplish in the game you're a player in, it gets pretty simple. You buy skills that you don't have. You recruit people who give you a competitive advantage because of the skills they have, and the people who have those skills might not be in your industry; in fact, often they are outside your industry, and that alone can be a competitive advantage, given how quickly the competitive landscape can change these days. When we inventoried our skill base through our formal talent management process of evaluating the types of leadership we have, and we saw where there were gaping holes, where we needed different types of people, where we had not moved as we should have—those are the areas in which we sought the skills and experiences.

- **How do you integrate new people into the organization so they are quickly, in your phrase, "additive" to the team, performing beyond an individual level?**

Our approach to human capital is that it is an investment in people. Because our new people have to understand the size, scope, and scale of what we are trying to do as a company, it is to our advantage to provide a structured orientation program as well as mentoring. We create individual developmental plans for people. We monitor their performance for traction or slippage, and perform 360-degree feedback. We give them as much autonomy as possible, allowing for mistakes because that's a great way to learn. They must accelerate and flourish from Day One because we can't afford to lose people we've invested in. This is not new magic; it's just putting the pieces together as a package.

- While you're focusing on business transformation, new leadership models, and recruiting, you run the risk of losing focus on retaining your existing talent. How can you balance the integration of new skills and talent while at the same time cultivate either a new set of skills internally or give the embedded leadership team a platform to move forward?

We look at both a person's current performance and his or her potential to take on more responsibility. If a leader is not expandable, that is, able to take on more responsibility or an expanded role, then he or she has to be performing at an excellent or distinguished performance level. As long as the performance is strong, a person will have a long and fruitful career here. In fact, what we're finding is that our existing talent is energized by new teammates. Conversely, our new talent is impressed and energized by our existing talent, our culture, and our passion for winning. While we'll never forget what got us here in the first place, top-grading is now a way of life here. Everyone simply has to perform better. We value our meritocracy, and it's part of our commitment to ourselves and to the market that we're going to do certain things.

- Competitive advantage today is gained through people, innovation, and the ability to change dynamically with the marketplace. How do you create an innovative culture that's designed to change?

Because of the way we are spread out geographically, we've made investments in select technologies that serve as communication mediums. For instance, we've built an Associate Portal to facilitate customized information sharing among our associates. We are rolling out our Investment Cafe concept in select locations. One of the most effective ways to create this kind of culture, though, is to celebrate and reward people for solving problems. We've looked for people with cognitive skills via specific disciplines they have through academic training or their innate ability to think multidimensionally—people whose abilities lean toward problem-solving. With respect to a culture where people are motivated to win, there's always something you should stop doing because it's either run its course or it doesn't add value anymore, either because the game has changed or the mix of what we've got to do has changed. So, if you have a standard of excellence, you need to be very clear about what you're intolerant of. We'll be intolerant of office politics, intolerant of people who don't want to participate, intolerant of people who take advantage of their teammates, intolerant of people who are rude and unprofessional to their teammates and customers. In addition to a very clear and great rewards system, there should be an equally understood and strong disciplinary system.

- Napoleon said, "I tell people 'Go into battle' and they go into battle. But if I give them a piece of the yellow ribbon, they'll go into battle and die for me."

Yes, Napoleon had some interesting thoughts on leadership, which have played through historically to be more profound than people might have thought. He also believed that leaders are simply merchants of hope. They provide hope, they sell hope, and with that hope, leaders are responsible for defining a purpose, a means to achieve goals, and the rewards for results. That piece of yellow ribbon is nothing more than hope. And nothing less.

Leadership by mentoring

Linda Sanford
IBM Corporation
Senior Vice President and Group Executive, Storage Systems Group

- What is your leadership philosophy?

I really am a strong believer that you have to very quickly and proactively put the right business strategy in place. The team needs to know where it's headed. Once you have that strategy in place, you can realign your systems and your processes to support it and ensure that the things you're doing on a day-to-day basis are going to lead you to that end game there. Another key element in my view is making sure that you have the A-team on the field and that you focus its attention to the correct measures and data that let you know on a real-time basis how you are progressing against that strategic road map. Once you have all the fundamentals in place, it becomes a matter of constant coaching—coaching, coaching, coaching along the way. My leadership approach is a very open one. I have candid dialogues with my senior team on a regular basis. I try to take advantage of the specific talents of the team members. I choose a team for the perspectives, experiences, skills, and knowledge the individuals bring to the table and, very important, their ability to integrate with each other. I also try to be supportive of folks, especially in stressful times. I'm not a crack-the-whip kind of leader; I treat people with dignity and respect. My teams are held accountable for the end result. This really does motivate people to get the job done.

- **Have the skill sets to be successful as a leader changed over the past few years?**

There clearly have been some changes, and there is a need for more skills in today's world. Some leadership skills are fundamental and unchanging throughout time, no matter how business changes: good coaching and good mentoring of people, for example. Now, leaders need to add to their skill set a knowledge of technology and how to leverage technology to enable you to do your job more effectively and efficiently. From my experience here, there's a lot more focus on working across organizations and therefore needing to manage what I would call organizational interfaces and integrations—not only within your company, but also extending your influence beyond that into alliances and partnerships. Also, today's businesses are much more global. Whether in terms of your business operations or your customers, you need to able to address and accept differences in culture, in work habits, and in customer demands.

- **IBM is right up there with GE, American Express, Procter & Gamble, and others in developing great leaders. What is the role of the HR department in today's organization?**

We made a transition in the way we think about people and developing people. For example, in my storage systems group, we have a team of very bright and highly skilled HR professionals whom we deploy in each of the storage systems business units to partner with our line executives so that they can get a very good sense of the business issues, the business challenges, and the business priorities. They focus on four things. One is what we call organizational climate, whereby you create the environment that fosters the type of performance for which you are looking. The second thing they focus on is talent, and our HR team helps us identify sources to fill gaps in skills. The third thing the HR team will focus on is leadership and how we can continue to identify and develop our leaders. Finally, the HR team helps us measure the performance of our entire team against the objectives we set. None of these steps is done in a vacuum; we have integrated the HR community with the business line leaders. The transactional HR stuff like benefits, compensation, and administration is handled in a centralized fashion by three groups, one in the United States, one in Europe, and one in Asia. That leaves my HR team focused on the strategic partnering with our business leaders.

- Have you identified positions within your group or within IBM that are truly developmental positions?

Leadership potential and development depends on the individual in many respects, and on what experience and skill bases he or she has. We try to nurture professionals with specialist skills into more general managers and, in the process of doing that, we try to give them experience that helps broaden their skill bases. Often, this means putting them in a variety of functions. My background, for example, is in product development. Then, along the way, I moved into strategy for one piece of the business, our worldwide sales team. That gave me a better appreciation of the products because it helped me understand how the salespeople sell them day in and day out.

- What is your advice to people who want to pursue a career as a leader?

I was very fortunate early on in my career because I had a mentor. All people who are striving to run significant pieces of a business need to have a mentoring relationship, and it should start as early in the career as possible. Your mentors can change over time. I've been here for 27 years now, and, at one point, when I had taken over the global sales job, I was meeting on a monthly basis with [Chairman] Lou Gerstner himself, getting valuable coaching and mentoring. Mentoring is very, very critical because it is another mechanism to get feedback and input on different styles and approaches of business kinds of issues. I also think it's important to be proactive in asking your boss for a coaching relationship. You never know everything clearly, so establishing a give-and-take coaching relationship with your boss in addition to a mentoring relationship—which tends to be from someone outside your direct line—is a wonderful way to learn. As we progress in our careers, there's a human tendency to believe that we are deemed successful only if we have the authority to run something. It's important to recognize that a person can lead from any position. You don't have to be the boss to make an impact. Younger executives need to realize that you can have a significant influence on the direction of a business from any position. It's all about your behavior and the leadership skills that you demonstrate on a particular project. There is no replacement for having self-confidence. Set examples and be responsible.

- What trends do you see in terms of leadership?

There is an interesting dynamic that has been going on relating to leadership. Leadership going forward is not focused on one individual; group leadership or team leadership will become the critical game-changer. Business today is integrated across a value chain of partners and customers and suppliers, and it has become very complex and fast-changing. Our reach is now very extensive, and as a result, a new paradigm of distributed leadership is most effective. We won't have one very strong person leading the charge; there will be leadership across a team of senior executives who are going to be bringing the experience, the talent, and the expertise to the business.

The difference between leaders and managers

John P. Kotter
Harvard Business School
Retired Konosuke Matsushita Professor of Leadership

- What is the difference between leadership and management?

Management is a set of processes designed to make something work over time. In business, that means management is designed to help you produce a product or a service on customers' expectations, day after day, week after week, month after month. Those processes may involve planning, budgeting, building an organization, measuring, testing, investing, executing on plans, and problem-solving. The more people you involve, the more difficult it is to execute these processes efficiently. Leadership is very different. Leadership is, most fundamentally, about change. What leaders do is create the systems and organizations that managers need, and, eventually, elevate them up to a whole new level or, more often these days, help them change in some basic ways to take advantage of new opportunities. Most often, leadership creates a picture of the future or a vision or some sense of strategy, a primary strategy for achieving that vision, of making sure enough people understand it and buy into it and then creating the conditions that motivate them to act.

- What are the key skills of a great manager and a great leader, respectively?

It's hard to be a great manager unless you're a very systematic person who has at least a minimum capacity to think in structured, linear and logical ways. You must have a lot of discipline because to keep the system working well means to create discipline within it, which requires discipline within you. It requires great problem-solving ability, too. Leadership is, again, very different from that in the skills needed to be successful. Foremost is the capacity to see ahead and to grapple with very basic questions such as "What's the point?" Great leaders have the capacity to communicate broad notions about purpose and direction so that people not only hear and understand, but connect on some deeper, emotional level as well. Emotionally related skills associated with helping people tap into their sources of energy and helping them to break through boundaries are also very important for great leaders.

- **Why do many companies find it difficult to institutionalize leadership?**

There are enormous pressures on firms—from employees, from customers, and from the financial community—to be well managed. These in turn place huge pressures on companies to find, promote, and train people who have managerial skills. If you just give in to those pressures, you won't end up with much in terms of leadership behavior or leadership skills. What some smart companies have done—especially in an age of change—is create mechanisms that allow them to bring in and develop people who make great leaders while also meeting the demands for managerial skills.

- **Can people be great managers and great leaders, or are they typically different individuals?**

Almost everybody has potential for both, but some people are a lot more skilled in one than the other. Some people who do very well in life develop their potential in both areas as far as they can, and that means they end up fabulous managers and pretty darn good leaders. Fewer people, probably, end up as fabulous leaders and pretty good managers.

- **Should companies distinguish between management and leadership in creating their education and development programs?**

If you look at the formal educational efforts, or the criteria and processes for promotion, or if you look at the informal processes of how people are coached and mentored, for example, you will find, in a whole lot of companies, that 80 percent of the efforts are applied toward management skills and 20 percent to leadership development. Believe it or not, that's better than it was 10 or 15 years ago, when there were protected bureaucracies—protected in the sense of large market shares in capital-intensive industries where entry barriers are high, and the spilt was more like 95 percent management and 5 percent leadership. However, as pressures mount from the outside world, companies are forced to change, and this starts the shift to a deeper focus on a company's ability to nurture great leaders.

- **What role does the trusted advisor play for CEOs or someone emerging in a leadership position?**

One of the things that people learn when they start developing their leadership potential is that it helps enormously to have a broad network of relationships from which they can draw for lots of reasons. I don't mean having a full Rolodex—because those are just people whom you barely know—but true relationships that help you learn. Possible advisors would include people within the organization as well as external mentors such as university professors or other CEOs, but people who are seen on a regular basis. A great example is Jack Welch using Scott McNealy, the chairman and CEO of Sun Microsystems, as an advisor. Here is an example of a seasoned leader learning from a member of the younger generation who has some real wisdom about how to do things in today's world. It is okay, even desirable, to ignore age boundaries and other social hierarchies. It doesn't matter who your advisors are, as long as you build a web of relationships in which you can be nourished and learn. The true leader looks beyond status incongruities and strives to learn from the richest sources.

Leading by creating a values-based culture and inspiring commitment

David S. Pottruck
The Charles Schwab Corporation
President and Co–Chief Executive Officer

When I was asked to contribute to this book on the subject of leadership, I thought immediately of a remark that master strategist Gary Hamel made to the Schwab executive committee several years ago. We were discussing the ingredients for the success of new business ventures. Gary said that since all business plans and spreadsheets look pretty much alike, good venture capitalists ask a new entrepreneur only three critical questions: "What is the value to the market?" "Can it be scaled for profitability?" and finally, "Is this the most important thing in your life?" According to Gary, if the answer to the last question is not "Yes," then the answers to the other two don't matter much and the start-up should not be funded.

To me this observation is a memorable commentary on the importance of leadership in this new exciting commercial world we are part of. Leadership has become more personal and at the same time more public than ever before, and the Internet and its technological cousins have created an environment that places a premium on inspiration and commitment. Of course, competence is still required, but competence alone is no longer enough to create and sustain competitive advantage.

Not long ago, the founders of first-stage companies could sustain commitment from their employees with a "garage-to-penthouse" dream, at least for a little while. But the penthouse staircase has become much steeper in the last few years. The new, more sobering reality finds technology workers asking for more cash than options, and acting again as if they are merely bundles of skill, for sale to the highest bidder. In the absence of the promise of getting rich quickly, the importance of real leadership has again been magnified. In our book *Clicks and Mortar*, Terry Pearce and I explored the characteristics of leadership in this environment, and we have continued to add to our understanding since the book's publication at the turn of the century. As a context, we believed that a leader had to institutionalize the ability to change by building loyalty so strong that employees would take risks and contribute every single day, and customers would stay with a company because their overall experience of that company was superior, in a qualitative way, to others. This new leadership even requires the alignment of traditional business disciplines so that they are not just business functions but tools to inspire everyone to contribute even more. At Charles Schwab, we have managed to create a company that is close to this model, and we believe our ability to continue to do so is our fundamental competitive advantage. The leadership characteristics that I view as most essential have to do with building culture through character and communication.

The Ability to Create Culture on Purpose

While we might disagree on what is fundamental to a culture, we know for sure what it does. Culture binds people together as a group, causes them to defend that civilization over time, and makes it thrive as an entity. A civilization's culture evolves over decades or centuries and is usually resolved by wars and successions. In a twenty-first-century company, culture has to be created and sustained on purpose by its leaders, and, as we have discovered, it has to be able to survive and be tempered in tough times, including times that require rapid fiscal adjustments and downsizing.

In the corporate world, many mistake culture for style. Culture is not style. Culture is not beer busts on Friday and casual dress, nor is it suits and ties and conservative offices. These can be the images that reflect the culture, but they are not themselves the culture. Culture is rather a set of values, a purpose that focuses on something greater than the individual, a common language that expresses those values, and the actions that make them real. It is vital in today's world, as it provides four functions, as follows, that institutionalize the ability to change.

Culture Transforms Change to Progress.   First, culture provides a foundation of what does not change to allow everything else to change rapidly. People hate change, but they love progress. The difference between the two is purpose, and culture provides that purpose. Without a stable culture, change can seem negative, random, and meaningless. With a stable culture, even the most difficult change can be seen as positive, targeted, and meaningful.

Culture Is the Reason We Work Together.   Second, culture provides a basis for alignment. One of the truths of the fast-paced world is that working together is more effective than working alone. Whether you are an independent contractor or an employee of a firm, you have to be aligned behind a common understanding in order to take a role among many rather than trying to go it alone. The former GE chairman Jack Welch claims that his success was built largely on his ability to create an environment in which people will share best practices. When people are united around a purpose and a set of values, they are less inclined to overvalue their own agendas. Culture provides that alignment, that common goal that is larger than the individual.

Culture: A Virtual Procedures Manual.   Third, culture provides a filter for daily practice of the business, a quick decision tool for action at a time when we certainly can't write procedures fast enough. "Doing the right thing" is a powerful measuring stick for everyone to use as they make quick, effective decisions. We know from research at the University of Santa Clara that people who know their own values are more likely to become strongly committed to the goals of the company and will make decisions that reflect them. Culture encourages the discovery and application of values every single day.

Culture: Creating Loyalty Rather Than Satisfaction.   Finally, culture provides a way for the company to export the values of the firm to its customers and to its employees, and it creates loyalty in both. There is a distinction between satisfaction and loyalty: Satisfaction comes from what you do; loyalty comes from who you are. When customers and employees believe in your company's values, its integrity, its intention to serve them, its trustworthiness, they don't want to change firms because of a transaction; they want to stay with you and help you fix your problems. Loyal customers and employees will not only forgive some mistakes, they will help you do the repair because of their belief in your values and purpose. This is particularly important in difficult times, when decisions frequently create hardships for employees.

So the new leader has to first know the importance of creating culture and make it her priority to build a field where others will be able to do their best work. Then she has to develop the personal traits, skills, and behaviors that it takes to inspire others to actually contribute, an ability that requires a combination of character and communication, and the willingness to deploy herself liberally throughout the organization.

Character: Who You Are Counts More Than Ever

The Internet makes it possible for everyone to know nearly everything, including people's opinions, unsupported or not. It's not just politicians who have their integrity scrutinized, it is anyone who exercises any authority. Last year, if you wanted a lesson in vulnerability, you could have visited mybosssucks.com. This site did not survive the "dot bomb," yet its function was a portent. On this site, anyone could enter comments about his boss, by location, by company, by name. In the same way that the Internet holds our companies' brands to the fire, it holds our personal character to the fire as well. Prior to the Internet, only media and word-of-mouth spread the news. Now, anyone can publish anything, worldwide, instantly.

Building character is not just a matter of managing the news. It is a matter of personally discovering what matters, and making a constant and conscious effort to act in a way that is consistent with the values that you espouse. I refer to this process around three characteristics: responsibility, integrity, and generosity of spirit.

Responsibility simply means interpreting your espoused values spiritually rather than legalistically. The body of ethics behind the law is infinitely more important than the law itself, and people recognize and despise deceit draped in a defense of "wordsmithing." Conversely, responsibility does not mean rigidity or never changing. It really means being "able to respond" to the values, regardless of the situation.

At Schwab, we are constantly looking for new ways to express our values without compromising them. For example, we have built the company on the principle of "no conflict of interest." For many years, we defined that principle as "we will not give investment advice," because we equated advice with the old-line practice of selling hot stocks to maximize brokerage commissions. When we found that our customers were demanding advice from us, we realized that our business model, one that did not compensate brokers for sales, made it possible for us to give advice and continue to avoid conflict. We changed our practice to give the customers what they wanted, expert advice that is "objective, uncomplicated and not driven by commission," and at the same time we strengthened our commitment to our values. We feel that was a highly responsible change.

Integrity is the follow-through to responsibility: putting the values into action, even when no one is looking. Integrity is important, of course, to avoid being mentioned in some version of mybosssucks.com, but it is even more important as a personal way of life, as a way of modeling the kind of behavior you expect from others and from your company as a whole. It is a never-ending process.

Generosity of spirit means simply assuming goodwill and good intentions in other peoples' actions and communication. In an atmosphere where we are compelled to delegate, where we want to inspire people to act on their own in alignment with our values, such a default can make the difference between developing trusting, inspired employees and driving yourself and others absolutely crazy with second-guessing, doubt, and control. Generosity of spirit produces huge dividends, so naturally it is the most difficult aspect of leadership to develop. Our tendency as leaders is to look for problems to fix, to find what is wrong rather than what is right. But the assumption of competence and goodwill generates an optimism and trust that will fuel teamwork, loyalty, and, ultimately, tremendous growth in those we lead.

As email, voicemail, and other impersonal forms of communication become the norm, the assumption of goodwill becomes even more important. These new forms of communication are fraught with the potential for ambiguity. In fact, such ambiguity was the focus of an insightful article in the *Harvard Business Review*, written by the psychiatrist Edward Hallowell. He makes a compelling case that techno-communication from people who otherwise do not know each other may well actually spread tension and misunderstanding. These channels provide little visceral feedback, little experience of the real person who is communicating. Given the dominance of these new ways of connecting, personal leadership communication has taken on greater importance than ever before. The twenty-first-century leader will have to match the increase in volume of information with his or her own ability to communicate personally.

Leadership communication, to actually move people to act, must be both authentic and frequent. It is a rare combination of listening and speaking that lets others know you care, and inspires them with possibilities that they may not, without you, be able to see.

Inspiring Commitment Rather Than Requiring Compliance

"Inspire" means to "breathe life into," and since it is impossible to breathe life into anyone else unless you have it in yourself, the leader's first task is to align his own passion with the business. If his personal legacy is connected to the business, and if he is able to communicate his passion and conviction, he will be able to inspire commitment in others. Ask any group to name leaders who meet the criteria of inspiring change, and you will hear names like Gandhi, Martin Luther King, Nelson Mandela, Abraham Lincoln, and Anwar Sadat. These leaders also share other commonalties: They either spent a great deal of time in jail, were killed for their trouble, or both. Their conviction energized everyone, even their enemies, who appropriately feared the power of their character and communication. While few of us will have the right venue to change the world at the scale of these leaders, we can clearly take a lesson from their own communication. It was grounded in their personal commitment to the cause.

At Schwab, we see leadership communication as a special skill. It is not merely the passing of information but also the transmission of inspiration. Leadership communication is about change, and it includes links to both corporate and personal objectives, both strategy and values, both clarity and depth, both purpose and meaning. The new leader is both decisive and empathetic. She speaks from both the head and the heart, but she also listens better than ever before.

Trust is built through knowing that a leader cares about you. A leader simply has to be able to see and acknowledge other points of view, value them, and communicate appreciation for them. The focus is not merely on answering questions but rather on responding to people. The effective and authentic communicator knows the difference between the questions "Did he hear you?" and "Do you feel heard?" One is a transaction, the other is a connection; and it is connection that inspires people to do their best work.

The twenty-first-century leader is surely different from the leaders of the last two decades. The Internet has placed real power in the hands of people around the world. It has increased the possibilities for millions to do the work that enlivens them. There will be little loyalty to people or to organizations that are not worthy. No longer do pension plans and benefits create chains that hold people in one spot. To create loyalty in such an environment, the new leader will understand how to create a compelling culture, one that will allow people to contribute their best. He or she will then communicate meaning and trustworthiness in every word and action. Culture, character, and communication are the cornerstones of today's new leadership.

Chapter 2

Managing Human Capital

Integrating human capital strategies
into the overall business strategy

John Hagel
Business Consultant and Author

Three trends are converging that explain the abundant demand for qualified talent today, as follows:

1. *Performance demands—especially growth demands—on business are increasing.* Technological and regulatory forces are combining to create more demanding markets. Technology, especially the growth of electronic markets, inexorably shifts power from vendor to customer, leading to the emergence of reverse markets in which companies must deliver more value at lower prices just to stay in the game. Technological and regulatory forces are also restructuring financial markets, creating more demanding investors who richly reward companies that deliver higher levels of performance and severely punish those that don't. In this kind of environment, companies must increasingly focus on growth in order to continue to create value. Cost-cutting is necessary but not sufficient, since the cost savings will be competed away in reverse markets and captured by the customer.

2. *Surplus is shifting from a structural advantage to a human capital advantage.* As corporations strive to deliver higher levels of performance, they are finding that the conventional ways of generating surplus are eroding in power. Sheer scale, which used to be a "game over" advantage, is shifting from an asset to a liability for many companies as nimble attackers slice and cherry-pick the most profitable business opportunities. Other structural advantages such as geographic position and regulatory protection are similarly eroding. In their place, we are seeing companies recognize that human capital often turns out to be the winning variable. Strategies based on privileged insight or

superior front-line execution tend to be more powerful in dynamic markets where structural advantages lose their power. Technology and regulatory discontinuities are prying open once stable markets and rewarding companies that mobilize human capital effectively.

3. *Shortages in key skill sets/experience become the bottleneck to value creation.* As companies begin to recognize the importance of human capital in implementing more aggressive, growth-oriented strategies, they are also confronting the shortage of executive talent necessary to provide both insight and executional experience. Executives who have spent a lifetime in stable industry settings often bring mindsets and habits that are difficult to adapt to more dynamic, growth-oriented environments. Conversely, executives who have achieved success in such environments often lack the breadth of insight or experience to ensure success on a repeated basis. In an environment where discontinuities create many opportunities for growth and where investment funds are plentiful, executive talent increasingly represents the bottleneck, making it difficult for the investment funds to connect most productively with the opportunities.

What can companies do about these trends? As talent increases its ability to capture value, companies will need to rethink their businesses on a profound level. This includes even the most basic question of all: What business are we really in? Perhaps the most significant challenge involves the need to adopt a different mindset. Rather than looking at cost-cutting and automation as ways to cope, businesses will need to focus on accelerating growth as a way to reward talent and increase returns to the business at the same time. Rather than focusing on attracting and retaining talent, companies will need to concentrate on developing privileged relationships with talent, wherever it may reside.

Arbitrage Talent

Companies will need to become adept at talent arbitrage as a way to reward and develop talent. Talent arbitrage involves creating aggressive growth platforms and shifting talent from low-growth to high-growth environments.

In order to maximize rewards for talent, talent must be positioned to create as much value as possible. Low-growth environments inherently cap the value-creation potential of talent—no matter how much effort they apply, the "headroom" available for value creation will be much more limited in low-growth environments. Some businesses can be reconfigured to provide higher growth potential; in other cases, talent arbitrage may involve shifting talent out of a low-growth business and into a higher-growth business.

Why are aggressive growth platforms so important for talent? First, growth increases the value that talent can add to the business, thereby providing an opportunity to increase the financial reward for talent. Second, growth accelerates the development of talent. Talent gains exposure to a broader range of experiences in a shorter period of time. Growth also demands more hiring, so existing talent gains an opportunity to work closely with other talent coming from the outside with a different set of experiences. Third, talent can advance more quickly in high-growth organizations, giving talent an opportunity not only for additional financial upside but, equally important, an opportunity to develop even more rapidly.

New entrants into relatively stable markets often owe much of their success to the opportunity to engage in talent arbitrage. By targeting talent in lower-growth incumbents and providing them with much higher-growth business platforms, attackers can significantly increase the rewards, both financial and developmental, for talent. Low-growth companies become very vulnerable to talent arbitrage, a vulnerability that can only be addressed by creating higher growth platforms of their own.

Leverage Talent

Companies must also become more and more creative in accessing talent that does not reside within their own companies. In a world of talent scarcity, the notion that a company can hope to attract and retain all the world-class talent it needs must be aggressively challenged. Other mechanisms must be found to provide privileged access to world-class talent. Senior management must broaden well beyond attraction-and-retention talent strategies to focus much more attention on mobilization-and-alignment talent strategies.

Outsourcing options can often be powerful ways to gain access to the best-in-class skills and experience. The outsourcing trend is still relatively new. As electronic networks make it easier to coordinate activities across corporate boundaries and as performance pressures increase the need to deliver higher levels of performance, companies are starting to outsource not only specific activities but also entire business processes.

Mindset again becomes a barrier to more rapid growth of outsourcing activity. In too many large companies, senior management puts the burden of proof on the outsourcing proponent and insists on cost reduction as the only basis for proving that outsourcing is a superior option. Instead, what is required is a shift in the burden of proof: activities should be outsourced unless opponents can prove that their company has unique capabilities in the areas involved. Rather than looking to cost reduction as the only rationale for outsourcing, senior management must recognize that outsourcing can often be a powerful way to accelerate growth.

Outsourcing is only one option for leveraging talent residing outside the company. Even more powerful means are available. Few companies understand, much less have harnessed, the power of business webs to create privileged access to talent. In contrast to more conventional alliances or joint ventures, business webs rely on economic incentives to mobilize large numbers of companies (often in the thousands or hundreds of thousands) to support the strategies of web shapers. By understanding what economic incentives are necessary to motivate action and then building platforms that create these economic incentives, a web shaper can gain privileged access to a very broad range of talent. Microsoft is the classic example of a web shaper, but business web opportunities exist in a broad range of business contexts.

Other examples of talent leverage involve the development of user groups and alumni networks. In the computing and software industry, user groups are well-established mechanisms to harness the insight and experience of customers to help technology providers focus their innovation efforts on the most promising unmet needs of the market. Alumni networks tend to convert employee turnover from a liability into an asset. Rather than focusing exclusively on retention, senior management should determine what they could do to build relationships with talented executives who have left the company. How can the talents of these departed executives be harnessed to provide continuing support for the company? In the professional services arena, McKinsey & Company has demonstrated considerable initiative in building and maintaining a robust alumni network.

What Business Are You Really In?

The increasing need to access and reward talent provides a catalyst for many companies to redefine their business in order to become more attractive to talent. For example, in order to identify more aggressive growth platforms, many companies are being forced to challenge traditional definitions of their business.

Companies seeking to leverage third-party talent more aggressively will also be motivated to redefine their business. Deciding whether to hire and develop internal talent or to access third-party talent hinges on the ability to decide what is truly unique to the business and what is secondary for the business. This in turn depends on management's definition of the business. Computer hardware companies used to invest substantial assets in manufacturing facilities. Increasingly, they are outsourcing manufacturing operations while focusing more on the design and marketing of computer products. Some of the more advanced, such as Dell and Gateway, are using the Internet to concentrate on building customer relationship businesses that eventually may become their primary business focus.

Business webs are perhaps the most powerful mechanism available to leverage third-party talent. In order to succeed, the web shaper must have a clear business focus and communicate this effectively to potential participants. In the early days of the Local Area Network (LAN) business, Novell took the radical step of redefining itself from a broad-based LAN product vendor to a more tightly focused LAN software business, and in the process divested more than 80 percent of its existing revenue base. By focusing more tightly, Novell increased economic incentives for a broader range of participants in its business web and deepened its ability to lead the market.

The need to access and reward talent will lead to a redefinition of existing businesses, but it will also lead to the creation of new kinds of businesses. Talent agents, representing talent to extract more value from employers, will spread from the world of entertainment and sports into the broader business world. Talent arbitrageurs, acting as third-party agents akin to today's venture capitalists, will work on extracting talent from low-growth organizational environments and will help build high-growth business platforms to reward talent more effectively. Talent accelerators will develop specialized businesses focused on building lifetime relationships with talent in order to implement talent development and coaching programs designed to make their clients even more valuable over time.

More broadly, we are likely to see new forms of operating companies emerge, seeking to mobilize, align, and integrate talent across a portfolio of companies in order to maximize value for the companies as well as the talent. Unlike the financial conglomerates of the past, which largely focused on redeploying financial capital across a portfolio of businesses, these new operating companies are focusing on addressing the growing bottleneck of management talent. The recent craze around incubators provides a glimmer of the opportunity available, even though many of today's "incubators" lack the depth and breadth of talent required to deliver on the potential.

The growing pressure to attract and reward talent will accelerate all of these changes. It must be emphasized, though, that these changes are not only in the interests of talent—they are in the interests of all businesses. Just as the greater liquidity of financial capital is forcing companies around the world to raise the bar in terms of operating and financial performance, the increasing shortage of management talent will force companies to leverage assets (especially human capital) more effectively and to identify and pursue new sources of growth more aggressively. We will all—as talent, as customers, and as stakeholders in companies—benefit from the rewards created by higher levels of corporate performance.

The leaders featured in this chapter emphasize the importance of aligning a defined human capital strategy with an organization's overall business strategy. As corporations continue to unbundle their physical assets and shift toward leveraging intangible assets, we are going to see an accelerated trend of companies establishing competitive advantage through their knowledge workers, both as full-time employees and, increasingly, as outsourced talent. As this trend continues to evolve, so will the importance of the human resources function. Two overarching themes in the chapter are diversity of talent and the growing strategic importance of the people function.

Diversity of Talent

Diversity of talent in this context takes a broad view, including diversity of ideas, diversity of thinking, diversity of experiences and backgrounds, and cultural diversity. Steve Reinemund of PepsiCo says: "Not only is diversity the right thing socially; it can be quantified as a good business decision." Ken Lewis of Bank of America has looked outside the traditional financial services for talent, bringing in best-of-class people from the consumer products, logistics, and manufacturing sectors to push the boundaries of thinking inside his firm. Bill Coleman of BEA Systems declares that "strategic external hires can take your company to the next level," and in fact, several of these leaders may continually seek talented people even when no formal position is open.

Strategic People Management

The relationship a corporation has with its talent will continue to evolve as the information- and intellectual capacity–driven service economy unfolds. Given that reality, it is critically important that the people functions inside an organization are elevated to a position of strategic importance. Henry Mintzberg of McGill University abhors the term "human resources." He asserts, "As soon as you start thinking of people as human resources, you've taken the people level down to the information level and you're treating people as data or as things." Jeffrey Pfeffer of Stanford University points out: "There are countless examples in which a company has loads of amazingly talented people, yet they operate in a system where people aren't permitted to use their talents to the fullest." These experts agree not only that an effective people strategy incorporates values and philosophies that emphasize the importance of the workforce but also that it is essential to have a set of management practices that make those values real through actions as well as words. One way to achieve this is to have the HR function tied in at the operating committee level.

Steven Kerr of Goldman Sachs and Heinrich von Pierer of Siemens advocate strategic executive education and shaping a company into a "learning organization" to connect individuals and increase the exchange of tacit knowledge, a clear competitive advantage in the information age.

Steve Reinemund
PepsiCo
Chairman and Chief Executive Officer

• What is your approach to leadership?

A leader's job is to define an overall direction and motivate others to get there. Most companies have relatively few people doing a lot of the important work, but in an organization such as ours, a lot of people are involved in everything we do. PepsiCo's heritage is that we've only had four CEOs in 40-some-odd years, but each of our businesses is autonomous, with many leaders running each one. My leadership style has changed over time because what needs to be done continually changes. When I was running a division, my role was very different from running a corporation of our size and diversity; so, along the way, I had to re-evaluate what leadership characteristics were needed for the job at hand. Few people recognize that when their job changes, their style should change as well. As a division president, for instance, you can be more direct and tactical; as a CEO, your role is more like that of a coach and a coordinator of other leaders. You are motivating and enabling a larger group of people who are running the business.

• What will be your contribution to PepsiCo's heritage?

We've evolved over time as a place that develops people. My predecessor, Roger Enrico, spent a lot of time on executive development programs. By the time I finish here, I hope to have added some real value in that area as well, but one place in particular I believe deserves more emphasis is workforce diversity. If we fail to arrive at our goals in the next few years regarding diversity and the ethnic and cultural diversity of the organization, we will not continue to be a world-class consumer products company. If we achieve our goals, we will do so by virtue of our ability to replicate within our organization the demographics of our consumers in a way that no other company can. Several years ago, we were not unlike a lot of other companies in that our senior executive team was not very diverse. In effect, we were recruiting from a pool of only 34 percent of the [U.S.] population. While we did a pretty good job of attracting qualified people, we were limiting ourselves to a small portion of the available talent. We also had perspectives that allowed us to be successful only in certain marketplaces. For example, Frito-Lay had roughly 60 percent market share in the

United States as a whole, but, in urban markets, it was down in the thirties. When you get 60 percent overall market share, there are not a lot of avenues for incremental growth on a marketwide basis, so you try to figure out where else you can target. Urban markets are growing two to three times faster than suburban markets, and we basically weren't competing there because we didn't understand that consumer base. We were missing a huge opportunity. For us to win in that market, we have to have senior executives who have an appreciation for how to succeed with these consumers. With a diverse senior management, we also have the ability to attract other highly qualified people to come into the company by drawing from a larger talent pool. Not only is diversity the right thing socially, it can be quantified as good business. We have been recognized as a top place to work for minorities and women, but we still have further to go. To follow Roger's passion about developing people, we are augmenting our executive development programs with a diversity component. For example, we have developed a one-week leadership training course with UCLA where external and internal senior executives—myself included—teach and mentor minority executives.

- What role does learning play in your organization?

The great companies of the future depend on the outcomes of their learning programs today. I believe that learning goes beyond formal programs: it's really about how companies can get the best from their people. What most companies do is reward people who do well with certain businesses so that, over time, you keep getting rewarded until you stop performing, and you can stop performing for any number of reasons. What can unfortunately happen then is that a company will discard you rather than finding or creating a new role for you within the organization. Learning helps those executives continue to perform and add value when the roles they held previously no longer apply. That can only happen if you create a culture where it is accepted and rewarded if you take a different direction—across, down, over—and are successful there.

- Do you have a formal process in place for assessing the talent of an acquired company, and if so, who makes those decisions and reviews?

We all play a part in this, but I look to our human resources staff to take the lead. It is part of our acquisition intelligence-gathering strategy to assess the talent to some degree before we make the deal, as we negotiate the deal, and then certainly postacquisition, as well as to ensure that there is a good transition. We ask our search partners such as Heidrick & Struggles to give us a read on the talent in the target organizations, to identify the gaps and to help us evaluate and gather intelligence. Once we are able to actually meet the executives, we all spend a lot of time one-on-one to get to know their issues and aspirations—professional, personal, and financial—in an attempt to find the best possible fit for us all.

- Can you discuss innovation at PepsiCo? You have crafted a recent deal with Big Boy, which includes PepsiCo's developing and maintaining an extranet site to manage the relationship. Your introduction of Code Red has been an overwhelming success in the marketplace. Can you talk about building a culture that thrives on innovation and change?

First, it's a reality of the categories we're in. Fortunately for PepsiCo, the convenient food and beverages sector is very much the growth segment of consumer products. However, consumers are constantly looking for innovation and news and, of course, there are a host of fine companies who would love to fulfill their needs. We can only maintain our leadership position and continue to grow the categories if we are at the forefront of innovation. This means that we have to have a finely tuned understanding of emerging trends in our consumer base and an ability to develop new products and packages to meet these needs. It also means that we have to change the way we think and work to build new capabilities. Some examples of this include breaking down internal barriers between functions to improve our speed to market and bringing together different pieces of the organization to create new product and distribution opportunities. We need to focus on consumer needs and be nimble and creative in meeting them. Also, the answer doesn't always lie within the internal organization: some of our most successful innovations have come from alliances with external partners.

- Many companies are moving away from transactionally oriented human resources departments to a more strategic human capital management model that includes the transactional component but also leadership development, coaching, mentoring, executive education, career planning, talent acquisition, and retention. Is this the future of the HR function, and if so, why?

I believe it is the future of HR. One of the distinguishing features of PepsiCo is that our human resources function has played this kind of strategic partner role for many years. However, the competition for talent will only increase over the years to come, and this will place even more of a premium on excellence in this area, so the bar will continue to rise.

- Peggy Moore, your worldwide head of HR, is not a traditional HR executive; she has held very senior positions inside PepsiCo. Can you talk about this appointment and what it means for PepsiCo's human capital and leadership strategy?

Peggy did in fact spend several years in our HR function earlier in her career. However, she went on to build a very successful career in our finance function—first as one of the most respected investor relations heads in North America and then as treasurer of the PepsiCo Bottling Group. In appointing Peggy to this key role, I was getting the best of both worlds—a world-class business executive who also had depth in HR and could help to forge an even closer strategic alignment between our business goals and HR strategies. It also helped that she had enormous credibility with our senior business leaders. So far, I'm delighted with the way in which the HR function has driven new levels of innovation in our efforts to make PepsiCo an even more compelling place to work.

- What are specific elements of your leadership development plan for 2002?

I have two priorities for 2002. The first is to drive a stronger focus on talent development throughout PepsiCo—we need to be more rigorous in our succession planning and ensure that we have a rich pipeline of talent coming through to take on our senior leadership roles. I want to spend time with our emerging leaders to get to know them, understand their career aspirations, and help to provide them with the right developmental challenges. Second, at PepsiCo we believe that "Leaders Develop Leaders." As part of this program, I am planning a one-week leadership development program with some of our high-potential leaders in 2002; we're partnering with the Darden School of Business at the University of Virginia to develop the program, and I'm really looking forward to it.

Leadership by a holistic approach

Kenneth "Ken" D. Lewis
Bank of America Corporation
Chairman, President, and Chief Executive Officer

- When hiring or allocating talent, which takes priority, brains or business experience?

What perplexes me at times is the disparity between IQ and business acumen. I've seen many examples of smart people who don't have good sense about the business world. I don't know what combination of instinct, intuition, intellect, experience, or interpersonal skills is perfect, but an individual's package of skills doesn't necessarily predict that the person with the highest IQ is going to be the best businessperson. I see this time and time again: very well-educated, well-heeled people who lack the proper business know-how. Having said that, within an executive's package of skills should be a passion about the business, a high energy level, a sense of competitiveness, street smarts, good intuition, common sense, and then a reasonable level of intellect.

- Using this approach to talent, Bank of America has built itself into one of the most admired companies, not just in financial services but across every industry. How do the passion, energy, intellect, and other qualities you seek in executives translate into making your organization a most admired employer and a most admired company?

We brand ourselves as the best place to work, the best place to bank, the best place to invest. We are making more than a casual attempt to approach this in a holistic way. You can't *just* talk about financials. You can't *just* talk about risk. You can't *just* talk about associates. You can't *just* talk about clients and customers. You have to think about your company in an integrated fashion and consider the interdependency of all the pieces. We and many other companies have a tendency to talk about financial results separately, or as something that just happens. The reality is that it's all tied together. Simply put, the associate has to interact with the customer or client and that drives revenue and income. So the first thing to do is focus in on actionable things that drive results as opposed to ethereal things like accounting results. Then, acknowledging and incorporating risk—not just credit risk as it relates to our business—but market risk and brand risk. Finally, the task of making a promise and then—here comes the hard part—delivering on it. That's what this integrated approach is all about because we can spend enough money and do enough research that we can make the promise pretty effective, but delivering on it means you have to be very focused on what your associates need and subsequently what your customers and clients need. That's a different way of looking at it from in the past, and it all gets back to measuring and reacting to things that are actionable.

- How do you disseminate your message throughout the organization?

One of the main duties of a leader—in particular, a CEO—is the ability to see the need for change, to articulate that need, and then to create excitement and buy-in about that need so that the team then can do the most important thing: execute. In the last two years, we've gone from a bank that grew by buying other banks to one that grows organically through deepening and improving relationships with our customers and clients. To deliver that message successfully, a leader must leverage the management team and make sure those leaders are committed and excited about the message, too. And the management team needs to communicate with you just as much as you do with them. You are only as strong as your weakest link, and a manager who doesn't communicate upward, downward, and sideways is a weak link. In the end, collective buy-in and support from your line managers is critical. Then you show results as early as possible that support the organization's progress in the new direction, and all the elements should come together, and it feeds on itself, becoming a successfully communicated and executed message.

- Speaking of your evolution, going from a company that has grown through acquisitions to a company that has grown organically, are there different leadership skills required of the CEO in this new environment, and also among the leadership within the company?

The previous model valued charisma. Being a charismatic leader, having excellent communication and negotiation skills, is still immensely important, but now you also have to be a good manager by knowing the business, paying attention to detail, and finding beauty and excitement in getting it right for customers and clients. You also have to find beauty and excitement in doing it better than before, day in and day out. The big excitement can't just be the episodic event of an acquisition, merger, or alliance of some sort. It has to be these day-in and day-out, grind-it-out things, which probably call for a different personality, a different person. Consider also that in the former model, a relatively small group of people had disproportionate influence on the success of the company. First, there was the negotiating person or team, and then there was the execution of the event and finally of the operational conversion. Many times, the way you succeeded was to get the deal first, and then do draconian things to cut enough expenses to make the numbers work. You rarely talked about revenue and, ironically, even built into your model how many customers you were going to lose that you found acceptable because you knew that during the operational conversion that was inevitable. Now, growing organically, you have a situation where there's not that disproportionate contribution by a small group, which means we all have to contribute on a more equitable scale. And all the soft things that leaders have to focus on become very important—those areas such as professional and leadership development, work and family and quality-of-life issues, whatever it is that gives your people a reason to be excited about waking up and going to work every day.

- You've gone outside the banking industry—to FedEx, GE, and
  Honeywell, for example—for some key people, bringing in world-class
  talent as opposed to just looking in the financial services industry.
  Why go outside your traditional industry for talent?

We want to be one of the world's great companies, not just one of the best companies in the financial services industry. Therefore, inherent in that goal, we believe there are standards and benchmarks that are higher in certain industries and in certain areas than in the financial services industry. We also, as we began to look at our processes from end to end, realized that we did not have enough talent internally, particularly people with engineering and Six Sigma backgrounds and qualities to really achieve the amount of change we needed or improvement we needed quickly enough. We clearly had embraced the importance of process and of breakthrough improvement, but we didn't have all the expertise or experience to get us where we needed to be. A lot of that kind of talent was found outside the financial services industry. Once on board, those new teammates with new skills made us more attractive to other top talent that we brought in and set world-class standards beyond the financial services industry. You end up with a set of people who push others out of their comfort zones and out of the inertia of doing things the old way. This is the catalyst for change.

- The risk associated with any change is the threat to your culture. How
  do you do inject new talent into your organization and yet sustain the
  part of your culture that people have always been able to recognize
  and thrive in?

It's salting the organization with new talent that strengthens your culture. Bringing in new perspectives augments the world-class talent base that has been with you for some time.

- Building your talent pool is an ongoing process. However, once
  your top talent is in place, how do you take it to the next level
  in terms of education, leadership training and development?

We have several ways we develop talent. First and foremost, we realize that an underlying part of leadership development is ongoing communication and dialogue among senior managers. We meet on a quarterly basis as a group to identify the specific need at the various levels, to talk about success stories and failures, and to talk about the process for change where change is necessary. It is important that my senior managers have my support in meetings for this purpose and for prioritizing this, and that they are allowed to network and meet people out-side of their areas and functions so they can continually be in a recruitment-and-development mode. We have leadership sessions all over the country. We spend a lot of time on talent planning to make sure we identify the high potential execu-tives, manage their assignments, ensure they're getting candid feedback and coach-ing, and get them involved in something developmental: for example, getting a cross-functional team of high-potential people together and then attacking a real business issue. This exposure to the top management team energizes the whole group. Also on a quarterly basis, I meet with the direct reports of my direct re-ports and talk about their financial results, their business, and the future of the business. We address talent-planning issues with them as well. We have town hall meetings and meetings with our knowledge channels that address these issues, too. We do all this for many reasons, but if for no other reason, to have things out in the open, unfiltered, or open for misinterpretation.

- **In terms of institutionalizing leadership development, what are your biggest challenges?**

Even though we are all in agreement on our leadership goals and objectives, com-municating those shared goals in a consistent manner across the company is a huge task. It is a combination of identifying and articulating our values and then bringing the right people together to communicate and execute. With so many of our as-sociates located around the world, it is all about leveraging talent, which in reality is what leadership is.

- **What role does technology have in financial services, and how does it change the competitive landscape?**

Banks and financial services companies have a chance to leapfrog some other in-dustries because of the nature of our business. We're in the business of providing information and service, which is now done primarily through technology. Con-trast that with a retail company, which can be technically proficient on the front end with all the bells and whistles but on the back end is a forklift and a truck delivering the product to the customer. Ultimately, technology is an enabler, not a business unto itself. For example, there has been a false assumption that one channel, if provided through cool, new technology, was sufficient, but Internet banks have not done very well by and large because customers all along have had and expressed a desire for convenience in a multichannel fashion. So you find us now gaining more customers each month than any Internet bank has in total. Technology remains one of our bigger challenges. I think back to early in my career when one could easily identify and pick one or two competitors and really grow to hate them; whereas, now, you almost have to talk about competition regionally or by type of business before you can narrow it down. There are the large, obvious competitors you go at head-on. Then there are new, emerging competitors you never dreamed would be competitors. For example, GE, a company traditionally associated with making everything from light bulbs to jet engines, now has the largest core of its business—GE Capital—acting like a bank. Then there are the niche players who target the same customers and associates that you do, and while these competitors don't matter individually, they sure do in the aggregate. The only way to beat them is to be as nimble as they are and react to the market quickly and uniquely, very often by showing your technology, prowess, and innovation. Then, take advantage of your buying power and your economies of scale to overwhelm them on pricing and other issues that customers deem important.

- What do you think the financial services landscape will look like in years ahead? What types of skills and qualities will the leaders of tomorrow's financial services companies need to have?

I think you'll have fewer of everything: fewer insurance companies, fewer investment banks, fewer banks, fewer asset management companies, fewer qualified people. The banks will probably survive because of the sheer size of their equity bases and the power of their earnings strength. As this begins to happen, a global perspective becomes more and more important, as does the idea that you cannot be limited to any one country or any one region within the world. Managerial skills will become even more important because you've got to be paying attention in a lot of different ways, and controlling risk as you become much more multifaceted. Endurance will be important as you enter new and emerging markets. But other things that make a successful company will never change, such as creating a caring environment, making your organization a place where people want to come every day, and instilling a sense of pride in your associates.

- What's the toughest part about being a chief change agent?

Managing passive-aggressive behavior. It's hard to identify because people who practice passive-aggressive behavior get very good at it. You see people nodding their head and acting as if they accept something but then doing things in ways to thwart the change. You have to constantly seek that behavior out and destroy it. If you don't, it's like the southern weed kudzu; it grows uncontrollably and chokes the momentum. I feel the same way about bureaucracy. There's some correlation, in fact, because passive-aggressive behavior is really in resistance to change and thus causes things to slow down and become bureaucratic. Blatant opposers to change you can deal with; it's the passive-aggressive behavior cloaked in professionalism that is difficult to identify and thus do something about.

- What is your perspective on top-grading talent, and to what extent does that affect decisions regarding development of the leadership team and its direct reports?

We all know that "A" players produce disproportionately, and to the extent that you have "C" players blocking "A" players beneath them, that's the worst of all worlds. So you have to be very focused on the top-grading issues and have a very good process about going after it in a company, especially one of our size. It can be disastrous to have disconnects with rhetoric and implementation, or to have disconnects between rhetoric and the measurement/reward systems. Those are the pieces to top-grading: measure actions, reward appropriately, and insist on consistency. You cannot have a great company without a serious commitment to top-grading.

- As a leader, what most excites you and what most worries you?

The thing that excites me the most is that I know we're going to become a great company and I view this as an opportunity and a responsibility. What worries me the most is, interestingly, not problem loans or growth in earnings per share; it is that we would somehow find ourselves in an environment where our people thought we didn't care about each other anymore, or that what they did wouldn't matter because of our size. If a company finds itself in that environment, then it is on its way to mediocrity or maybe even out of existence. That is much harder to deal with because it is like trying to grasp smoke, something not as quantifiable as some other things. So we have to work at it all the time to make sure our people know that what they do makes a difference day-in, day-out and that we care about them.

- What are the key ingredients of being an effective leader?

Honesty, straightforwardness, and clarity. I believe that leadership is a privilege bestowed on you, and it can be taken away very quickly. You can manage someone or a group of people, but you can't get to a real level of performance through leadership if it's not bestowed on you by people who believe in you. The critical link here is trust. If you don't establish that bond of trust and you're not always credible, then you will eventually lose the ability to lead.

Leadership by creating the right environment

Eugene V. Polistuk
Celestica
Chairman and Chief Executive Officer

- What is your management philosophy and how does it relate
  to a human capital strategy?

I have always believed in a highly empowered enterprise, a real meritocracy with a flattened organization, a high respect for individuals, and a minimum value on bureaucracy. In our various businesses, we value our intellectual assets to the extent that the value helps construct the right environment for all our assets to be as effective as possible. We have a value-based culture, so anybody who is a part of it has to have a skill set to operate in this kind of environment. A high degree of integrity, interaction, and differentiation is required. We don't have a culture that supports people throwing their weight around and leading by intimidation. Part of real leadership involves creating an environment in which supervisors take the time to develop employees and get them aligned. If you provide the right environment and the right resources, your employees will be more effective, more efficient, and more responsive than you could ever achieve with a highly centralized model.

- Do you view your human resources department as a strategic
  component of your business?

I have always considered HR strategic in nature and, as a result, of my eight direct reports, one is Worldwide HR. I work very closely with my HR team, possibly as much as I do with my financial team. It all ties together: positioning the culture of a company; reinforcing the value system; strategically developing intellectual assets; acquiring all the tools, resources, and assets that are required; building recognition programs and management training; and maintaining a harmonious balance within the company.

- In developing your HR team and strategy, what approach
  worked best with Celestica?

Not all HR teams are equal. Some HR departments are passive-aggressive and purely transactional. We've grown Celestica in a way that values people, so we are able to attract and retain some of the best talent, much more successfully than many of our competitors. Because of our working closely with the HR team early on, they have become facilitators, builders of the architecture, and are very, very involved in our operational thinking.

- **When you make an acquisition, do you have a process in place for assessing the acquired company's talent base?**

It is actually our first criterion when determining whether we want to acquire a company. If we don't think we can integrate the people well, if it's not a cultural fit, we don't do it. We look at the quality of management and the quality of people, as well as their track records. Can they adapt to this new environment? Can each side establish a level of trust? Can we work with each other in an informal environment? With every acquisition, we have our version of a SWAT team that goes in and applies these criteria. When you have a flattened organization that is not driven totally by a "Command Central" paradigm, people have to be able to work with each other very well. They have to feel comfortable in sharing challenges and solutions. If the acquisition target's culture is one in which people are extremely preoccupied with potential consequences, we are cautious about doing the deal.

- **How do you attract, develop, and retain the best and brightest people?**

By creating the right environment. The question is: Do we have adequate feedback groups to figure out whether we have created the right environment? Many of the best practices among our senior managers have been adapted from our experiences at IBM and other companies and then supplemented with ideas from other cultures. Our value system was developed by 2,500 employees, and it hasn't changed over time.

- **Are there things besides money that are effective instruments for retaining people?**

Any company would be foolish to try to maintain noncompetitive salaries over time. However, people don't jump ship because of poor compensation alone. In fact, in some cases, people have stayed with us for less money because our environment is one of trust, appreciation, integrity, and excitement and it is a place where they feel they can contribute. It takes a long time to build this kind of environment, but it is a tremendous deterrent to turnover.

- Is it important to identify your top performers and then treat
  them differently?

We have a meritocracy, so everybody gets evaluated, ranked, and treated fairly and consistently. However, we do reward merit. Peer influence is part of the evaluation. We have very comprehensive opinion surveys, and the rank and file tend to be more critical than management, in many cases. We expect the bulk of our people, maybe 80 percent, to be effective team players and reside in the middle. Then, 10 percent of our population make up our group of superachievers, and we go to great lengths to retain and recognize them. The bottom 10 percent we work with to retrain and develop in an effort to enhance performance. Ideally, this group would have been screened out prior to the recruitment stage, and if they are unable to bring their performance up to standard, then we have to screen them out after the fact. It is just as important to manage the bottom 10 percent as it is to manage the top performers.

- Many companies are in the process of institutionalizing leadership
  development. What do you do to develop your company's next
  generation of leaders?

Our goals are to select the right people, recognize and augment the talent gaps, and plan ahead for continuing development of our top performers. It takes courage to move them into other jobs when they are performing well in their existing positions, but you have to do that to build bench strength. Your management development sessions must involve all senior managers. For instance, we have courses in which our top two hundred to three hundred leaders across the company spend time with the top four executives, including me, engaged in strategic brainstorming, not unlike Jack Welch's bear pits.

- Do coaching and mentoring play a role in these activities?

They are very critical. There's no new science here, no breakthroughs. It's purely a question of deployment, and it has to be honest deployment. If a leader stands up and talks about this, glows about that, but doesn't walk the talk, it's of no benefit. If you honestly believe in what you are saying, you'll create a healthy enthusiasm that spreads throughout the organization.

- How do you manage to maintain the culture while infusing it with new energy?

That is one of our challenges. We have to keep monitoring the culture to ensure that it is intact and positive, and we do this through surveys, feedback, management meetings, site visits, and so on. We're constantly spot-checking. The method itself is not magic, but the results can be quite magical. It is worth the effort. What I love most about the whole human capital equation is that you can't create it overnight, and it only works if it is an integral part of the cultural fabric of a company, not just a superficial posture. Fortunately for us, some of our competitors don't understand that.

Leadership by developing complementary talents

Stephen L. Baum
Sempra Energy
Chairman, President and Chief Executive Officer

- **What experiences in your career have helped most to prepare you for your current position?**

I was an officer in the Marine Corps, which was a very interesting and formative experience for me. I learned a variety of things about how people perform under stress and what leadership is like under stress. Much of the way I look at things now has been influenced by that training and experience. Then, being a lawyer gives me a certain turn of mind about business analysis and problem-solving. I tend to look at business opportunities and challenges as a series of risk management problems. Throughout my career, it also has been very useful to have been placed in a variety of roles and to be exposed to many different environments. Cross-training is valuable to introduce in any organization, and it has been important to me in the formation of my experience and abilities.

- **Is there a management philosophy that surfaces from all of your experiences?**

What comes to mind most clearly is the importance of assembling the best team possible. That is one of the principal roles of a CEO, in addition to providing strategic direction and creating an environment in which strategic thinking develops within the organization. It is also critical to assure that the team is well-trained, well-motivated, and highly intelligent and that its members understand the business and the financial model on which the company is based. A corporation is people, and the people are infinitely more important than the physical assets. Another view I like to take—and this would probably get a big "duh" out of a lot of industrial CEOs, but in my business it really bears talking about—I believe in big rewards for people who show results and make money for the company, in an ethical and positive way, obviously. There are three things that I think we ought to say about ourselves. We ought to say we want to have fun, that we want to make money, and that we want to be proud of what we do. I emphasize making money a lot, because in the old utility model, that concept was really constrained by regulation. Regulation created a mentality in which the idea of profit and the idea of thinking how to make more money was repressed by the environment. I really believe in infecting—and I'll use that word—an organization with a real desire to make money.

• **What skills do leaders need to manage people successfully?**

There's an interdependency and hierarchy of skills. Intelligence and IQ aren't necessarily the same thing. High IQ is a sine qua non. However, an organization can have socially intelligent people who also happen to be great people managers but lack the IQ to make the right decisions. What we attempt to do at Sempra is start with the smartest people we can find, who can relate well with others. In most cases, smart people who don't have good interpersonal skills are not effective; the intelligence is wasted. The execution of strategy is dependent on teamwork, so people skills are critical to maximize the value of an organization's human resource.

• **What has been the progression of leadership challenges in the energy industry, and what skills are now important?**

For a long time, the utility industry was very much an engineering culture, an engineering business, driven by engineering skills. The utility culture of old was thoroughly and completely disrupted in the 1970s by oil shocks and a rapid rise in energy prices. The changed scenario called for strong financial leadership, because the utilities were put under terrific financial strain. Merging into the 1980s, the demand for financial leadership started giving way, to some degree, to legal skills, because the industry became much more of a regulatory game and continued as such into the nineties. Today, we're seeing yet another transition, one that calls for skill in risk management, broadly defined—meaning the ability to understand businesses—a portfolio of assets, risks and potentialities—and to manage them by the way the pieces integrate. The pendulum is inching away from a legal, regulatory environment and toward a modern version of the financial management skill set. For example, in Sempra Energy Trading, we acquired a very accomplished trading operation and made it part of our business. This gave us a whole different way of looking at what we do. When we buy an asset or we enter into a contract, what does that mean for the long term? What are the risks inherent in that? How does one hedge those risks? We look at the balance of risks across the entire organization and run it more like a portfolio, almost like a trading operation. This is a nontraditional way of looking at the utility business. Traditionally, we only looked at hard assets. Now, we are constantly building a long position as kind of a guaranteed market. Since there are very few guaranteed markets anymore, you really need to evaluate the short side, the demand side, of the equation very carefully. That brings one to much more of an emphasis on customer relations. In terms of leadership skills that are important in this industry *today*, however, it's more a portfolio risk management business than it ever has been.

- How do you establish a high-performance culture
  and work environment?

It has been said that a leader casts a long shadow. I believe that's true; one leads by example. Culture has been a major issue for us because Sempra is relatively new as a company. It was created by the merger of two large companies with different cultures and different histories. We've had a cultural integration issue of the first magnitude; in working through that, we have attempted to create cohesiveness and a new, consistent standard for the organization by, first and foremost, communicating regularly with our employees about the new standards and aspirations. We developed a new vision, strategy, and goals and communicated them throughout the organization. We established a corporate learning center to enhance the financial skill sets of our management team, which are an absolutely essential skill set. There simply was no way we would be able to communicate effectively with one another until we all spoke the same financial language. Now, all director-level and above employees receive financial training to ensure that they understand discounted cash flow calculations, how to value an investment, and the concept of cost of capital. I wanted people to understand the financial consequences of their decisions or of others' decisions and inculcate this risk management philosophy and the proper calculation of exposures in a broad way. We took a less traditional approach to getting a singular culture in that we didn't go about it in a soft way. We wanted to create more of a common environment for communications and skills, and then we added to that a series of very clearly defined financial goals and rewarded people for meeting them. We introduced a fair amount of cross-training so that there was a line of sight to success.

- How do you identify, develop, and retain high-potential people
  at Sempra?

We have a formal process in which each of the responsible officers and his or her direct reports identify their "A" players. That information is in a database in Human Resources, which in turn analyzes the talents in-house, based on the information contributed by the supervisors. Partly as a byproduct of the review processes that exist for evaluating performance and partly just because stars tend to stick out, we formally identify those people and we have a succession-planning process that indicates when people are moving forward, when they are ready for the next job, and what additional development could facilitate the process. This is a relatively formal process, and we encourage the up-and-comers to pursue additional training, even to the point of going off to academic business programs or specific training. These evaluations are reviewed by the management group periodically so that we get a bit of a cross-check. Sometimes somebody's protégé might not be viewed that way by the rest of the group. When a high-potential person is up for a significant promotion, the management team completes a 360-degree review. We also conduct psychological evaluations as part of the screening and recruiting process. The purpose of that is not so much to rule out, it's more to be sure we have identified the strengths and weaknesses in people as well as other areas where the person might be helped by either training or counseling.

• **What keeps you awake at night?**

The political and regulatory situation in California and in other major markets. The fact that we tried a form of deregulation and free markets that hasn't worked well. How we'll navigate what I would call the minefield of current laws and regulations to get results that are acceptable to the public as well as workable for our industry. In our case in California, the two other publicly held utility companies (P G & E and Southern California Edison) are either bankrupt or in financial difficulty. We've maintained our solvency and our good credit ratings, and so we've been able to maneuver properly in the political process. It comes back to risk management. When the law put a retail price cap in place back in 1996 for all three utilities in California, the risk of that price cap was, I believe, inadequately understood by the other two companies. We looked at it precisely from a risk management perspective. We asked ourselves, Can we hedge it? Can we hedge this retail cap? We did a lot of modeling about how we would work with the margin that existed between the cap and our costs to move to a time when the cap was no longer there. For example, we asked the California Public Utilities Commission if we could have a risk management function, that is, a hedging function within the utility. They said they didn't want us to be in the longer-term contracting business. They wanted us to get out of that mode and expose our customers to a spot market where they could make a choice of supplier. Well, in that environment where we couldn't hedge the cap by buying forward, we concluded that the only way to manage it was to get out from under the price cap as quickly as possible. The other two utilities thought that they could work through it or didn't properly appreciate the risk involved in having a retail price cap forward for four years. We did what are called value-at-risk calculations. These are statistical analyses that use game theory to figure out what the exposures and potentialities are. That's a different kind of management style from what most of the industry has engaged in the past, and we were successful by taking a cautious and calculated approach.

Leadership by creating an environment of learning

Steven Kerr
Goldman Sachs
Chief Learning Officer

- You are widely recognized for your work as chief learning officer (CLO) and vice president of leadership development at General Electric. You are also credited with developing GE's world-renowned leadership education center at Crotonville. You joined Goldman Sachs in May 2001 charged with a similar mandate to help the investment banking behemoth build out its next generation of leadership. Why do you think companies have trouble institutionalizing leadership development?

I expected this question and I've thought about it, and the truth is that I really don't have a great answer. At Crotonville, we got several requests daily from other organizations that wanted to study and benchmark what we were doing. The alternative is for organizations to send their people to a nonaffiliated, expensive, multiweek classroom setting to learn leadership. We ran Crotonville very lean: 44 people—28 U.S.—to train 360,000 people. We didn't have our own vendors. We didn't have our own instructional technologists. We didn't have secret theories on leadership. In other words, throwing money at a problem doesn't always work. People credit former chairman Jack Welch with GE's success. Welch was as much an example of what GE produces as the opposite. He certainly improved it and supported it. But in fact, it preexisted him. I tell people at Goldman Sachs that I'm really just a plumber. I don't have secret theories or vendors or anything that isn't already known. I learned how to do this because GE is very, very good at hooking everything up. They are no more interested in leadership development as a dependent variable than any other company, but they have hooked it up to compensation, hooked it up to manpower planning, hooked it up to career backups and all the things that surround the so-called war for talent. It's plain good business to do ongoing leadership development. When people left Crotonville, I could always predict their first two sentences. The first is: "I expected more than that." The second sentence is: "I can do that." And yet history says very few will.

- Would you agree that, more than just structured training, leadership development involves stretch roles, cross-training, coaching, and mentoring?

There's an old saying, "Misery loves company," but when you do the research, it turns out that misery loves miserable company. Regarding leadership development, all GE did was connect the training to career stages as people transitioned into new roles, all the way down to the lowest levels. As you transition into new roles inside GE, for example, if you are a new manager, or a new global manager managing across time zones, you are put into a room full of other people who have the same general problem and you discuss the issues and make connections and at the end everything is connected better than it was at the beginning. GE understands that when people go through career transitions they can use some targeted help. I think this is why GE is so successful, and for the life of me, I can't tell you why other companies don't copy it.

- What is an ideal framework for institutionalizing leadership?

Predictive leadership is the right approach. The best way someone is going to be a better leader is to let him or her lead something, and the best way you're going to be able to know if you have a good leader on your hands is to watch him or her lead something. The notion of the framework, or the overall theory here, is popcorn stands, as Welch calls them. Popcorn stands are business units not directly impactful to the core business. You put people into leadership positions when it's far from clear they will do a good job in those roles, but those roles will let you know whether they are capable of doing a good job and will teach them. It's like pre-season or spring training. If you aren't sure somebody can hit left-handed pitches, you don't wait until the third game of the World Series to find out. You find out up front, when it's cost-free. GE has, as other companies should, places and roles that act as incubators of talent.

- Many leaders want it done right the first time and don't want to let their people make mistakes, but so much learning happens when you make mistakes.

Mistakes are a fundamental part of learning leadership. A few little mistakes are good. It's ironic, because nobody likes to fail more than GE, but you have to permit failure in the popcorn stands in order to guard against failures in the main businesses. Nobody knows how to prevent the first leadership experience from being mediocre, but everybody is mediocre when they do something new. What we can do, though, is keep the first leadership experience from being important. You don't label it as a popcorn stand because you don't want to denigrate the people leading and working in it, even though everybody learns in the popcorn stand, everybody benefits, everybody appreciates the natural experiment. Think of it as an experiment and build in feedback loops, perform 360-degree reviews, build controls, protect from risk. It is essential for companies that are serious about leadership to figure out where their popcorn stands are before people start making mistakes in the core. Every company has popcorn stands, but few use them as beta test sites for leadership.

- **What are skills that good leaders have in common?**

They're great communicators—not necessarily charismatic, just effective at communicating. They have candor. They give a consistent message regardless of audience. Also, Welch would preach that there are three types of boundaries, and every action a leader takes has to break down one or more of these boundaries. First, you're always trying to blunt the boundaries between levels; those are the vertical boundaries. Second, you're always trying to blunt the differences between departments and regions; those are inside walls. Third, you're always trying to create synergies and remove barriers between you and the outside world, which is customers, suppliers, regulators, and so on. You do this in different ways depending on your position in the firm, but always tell yourself to break down boundaries.

- **One leadership expert recently noted that, with many companies reducing their middle management ranks, managers no longer have five people reporting into them—now, typically, there are 250 or 500 in their span of control. So the ability for these leaders to communicate effectively through all of the mediums is getting more and more important.**

We now see courses—or at least brief sessions—that deal with email as a communication mechanism. People just assumed that email was another form of written communication, but the early evidence is that people treat it as a different medium altogether. They take more risks; people say things online that they wouldn't say in a memo, as if the thing couldn't be turned into one. In email, they're more outspoken than may be appropriate, which can put the company at legal risk. Equally important is to match the communication medium to the message: a memo is quick and cheap and goes to everybody immediately. It won't, however, do you any good when it comes to changing people's minds. Alternatively, using the one-on-one medium is more labor intensive, so you shouldn't overuse it. These are the things that almost nobody gets taught—the rudiments—not nouns and verbs, but determining the purpose of the communication. What methods are effective in changing peoples' minds? Which methods work best to get something on permanent record? Illustrating the false dichotomy between high-tech and high touch, today's young adults go to parties and sit without talking to each other. Then they go online and share intimate experiences in chat rooms. As the younger set grows into leadership positions, their ability to develop social skills through modern media may turn out to be advantageous.

- **What are your thoughts on top-grading talent?**

Some of the notion of top-grading is opinion and some is not. The way to start looking at top-grading is to divide it into two parts: one is the ability to recognize your "A," "B," or "C" players, and the other is what to do with them afterwards. A lot of companies confuse those two parts. So you start with the fact that people are not machines. We don't all perform at the same level; by nature, we are not designed the same, intellectually or otherwise. Therefore, you can't choose not to have a first core, a second core, and so on, of talent. The only thing you can control is what you do with that information. You therefore must acknowledge that a system that does not permit you to know the difference between your top tier and your bottom tier is a bad and useless system. No good can come out of such self-deception. Whether you are having a banner year or having to downsize in tough times, you should always know who your poor performers are and who your stars are. Once you have them identified, you get to the second part of the top-grading equation, and that's where opinion enters. Some companies, such as GE, make it very clear who their "A" players are and fire the bottom 10 percent every year. The argument for this approach is that if your customers and clients want 10 percent more every year, then the product or service should improve by at least 10 percent every year, so shouldn't your workforce make equivalent improvements as well? Another reality is that you can predict more from selection than from anything else. There are any number of sociometric scaling systems in which you put people together by common likes or common this or common that, but there is no system that causes top performance as much as hiring good people. Analysis shows us that very talented people in mediocre systems will outproduce average people in good systems. Some opponents of top-grading are quick to point out that calling 10 percent "high potential," in effect, lets 90 percent of the people know they're not perceived as high potential. This characterization could convince people they're not worthwhile; then, self-esteem goes down and performance follows. It never helps to drag self-esteem down. This is where the notion and process of top-grading becomes opinion. Do you want to have an elite group of people, your stars, treated as stars? Or do you want to bring in a more egalitarian system? Actions tend to follow the established culture. The key, though, is first accepting the fact that you can't choose not to have stars and laggards. That's part of life's normal distribution.

- Do you think that there is a trend toward changing the traditional, transactionally focused HR department to a business unit that executes a strategic human capital management plan?

Some of the changes that companies are making are merely semantic. The question is: "Does this change anybody's basic thinking?" The idea to call it human capital "something" may be more acceptable in a performance-driven company, but only to the extent that you build HR practices around results that are important to the organization and its major constituencies. It isn't like getting your karma together; it's about increasing shareholder returns, product quality, and so on. So, if that's the implication, then I think that is a meaningful change. We need to think of HR not so much as a series of transactions but rather in terms of outcomes and, more specifically, business outcomes. This is a real change in emphasis, with important consequences. However, some companies are just using the latest buzzwords and not intending to really change what they do or how they think.

- What are ways that companies can show an intention to change—that is, specific actions to support the words?

Just as an example—not that it's defining, but it is typical—Goldman Sachs went to a human capital approach late in 2001. For the first time in the firm's history—at least in recent history—the head of human capital is on the management committee. Other companies may chose to put their HR directors on the corporate executive council, executive committee, or operating committee to give those executives a higher place in the ranks so that they are at the table when it comes to strategic decision-making and are closely connected to the business goals and strategy. Therefore, the twenty-first-century human capital manager may have run businesses, had P & L responsibility, or worked in a variety of operational or managerial roles, as opposed to a traditional HR background. Every signal, including not being at a meeting, is meaningful. Every nonvote is a vote. Being hands-off is as much of a signal as being hands-on.

- What can you tell us about Goldman Sachs' Pine Street Project and what it is doing to change the culture?

It is Change Leadership 101. When you go to a very successful place, it's harder to initiate change. It is resisted because people are justifiably proud of what they've done. So, part of the plan is purely technical. For instance, as a firm, we may do 20 things that appear goofy. But the fact is that 15 of the 20 are probably functional. This place became the leading investment bank on Wall Street for 100-plus years despite having had some dysfunctional systems and processes, just like every company. So maybe 15 processes are functional, and of the other five, two are no longer relevant, and three are just plain goofy. The trouble is, you don't have any sign on things saying what is baby and what is bathwater, so the challenge is to save the one and throw the other out, identifying how the organization is different from what the research recommends. That is my job here. Take setting stretch goals, for example. There's a whole bunch of literature on goal setting that says that you set goals that are possible. People try; there are a lot of reasons they don't perform optimally. Welch would say an over-stretched executive is the best executive because he or she doesn't have time to meddle. So the overextended executive sits and tries to control 25 to 35 people, whereas the research is saying it should be around eight people. It's interesting when people do goofy stuff, especially when they're high performers.

- Is Pine Street an actual physical entity like Crotonville?

Yes, but the budget doesn't permit you to bring everybody in all the time, so we need to factor in online learning, videoconferencing, and traveling road shows, and we have regionally based centers of excellence. It has to be lean, and the best resources are what we call resources in place. They are people in your divisions who can add value to what you are doing. For instance, we'll create a Global Learning Council and have people from the business help build curriculum and test ideas on what should be done centrally and what should be done divisionally. Like Crotonville, we'll have most of our Pine Street faculty members come in for a set period of time, usually two years, and then leave. We call these global mobility assignments.

- How can CEOs use the role of chief learning officer or otherwise apply learning in their companies?

Maybe the place to start is with the old equation: ability times motivation equals performance. If you want something to change, you've got to make people able to change and you've got to make them want to change. Let's illustrate with two positions: the chief information officer (CIO) and the CLO. The CIO should worry about hardware and software compatibility, knowledge management, bandwidth, and these sorts of things. The CLO, on the other hand, should worry about motivation and incentive. You can build the best systems in the world, but there is no computer so sophisticated that it waits until its owner goes home at night and then it turns itself on and sends important information around the company. The basic reason people don't share information is because they don't want to. Now we are back to the idea of blunting boundaries so that these roles supplement each other. What is it about the company's politics and reward systems that prevent information from being shared? The CLO's role is to locate knowledge from outside— whether you call them good ideas or best practices—and bring those in. He/she also identifies best practices within a firm, and moves all these around and makes knowledge affordable and available. If you need a problem solved and there isn't the right knowledge around to do so, you create your own. You are creating, you are transporting information, and you are making it useful and beneficial to share. Learning is simply converting information into behavioral routines. This process changes how people behave and, ultimately, how companies perform.

Leadership by developing the people who can grow the business

William Coleman
BEA Systems
Chairman and Chief Strategy Officer

- What is your management philosophy?

My management philosophy is based on a set of timeless values so that people understand and trust me and my capability. First, I start with the fact that the company only succeeds if it brings real value to customers and shareholders. To create real value, there are really only three things a CEO can do effectively and must do personally. The first is to give a vision, a direction, for your company that will offer a true value proposition to all your constituencies. The second thing is to hire and grow great people, and the third is to organize the company to make those people effective. A guiding principle I use is that a CEO's job is to grow the people who can grow the business and to provide the metrics and resources that enable people to grow the business. Granted, as a CEO, you have a lot of oversight responsibilities for your senior people, but if you try to step in and do their jobs, you are not going to develop and empower them.

• Would you elaborate on how CEOs can hire and develop executives
  to grow a business?

It depends on the stage of a company. A company that is just getting started and
growing very rapidly probably doesn't have all the talent it needs. In fact, the
only way to grow a fast-growing company is from the top down. In this stage,
you should bring in top performers, people who have "been there, done that"
and who therefore know how to hire and develop other top-performing people.
These top people should also be specialists of the areas your business is growing
in; in that way, they'll really serve as change agents by raising the level of critical
parts of the organization. Strategic external hires can take your company to the
next level. Once you get to be a company of critical mass, however, it isn't fea-
sible to continue to grow at or above the industry rate without growing the
organization organically and through the ongoing development of your own
people. Once your organization is very large, you must develop your talent largely
from within; if you only go outside for talent, you'll constantly upset the culture that's in place, and your time will be spent retuning the company to adjust
for these disruptions. Managing growth is always a challenge, but to develop a
company from start-up to a complex organization, there is a paradigm. To do
it right, you have to grow the company from the top down first; then, those
people create the management infrastructure beneath. Once this process is in
place, it creates growth exponentially. At this point, if you rely entirely on a
bottoms-up strategic for organizational growth, you'll constantly be reinventing the company's workforce, at the expense of operational and other key areas
of growth.

• When you make a strategic external hire, what do you look for in terms
  of skills?

In many instances, we still need the "been there, done that" person. So, we look
for people with the right kind of experience. That's a given. But the two most
important criteria for these recruits is whether they fit in with the culture of the
company and whether they are likely to be effective managing in the environment that we have built over the years. I've seen companies bring in a ton of
vice presidents and division presidents without much regard for cultural fit, and
only about one in four stay on for more than a couple of years and become long-
term contributors. So, it's as much about whether their management styles and
philosophies work in the new environment as it is about how good their skills
are.

- Your business is all about intangibles and intellectual property because it involves both people and software. Is there a single skill set that is a strong predictor for success in this environment?

If you think about the industrial age, it was an era when humans were really regarded as just another resource: How many interchangeable people can you put on the production line? Then, we experienced a major shift in attitude as we started to develop a middle class and the knowledge worker emerged. When Alvin Toffler wrote *Future Shock* in the sixties, it was about a world moving toward a service economy. Well, we *are* going to a service economy, but it wasn't the one he predicted. Our service-based economy is at a much higher level: it is an intellectual capacity–driven service economy. In this world, people are your primary assets. So, growing people, teaching people, empowering people is how you succeed in our economy. I believe the priorities for companies are: first, a total customer focus; second, employee empowerment; and third, teamwork. Empowering people and fostering good teamwork are two things that don't happen without a lot of work because, often, empowered people don't look at themselves as the best team players. It's the teams that really win, not necessarily the individuals in them or the teams with the best positions.

- What kinds of teams are most effective in today's service-based economy?

There are two functional areas that historically have been buried way down in the organization but are now the keys to empowerment and growth in the twenty-first century: human resources and information technology, or management information systems (MIS). MIS is a powerful tool for productivity and change because it makes people more productive. The human resources field has taken some turns over the last century. It came about in the World War II time frame and it evolved in the late seventies and eighties as "personnel." "Personnel" was really about creating career paths. But career pathing as it turned out was not really a mechanism for promoting people; instead, it was a mechanism for controlling their expectations about how fast they could be promoted. Under this rubric, there were steps to advance and rigid protocols that were very uncreative but were useful, considering that in this era, most people stayed with one employer throughout their whole careers. Then, we went through a major attitude change in the late eighties through the nineties, when the "war for talent" started and the notion of personnel morphed into human resources—which is the worst thing to call it. If you think about it, it's like a throwback to the 1920s; these are not really people, they're just another resource, like cash and facilities. Human resources is a stiff term, but the focus has begun to be more about what we're doing with people. It is still in evolution; HR still handles all the maintenance things such as salaries and benefits, but it also tries to provide a nurturing environment in which empowered employees can fully develop their potential. An empowered employee should not look to the company for growth; he or she should look to the company to provide the facilities, the guidance, the path, and the opportunity to move forward. Ideally, it is a sort of bond between the company and the employee. At BEA, we don't want passive employees who wait for the company to say, "Okay, here are the things you need to do to become a district manager." We want to hire intelligent change-makers who can demonstrate leadership and who will seek out opportunities within our organization. Our part is to provide mentors and coaches and facilities and processes that empower these people to develop themselves.

- **Have there been times in your own career when you felt extremely empowered and really began to spread your wings?**

It's living through failures that has been the biggest influence on me. I've always been very goal oriented, and, after a failure, you are forced to think about goals, make decisions, and take action. For example, I was in the Air Force in 1976 and was distraught when I was not selected for the astronaut program. I had to ask myself if I wanted to continue in the Air Force or do something else. I had to find out what I was passionate about, and the answer was software. Software appealed to me because it is not restricted to any specific field, so I could participate in any business in any market in any organization. That eventually led me to GTE, where I had a highly successful career. The next major influence on me was when I left GTE to go to one of the first dotbombs, VisiCorp. I consider that the most technically challenging and interesting time of my life, and I built what I thought was one of the best development organizations of the time. However, Lotus 1-2-3 then stormed into the market, and Microsoft copied our technology to create the first Windows system. All of a sudden, our company went under. That was a real catharsis for me, and it helped me realize that it can't all be about technology; it needs to be about a lot more. I thought about what my goals were when I left the Air Force. My goal was to run software development for a *Fortune* 500 company by the time I was 45. So, I went to Sun Microsystems and, thanks to my 10 years there—which were much like a learning laboratory—I achieved that goal by age 41. At the time, the company was in the middle of an apocalyptic downturn, and I was asked to take over six divisions that competed fiercely with each other. That was a real lesson in leadership and, over time, helped me to realize I could apply those skills to something else, something of my own. That is when I came up with the idea for BEA Systems. Breakthrough ideas for me have come from being introspective at times of failure—not from times when I was very successful, because at those times I didn't have to think so deeply about my next moves.

- **Do you have a mentor or trusted advisor?**

There is a role for a trusted advisor, but I also think there is a role for a CEO network. I'm fortunate to have both. I have two people I rely on as advisors from different aspects. One is Carol Bartz, who is on my board and is chairman and CEO of AutoDesk, and the other is Bill Janeway, managing director of Warburg Pincus, who funded this company. I've known them for many years, and I know that I can call them as many times as I want and they are both willing to go out of their way to give their insight on any issue I have. I am also part of two formal CEO networks here. One is the Center for Creative Innovation, which is run by a group sponsored by McKinsey & Company, and it is made up of CEOs from Silicon Valley companies that don't compete with one another. We meet quarterly to discuss various topics, bring in expert speakers, and try to solve real business issues. When I joined the group, BEA had under a billion dollars in revenues, and it was great to get feedback and support from CEOs running companies five to ten times our size. The other CEO network I'm involved in meets twice a year, and it consists of CEOs or heads of software from the 30 largest enterprise software companies in the world. Over time, with both of these, you build a network of people you can call on for advice. The situations we all face are at once unique and not unique, so, no matter how good a CEO is, input from a variety of sources is essential.

Teaching leadership

Henry Mintzberg
McGill University
Professor of Management

- **You've studied and taught about the art of management throughout a long and distinguished career. In your view, what attributes make a great leader?**

We're living in the age of heroic leadership, of idealizing our leaders, but a lot of that is negative in effect and even dysfunctional. I'm a fan of what I call managing quietly—leadership that just stays in the background and gets things done.

- It's been said that the ultimate leader puts himself or herself
  out of business. Would you agree?

Not out of business, just out of people's hair. It's what I call engaging leadership. The job of a leader is to bring out the energy that exists within people and direct it toward the enhancement of the organization.

- You've written that leadership is practiced on three levels:
  the information level, the people level, and the action level.
  How do these levels interrelate?

You can manage through numbers and information, which is the MBA way of managing. You can manage through people, focusing on the interpersonal aspects of business, and you can manage action directly, meaning that you get down there and actually control what is happening, take charge of projects yourself. I think management has to happen on all the levels. My concern is that too much managing today happens at the information level only. That mindset is being at a distance. The term "human resources" is the worst term ever coined. I'm not a human resource, I'm a human being. As soon as you start thinking of people as human resources, you've taken the people level down to the information level and you're treating people as data or as things. The three levels have to be in balance; that is the challenge of leadership.

- What is your view of executive MBA programs as compared
  to the regular MBA curricula?

My view of regular MBA programs is that they train the wrong people in the wrong ways for the wrong reasons. The people who go through these programs, typically in their late twenties, are too young and inexperienced to appreciate the education. You can't create a manager in a classroom. You can only take people who are managers and understand management and help them improve their practice of it. And my view of executive MBA programs is that they train the *right* people, but in the wrong ways for the wrong reasons—because they take people who are experienced and then they do exactly what they do with the regular MBAs. They take a program that was designed for people without experience and they give it to people with experience. So it doesn't make sense at all. In our International Masters Program in Practicing Management, we have a different approach. Our philosophy is based on three principles: number one, you only take people who are already managers. Number two, they must be sent and sponsored by their employers. Number three, they must remain in their jobs in order to link theory and practice, so we bring them in for short bursts of time. And we draw as much as possible on their own experience in the classroom, so that, instead of focusing on other people's experiences, as in cases, they are able to focus on their own and apply the ideas to situations that directly affect them.

- Give us an overview of the program, if you would.

Employers select four to five high-potential managers to participate in our program, which extends over a 16-month period, in five two-week modules. The modules are held every four months or so, and each one is conducted in a different part of the world, as a partnership of schools in Canada, England, France, India, and Japan. It's a true partnership; there is no "lead" school. The first module, on managing self, is held in Lancaster, England, and is entitled "Managing Self: The Reflective Mindset." The second module, at McGill, is "Managing Organization: The Analytic Mindset." The third module, in Bangalore, India, is "Managing Context: The Worldly Mindset" and the fourth, in Japan, is "Managing Relationships: The Collaborative Mindset." The fifth and final module, "Managing Change: The Action Mindset," is held at INSEAD, the prominent business school. Various activities link theory and experience. After each module, for example, the managers do reflection papers linking what they learned with their jobs and the companies. So it's very personalized and built around their own work lives.

- It sounds as though there is a lot of emphasis on the so-called soft skills that leaders are increasingly called upon to employ.

There is a blending and integration of them with the more traditional skills. The softer skills are particularly emphasized in the Lancaster and Bangalore modules, which are on the reflective and worldly mindsets, respectively. The first one touches people very deeply because it really focuses them in on themselves. They're not just reflecting on their own experience and discussing the everyday dilemmas of balancing family and job pressures, but rather, looking at who they are and where they fit into the scheme of things. It tends to hit people hard, and is often a life-changing experience. The module in India promotes a real shift in that India itself is so different from what most of them are used to, and typically causes them to reassess their own world.

- A lot of companies are now making a real effort to institutionalize leadership; why do you think it is so difficult to do?

Because leadership is a personal chemistry, not some kind of technique to be "institutionalized."

- How are businesses and educators preparing tomorrow's leaders in the area of change management?

I have a very different perspective on this that some might find surprising. First of all, most things are not changing. Most things are staying the same. We just don't notice what *isn't* changing. You didn't get up this morning and say, "Oh, my God, I've buttoned my shirt." People have been buttoning shirts for centuries. You didn't notice it because everyone gets up and buttons shirts. You didn't get up this morning and say, "Isn't it funny that I'm driving to work in a four-cycle internal combustion engine?" So we notice what is changing, not what is unchanged. And now, as it happens, information technology is changing. So the Web and email get our attention, and we don't notice all the things that aren't changing. In fact, I think America is an incredibly change-resistant society. This is the only country I can imagine that would have an election where the winner got fewer votes than the loser, and yet there's no action being taken to change the Constitution. America is the only place left on earth, with the partial exception of the United Kingdom, that still uses a system of measurement that was outmoded two hundred years ago. We obsess about change. We get a lot of trivial change, a lot of cosmetic change, nonsignificant change. People get all excited about the new models of automobiles every year, but have automobiles changed significantly in decades? They are more comfortable, and we can put six CDs in now. But it's still basically the same technology that runs about the same speed and serves exactly the same function: It gets you from point A to point B.

- What about change management in education?

There's no change without continuity, so any management of change, any discussion of change, has to be accompanied by a discussion of continuity. Perpetual, unrelenting change is basically anarchy, and none of us would tolerate it for very long. The best change management curricula are those that teach about change within the context of continuity.

- What is the ideal path for young executives who aspire to be leaders?

There's the MBA route, which I believe is flawed for the reasons we've already discussed. The other approach is to get to know a business and an industry extremely well and hone your skills in something to which you are really dedicated. It's hard to be passionate about things you don't know really well, and it's hard to excel without passion.

Leadership by continuing education and networking knowledge

Heinrich von Pierer
Siemens AG
Chief Executive Officer

At the dawn of the twenty-first century, globalization is charting the direction and defining the dynamics of economies throughout the world. Traditional national markets are being superseded by a fiercely competitive global business arena governed by free and ever more complex flows of goods, capital, and people. In this almost Darwinian environment, knowledge has become *the* decisive success factor. More than ever before, a company's competitive edge in the global market depends on how well it trains and develops its people, networks them, and manages their pooled knowledge—or, in the rather dry language of economics, how well it leverages its human capital.

Surprisingly, this basic fact isn't reflected by reality in the business world. A recent study determined that only 20 percent to 40 percent of a typical company's knowledge is actually utilized. This wastefulness is enormous and alarming; in a world increasingly driven by new ideas and their speedy implementation, it can be fatal.

A global player like Siemens, with over 450,000 employees working in more than 190 countries, faces special challenges: recruiting the best people at every location worldwide, keeping their professional knowledge and skills state-of-the-art, and making sure this vast pool of know-how is networked, accessible, and used throughout the company.

Since our founding over 150 years ago, innovation has been our lifeblood. Today, growing and managing the knowledge that fuels this innovation has become an enormously complex task. We have research facilities in 30 countries, 56,000 employees dedicated to R & D, and over 120,000 engineers. Last year, we generated more than nine thousand inventions and continue to rank number one in patent applications in Germany and in Europe. In the United States, the most intensively contested market in the world, we currently rank sixth in volume of patent filings. About 75 percent of our sales come from products that are less than five years old. All of this is critically important for keeping a leading position in our industry. And all of this ultimately depends, in turn, on how well we nurture and network human capital and knowledge, our greatest assets.

Success depends not only on hiring the best but also on keeping your people state-of-the-art. Lifetime learning has become critically important in our fast-paced world, particularly in high-tech industries. At our company, lifetime learning begins with a worldwide apprenticeship program. During the past year, we trained 12,600 apprentices, 9,500 of whom were in technical professions and the remaining 3,100 in business administration. We have taken Germany's "dual system" concept—vocational training combining classroom education with on-the-job practical experience—and have had great success exporting this system to our operations in various countries throughout the world. The great advantage of this system is that it enables a company to adapt vocational profiles quickly and flexibly to changing industry needs. In recent years, for example, we have introduced new professional fields such as mechatronics—the combination of mechanics and electronics—applications development, project planning, and logistics. We also have founded five technical academies that train young people for two years (including six months' practical experience) in fields such as data and communications technology, automation, and mechatronic systems. As needs grow, we expect to extend this academy system to other locations around the globe.

In the past fiscal year, we invested over 500 million euros worldwide in vocational training and continuing education programs. Winning the "war for talent" isn't enough; one must be able to *retain* the best and brightest once they have joined the company. This means permanently updating professional knowhow and skills, as well as ensuring that our people have the necessary methodological, social, and intercultural competencies. In a typical year, more than one hundred thousand employees participate in programs ranging from management seminars to Web-based courses. In a business world in which lifetime employment with a company is a relic of the past, "employability," that is, keeping people qualified for future work either in the company or in the general job market, has become a must. It keeps people motivated and committed. And it is the best guarantee for sustained professional success.

One thing to bear in mind regarding vocational training and continuing education: the less effective the original educational process—in schools and universities—the greater the subsequent burden on a company. Continuing education should not—and cannot—be a cost-intensive repair program for deficient educational systems. It is thus not only a matter of good corporate citizenship, but is also a sound business practice, for a company to support the improvement of local educational systems wherever it operates. This is particularly important in developing countries, where company-sponsored school and university programs help raise general educational standards. These programs include research partnerships, international student exchanges, scholarships, graduate programs, awards for academic excellence, company internships, and project funding.

Having a global workforce of well-trained, highly skilled people obviously isn't enough: the workforce must be efficiently networked and leveraged to maximize benefits across the company. Thanks to the Internet, the flow of information has become instantaneous and universal. Our people now have unprecedented access to colleagues at every location throughout the world. Virtual teams, for instance, can now work on projects around the globe and around the clock, passing on data from region to region. In addition, we have set up a global knowledge management system called ShareNet, which makes a database of project information available to anyone who needs it throughout our operations. This eliminates duplicated work, speeds results, and cuts costs. A wealth of accumulated knowledge and years of practical experience is now just a mouse-click away.

Networking our workforce offers other advantages. An electronic international marketplace, for example, provides our people with an instant overview of what positions are available at a given location or in a specific region. At the same time, the system facilitates the search for internal experts needed for specific projects. This human resources development database provides maximum job transparency, promotes international transfers and stronger diversity, and helps optimize the filling of positions. As a true global player, we place a premium on having our managers gather extensive experience in a broad range of businesses and geographical regions.

The Internet also plays an increasingly important strategic role in recruiting. Our system currently attracts 120,000 applications a year, and those are in addition to what we receive through traditional recruiting channels.

Without close networking, without a global human resources strategy, no globally positioned company can effectively manage its business. In recent years, the international share of our total business has increased sharply, and our workforce distribution reflects this trend. In 1980, some 67 percent of our employees worked in Germany; today, only 40 percent do. We, like other companies in similar positions, now have to ensure that employees everywhere share a common corporate culture, common standards, and common goals, and that they are fully integrated into a global community. Only when our human resources system functions smoothly, only when it is backed by strong leadership at every level, can we hope to leverage our global strengths into lasting success.

Leadership by creating and supporting leaders

Jeffrey Pfeffer
Stanford University
Thomas Dee II Professor of Organizational Behavior,
Graduate School of Business

- What is the best approach for companies to institutionalize leadership development?

A lot of companies have gotten off-track in trying to substitute classroom experience for real experience. Classroom experience has an important role, but you also need to put people in positions with a lot of responsibility, where they can actually do things and make decisions and practice and refine their decision-making and leadership skills in the real world. The best model is to take relatively junior or inexperienced people and treat them as if they know something, because sometimes they actually do, and they will rise to the occasion. Leadership development really requires putting people in positions where they are able to make things and do things. There has been some valuable research conducted by my colleague, Charles O'Reilly, that shows that there are two basic guidelines for developing high-performance organizations. The first is to have a set of values and a philosophy that says your people are important. The second is to have a set of management practices that make those values real. There is an interdependent relationship between a company's values and its practices, and companies cannot build effective leadership programs and high-performance cultures without really believing in and acting on the underlying philosophy of putting employees first.

• How should CEOs determine who receives leadership development?

Everybody should be given the opportunity, until proven either not interested or incapable. A fast-track program is very demotivating to the people who aren't fast-tracked. If you want to grow your company at a good rate, you cannot afford to have a relatively small set of people prepared to take on larger roles. You need a large set of people who are prepared to take on larger roles. This is consistent with the concept that everybody talks about but very few actually act on, which is that everybody should be a leader at some level.

• So, you put a lot of people in stretch roles to test their leadership abilities. What level of tolerance is optimal for a new leader to make mistakes?

You should be given lots of room to screw up, because nobody is perfect. It's not just giving people stretch roles and objectives, it's also giving them social support. One of the nice things about team-based organizations and organizations in which there is less internal competition is that when people are put into new roles, there is an expectation that they will need and receive advice and help from people both higher up in the hierarchy and lower down. Think about how powerful that model is, in which people are recognized and rewarded for helping others succeed.

- What should the reward system be like to maintain
  a team-based organization?

It should be more communal, as opposed to an individual, pay-for-performance structure. You'd use elements such as pooled bonuses or profit sharing or stock ownership or some combination, so that people are rewarded for the performance of the company as well as of their unit, and then augment that with a smaller component for their individual performances. The reward structure is based on collective rewards so that people have an interest in seeing the enterprise as a whole succeed.

- What are the elements of a sustainable competitive advantage?

Human capital is the only sustainable element of competitive advantage. Financial capital is quite accessible. It moves with the speed of an electronic impulse. Technology doesn't give you very much competitive advantage, mostly because everybody has access to the same basic technical information. Once during a venture capital conference, somebody came up to me and asked, "What's all this human capital stuff?" and I said, "Well, where do you think competitive advantage comes from?" and he said, "Well, competitive advantage comes from the fact that we have this technology which is really unique and outstanding." I said, "How did you get such a unique and outstanding technology?" It was either taught in school by professors or it originated in someone's head. Ideas are relatively easy to find. Every day in the shower, you get ideas. If you've got the idea, probably thousands of other people have as well. The real competitive success comes from the ability to implement that idea, to get the team focused, to get the team working together. Competitive advantage comes not from ideas or concepts but from people, people who have the ability to actually implement ideas and concepts. Once you build a strong culture, it is very hard to duplicate it because of the values and philosophy ingrained in that culture. Instead of copying and benchmarking *what* successful companies do, you should emulate *how* they think and *how* they regard their people.

- What about going outside the company for leadership talent?

The grass is always greener on the other side; that is part of the phenomenon of companies looking externally for talent. True, we're in an intellectual-capital world, where the real source of competitive advantage comes from your ability to have smart people who can do great things for your company. But it is a fallacy to think that the only way to make that happen is by going outside for talent or hiring only smart people. If you look at competing companies where one is remarkably better than the other, the reason this is so isn't always going to be because the better company has smarter people. Likewise, there are countless examples in which a company has loads of amazingly talented people; yet, because they operate in a system where people aren't permitted to use their talents to the fullest, the company fails to bring products to market or gain market share or be successful in other ways. Many companies spend so much effort hiring experienced and talented people, then drop the ball once the new hires are on board, by telling them, "Just do what you're told, and here are the constraints and controls."

- **How should companies build a high-performance system that allows people to use their talents to the fullest?**

First of all, because it is inevitable that you will have to go outside for talent, hire people who share your philosophy and who fit the culture of the organization. You should not just hire people for their technical skills and experience. They should agree with and be congruent with the values and culture of the organization. You also need to help them understand how they are supposed to work in the organization and what the expectations are so that they are constructive to the culture. In addition to hiring right, get rid of the people who are disruptive to the culture. Companies do an equally poor or even poorer job of that.

- **What can CEOs do to turn around an organization, or to correct a bad culture?**

It depends on where the problems are coming from. If you're in an industry that's dying, there's probably not much you can do except get into another industry. The quality movement had within it a couple of good ideas, and one was that you tried to get down to the root cause of problems. It's called "root cause analysis," which means you ask "Why?" five times or more until you drill down to get at the basic problem. So, for example, when somebody says, "Our profits are down." You ask, "Why?" "Because our sales are down." "Why?" "Well, our sales are down because our customers aren't buying our products." "Why?" "Because our products are perhaps late or they're not fitting the needs of our customers." Why? And so on until, finally, you discover the root of the problem. Many companies are very superficial in their analysis of these issues, and therefore never solve the basic problems; and, since they don't fix anything or the right thing, nothing really changes.

- There is a shift in thinking about which skills ensure success
  for today's leaders. The consensus seems to be that it's not
  enough just to have business acumen and smarts, but that
  the softer skills of active listening and empathy are also essential.
  Is this a result of the intangible asset world we live in
  or something else?

That's one reason why the emphasis on soft skills has been elevated. The other reason is that hundreds of thousands of middle managers have been taken out of organizational structures; therefore, everybody has to learn how to manage more people. If my span of control is a few people, then I don't necessarily have to have any soft skills, because I can watch these few people every minute. However, as we've removed layers of management, people have had to learn how to get people to do things without direct supervision. You are also persuading many more people, and the soft skills are required for CEOs and line managers. By the way, the soft skills are actually much harder than the hard skills, since they're much harder to learn and much harder to duplicate. Anybody can read a finance book and learn how to do capital asset pricing models. The irony is that a lot of the things that people think are the hard skills are, in fact, easily learned and easily transferred and, therefore, cannot provide a sustainable competitive advantage.

- What is your advice to CEOs about knowledge management?

Knowledge management is not about intranets and Lotus notes and all the stuff around technology. It's about having an organization in which people are both encouraged to, and have the time to, talk to each other. The great paradox is that everybody talks about building a learning organization but no one wants a company where anybody learns anything—because learning, by definition, means having the opportunity to do things that you're not very good at, and that requires a large investment in people's development and a certain amount of inefficiency. Everybody talks about knowledge sharing and knowledge management, but if you had time to actually learn something from somebody else, in many companies, people would say, "Well, you know, we haven't fully loaded your work day, because how can you possibly have time to talk to and help out other people?" Few companies would support a whole day of nothing but brainstorming, and it would probably be considered inefficient to take a day or two off your project to help someone else, but these are some of the best ways to share knowledge.

- What are your views on the war for talent and how companies will compete for the top people?

It is certainly a demographic fact that there will be fewer qualified people in the job market; however, it is a fact completely irrelevant for many companies because, unless you intended to hire 100 percent of the workforce, you don't care what the workforce is as a whole. I have found that there is never a shortage of people in companies that are great places to work. For any given organization, all you need to do is make sure that you have a place where people want to be and want to excel.

- What two or three skills should CEOs really focus on and develop?

There are the obvious skills such as persistence and the ability to communicate. However, another great paradox of corporate life is that everyone wants to earn extraordinary returns, and they want to do it by benchmarking what everybody else is doing. But you cannot benchmark your way to the top. At best, you can benchmark your way to the middle, because you don't achieve exceptional results by copying other people; and that's true whether we're talking about products or organizations. The way you achieve exceptional results is by having the courage to listen to customers, listen to the marketplace, and do different things. If you do what everybody else does, you'll get pretty much the same results. And, courage, by the way, is in very short supply.

Compensation and reward systems based
on performance and business strategy

Pearl Meyer
Pearl Meyer & Partners
Founder and Chief Executive Officer

- What are the latest trends in compensation?

The most significant change in executive compensation packages over the past decade has been the shift to pay-for-performance programs that are focused on stock-based incentives to motivate and reward the creation of shareholder value. This evolution reflects the priorities of institutional shareholders and the corporate governance movement, as well as heightened scrutiny by the media. These trends and the historic rise in stock prices over the past decade have resulted in a sharp increase in compensation and extraordinary levels of executive wealth. For 2000 and 2001, 91 percent of CEOs pay at the top 200 U.S. industrial and service companies was variable, with as much as 70 percent based on the price of the stock and only about 20 percent based on business and financial performance. The top 200 CEO annual salaries have come to average over $1 million, despite the fact that non-performance-based earnings over $1 million are not tax deductible. A number of CEO pensions—income for life—are also in excess of $1 million per annum. At the end of fiscal year 2000, CEO equity holdings at the top 200 averaged $124 million, compared to $39 million at the end of fiscal 1996. That included direct stock ownership of $73 million and unrealized option gains of $51 million. Concurrently, shareholder return expectations during the 1990s rose to new heights, cycles have become more volatile, investor patience is more limited, and senior executives are accorded a very limited window in which to produce anticipated results. To illustrate, the number of new CEOs among the top 200 doubled from 1999 to 2000, and that pace continued in 2001. Executives rightly perceive themselves to be at risk for their jobs, their reputations, their pay, and their accumulated capital. This perception is reflected in the intense drive for financial and job security and a proliferation of escalating rewards, as well as employment contracts and change-in-control protections with platinum parachutes. Other special rewards, typically megagrants of options, have become commonplace as ways to recognize successful merger and acquisition deals, turnarounds, the sale of an enterprise, and other major transactions or extraordinary achievements.

- Going forward, what will be the trends in compensation?

For 2002, we see companies continuing to seek buoys for their underwater options and stock loans. Salary increases will slow, bonuses for 2001 performance will be cut or eliminated amid extensive layoffs, and there will be some shift away from options to long-term performance incentives and restricted stock grants. Looking ahead, companies' most critical compensation challenges will be focused around rebalancing their pay programs to move away from an overreliance on stock options and the stock market to fund their compensation and benefit programs. Redesigned compensation programs will reflect the true elements of performance, incorporating each company's specific strategy and goals. Such programs will reward executives for sound business management that leads to superior long-term financial results and that creates superior shareholder value. At the same time, companies need to reestablish their relationships with and trust of executives and employees. Companies will make a point of building "early success" opportunities into their annual and long-term incentive plans with increased leverage for exceeding targets. Such programs will incorporate some protection in stock market downturns, although companies will be challenged to do so without weakening the essential linkage to shareholder interests.

- What specifically should companies focus on?

Pay plans must be rebalanced to place more weight on incentives focused on business and financial goals and rewards for results achieved, rather than relying solely on stock prices to motivate and reward. Such incentives lengthen the performance horizon and recognize that management is a long-term job. However, we strongly recommend that companies also take action to ensure that key executives maintain a significant equity interest in the enterprises they run, without "giving away the store." The first step is correcting what we have long maintained is companies' overuse of opportunistic pay vehicles whose weaknesses were easily overlooked when the market seemed on a one-way ride north. Chief among those is overdosing on the standard 10-year stock option granted at fair market value—a misguided "one size fits all" approach. It frequently leaves optionees either highly vulnerable to—or beneficiaries of—stock market shifts beyond their control. More flexible option vehicles are needed—vehicles that can be tailored to meet each company's business strategy and human resources needs. The nonqualified option can be easily customized as to term pricing, participation, performance elements, vesting terms, and exercise rights. Among the many available alternatives are performance-accelerated stock options, performance vesting options, premium priced options, and truncated options.

- What is the role of the board in compensation?

The board has responsibility for compensation, which it generally delegates to the compensation committee. The compensation committee, depending on the charter of each company and the committee's charter, which is determined by the board, usually has total purview over executive compensation as well as overall employee compensation and benefits programs, and the administration of stock plans, including grants. However, during the last 10 years, boards have empowered their compensation committees to oversee performance as well as pay. This delegation has made compensation the most active and powerful of all board committees, meeting more often and having far more impact on corporate affairs than audit and finance committees.

- Given these responsibilities and authority, what are the desired skill sets of compensation committee members?

Integrity, sophistication, business experience, and human resources awareness are key requirements. Most important, members must understand business enterprises and economics from the perspective of the shareholder. Further, they need to exhibit backbone in recruiting, negotiating, and evaluating talent so they can withstand pressures and demand a high standard of performance from senior-level executives. Compensation committees and boards too often operate from positions of weakness, particularly when dealing with or even hiring chief executive officers who are critical to company fortunes. Some boards, looking for saviors because they waited too long to bring in great people, may respond by hiring a marquee-name CEO. In contrast, a smart board will apply stringent criteria to ensure the selection of precisely the right person in the role. It will look seriously at more than one viable candidate and be able to say, if necessary, "That executive is perfect for something, but not to be our CEO."

- **What are some of the common mistakes that companies make around compensation?**

My former mentor always said, "Say it with pay." A compensation system is a most effective way to communicate, yet many fail in this regard. Programs should be designed to reflect the company's vision, mission, value, culture, business cycle stage, and goals, as well as rewards that make it clear that producing winning results pays off. Yet, in establishing their pay programs, too many companies only focus externally on marketplace comparisons. They merely look at general practice or plan prevalence and price their programs at the average, median or seventy-fifth-percentile pay level among peer companies, rather than designing for the specific needs of their organization and its employees.

Chapter 3

- # Establishing Competitive Advantage in Today's Market Environment

Navigating in today's business environment: Companies with a "strategic principle" have a tool at the ready

Orit Gadiesh
Bain & Company
Chairman

Establishing a competitive advantage is vital to every leader's agenda. A competitive advantage is defined by a company's unique offer to specific customer segments, based on its cost position or capabilities that are superior to its competitors'. In order to be successful, a firm needs to communicate that advantage very simply to all stakeholders. Today, however, more than ever, a firm also needs to ensure that its strategic approach to achieving competitive advantage is understood and executed at all levels of its organization.

In this book's introduction, the editors outline some of the significant pressures facing businesses in today's market environment that affect leadership and the management of human capital, such as advances in technology, globalization, the war for qualified talent, the flattening of the organization, the importance of intangible assets, and the speed required to make and implement decisions consistent with a company's strategy.

The leaders featured in this chapter present their expert views on what creates, constitutes, and extends competitive advantage in today's world of intangible assets. They offer examples such as the need to create a culture where individual aspirations are realized, the increasing importance of people skills, using an operating philosophy to drive strategy and actions, establishing professional management techniques in an emerging marketplace, and creatively harnessing the value of relationships with all constituencies. All roads lead to how to best deploy people in an organization to differentiate and achieve break-away competitive advantage.

What I would like to focus on is an important tool for transforming a company's plan for competitive advantage, or its strategic direction, into specific, strategically grounded actions on the front line. This tool is relevant, be your business local, regional or global. It's called a "strategic principle." It's expressed as a clear, memorable directive that allows front-line operators to make trade-offs quickly in an era in which turbulence has become the steady state of business.

What does a strategic principle look like? When the "godfather" of strategic principles, Jack Welch, took the reins at GE two decades ago, he announced the conglomerate's new strategic principle: It would be number one or number two in its industries, or it would get out. "You can't reduce strategy to a formula," said Welch in his first major speech as CEO, and he quoted the Prussian general Helmuth Von Moltke: "Strategy was not a lengthy action plan. It was the evolution of a central idea through continually changing circumstances." So Welch evangelized his central idea, his principle, and he evolved it. In the nineties, as the economy picked up, he asked his business leaders to redefine their business boundaries so that they had only 10 percent of a given market, and then figure out how to be number one or number two in the newly defined market.

Such phrases may sound like simple slogans, but they actually encapsulate strategies at the heart of competitive differentiation. They have nothing to do with mission or vision statements. They are memorable and actionable directions that distill a company's corporate strategy to its unique essence. And they can be observed at a clutch of companies, even though those companies don't always label them as such. The phrases imply trade-offs in allocating scarce resources; boundaries for experimentation; and a litmus test for action.

At Wal-Mart, the phrase is: "Low Prices, Every Day." At Dell Computer, it's: "Be Direct." Because these phrases are easily remembered, they connect the hub of corporate strategy—a company's comprehensive plan for the effective allocation of scarce resources—to a broad rim of decision-makers, like spokes on a wheel. Indeed, during the recessions of 1987 and 1991, when consumers' concept of a "low price" went further south, Wal-Mart stuck to its principle and achieved its gains in large part through aggressive price rollbacks. At Dell, "Be Direct" forces trade-offs for every operator pursuing new products, markets, or even cost reduction. His or her decision must be in favor of maintaining direct sales to the customer. Dell's phrase likewise provides operators with parameters for experimentation and an acid test for new ideas. This principle fueled Dell's 10-year annual growth rate of 51.8 percent from 1990 to 2000. And Dell's brief abandonment of this principle to experiment with retail distribution led to its sole loss-making year in 1994.

Leading by Strategic Principle

Strategic principles have become particularly useful in today's volatile business environment. Over the past year, we have come to appreciate a strategic principle's ability to help companies maintain strategic focus while global economies have faltered and geopolitical landscapes have been threatened. Over the past few years, as the Internet has proliferated and industries have consolidated, we've seen how strategic principles have helped to foster flexibility among employees and therefore have permitted innovation and rapid response to opportunities and threats to occur. Strategic principles are likely to become even more crucial to corporate success in the years ahead as a means to:

- Force trade-offs between competing resource demands
- Test strategic soundness of a particular action
- Set clear boundaries within which employees must operate while granting them freedom to experiment within those constraints

Who Has Well-Articulated Strategic Principles?

Many of the best and most conspicuous examples of strategic principles come from companies that were founded on them, including American Express, Dell Computer, eBay, GE, Nestlé, Southwest Airlines, Vanguard, and Wal-Mart.

The founders of those companies crafted their strategic principles at a critical juncture: when increasing corporate complexity threatened to confuse priorities on the front line and obscure the essence that truly differentiated their strategy from those of their rivals. By espousing a clearly articulated, straightforward strategic principle that summarized the essence of what would become a full-blown business strategy, they attracted investors who believed it, attracted and hired employees who bought into it, and targeted and won customers who wanted it.

In the past, having a strategic principle could be more or less important, or more or less powerful, depending on the circumstances surrounding your business. But there are at least three situations in which strategic principles are critical to catalyze actions. In today's fragile world, these situations often exist simultaneously.

During times of retrenchment, for example, a strategic principle is crucial. Periods of retrenchment reduce the margin for error. A clear and precise strategic principle can protect your strategic trajectory and preserve your organization's flexibility and responsiveness while contracting. A strategic principle also anchors priorities for renewed expansion, a time when decisions and decision-makers tend to proliferate.

Take, for example, American Express (AMEX). In the aftermath of the September 11 terrorist attacks, which destroyed the company's headquarters, the CEO,

Ken Chenault, began charting a path through recession using AMEX's longstanding strategic principle. Chenault articulates the principle as "offering superior value to customers, continually driving toward best-in-class economics, and building the American Express brand." On the front lines, this principle challenges operators to push for product innovations in line with cost targets and look for cost-cutting opportunities that do not undermine customer value.

How are operators managing these trade-offs? AMEX is reducing costs by using technology to process more paperwork, and it's moving back-office functions overseas to places like India, where it can maintain high levels of service to customers at lower costs. On the innovation front, AMEX has launched products like the "Blue" credit card, whose enhanced services have allowed AMEX to reach a broader set of customers. As the first mass-market smart card in the United States, Blue allowed users to make secure Internet payments. But AMEX carefully targeted its investment in technologies embedded in cards.

AMEX's commitment to improve cost and value while enhancing its brand led management, post–September 11, to begin offering double miles on all merchandise purchased with its Delta SkyMiles credit cards. This was a costly decision that also created best-in-class economics by improving AMEX's ability to attract higher-spending customers and capture more of their purchases. In addition, the move is building brand loyalty for AMEX and its partners during a tough time—when friends in a foxhole can become friends for life.

In industries fraught with rapid change, strategic principles become very important. Radical changes in technology-driven industries over the past decade have been costly for firms without a strategic principle. Nowhere in business has there been more uncertainty combined with so great an emphasis placed on speed and such high odds of failure. Managers in these industries must react immediately to sudden and totally unexpected developments—both positive and negative—and the sum of the reactions around the organization become the company's strategic course.

Strategic principles—for example, Dell's mandate to sell direct to end-users—guarantee that the decisions made by frontline managers in such circumstances add up to a consistent, coherent strategy. Likewise, eBay, whose principle is "Focus on trading communities," might have been tempted, like many Internet marketplaces, to diversify into all sorts of services. But eBay has chosen to outsource certain services—for instance, management of the photos that sellers post on the site to illustrate the items they put up for bid—while it continues to invest in services like Billpoint, which lets sellers accept credit card payments from bidders. The company's strategic principle has ensured that the entire company stays focused on the core trading business, one that has profit built into every transaction.

In times of leadership succession, a strategic principle is a powerful tool to smooth the transition, and the need for such a tool has never been starker. A total of 2,045 CEOs in the United States left their jobs from November 1999 to October 2001, at an average rate of nearly three per day. In October 2001, alone, 80 CEOs exited, according to the outplacement firm Challenger, Gray & Christmas, including such industry icons as Jacques Nasser of Ford and James Goodwin of United Airlines. And the trend is accelerating. Exits in October 2001 were up 31 percent from September and 40 percent from August. Meanwhile, the average tenure of remaining CEOs shrank 42 percent to 4.2 years in October, from 7.2 years in August.

So how does a strategic principle render such transitions less rocky? Just ask GE, Southwest Airlines, or Vanguard, all of which passed the leadership torch with few ripples. Successors at these companies sometimes brought with them a change of strategy, but they stuck to their strategic principles. For instance, when Jack Brennan assumed the leadership mantle from the Vanguard Group's founder, John Bogle, the strategic transition was seamless. Brennan simply continued with the philosophy behind "Be lowest cost to serve the investor-owner." Managers knew the direction of the firm and could make trade-offs that would help them get there. For example, they made a relatively quick call on their Internet strategy: It would not promote online trading, which would increase costs, but would promote richer and more rapid fund and account information to investor-owners at the highest level of electronic security. Vanguard continued to pursue its strategic objectives without many of the distractions so often associated with changes in leadership.

Likewise, when terrorist attacks rocked the airline industry in 2001, Southwest Airlines' new CEO, James Parker, made quick decisions, in line with the company's principle of "addressing travelers' short-haul flight needs at fares competitive with auto transport." Although Parker had succeeded Southwest's founder, Herb Kelleher, only months before, the firm's employees quickly aligned, accepting pay cuts to avoid layoffs and maintain operations and low fares despite low loads. While United and other airlines reduced flights, Southwest kept a full schedule, winning customer and employee loyalty along with market share.

Strategic principles derive their power from grounding in a company's unique economic reality. Of course, just as a brilliant strategy is worthless unless it is implemented, a powerful strategic principle is of no use unless it is communicated effectively. It takes enormous discipline. Yet strategic principles do evolve over time. Just developing a strategic principle is not enough, especially in today's world of change. The onus on leaders who have a strategic principle is to review it—frequently—in tandem with their strategy, to ensure continued relevance. The onus on leaders who don't is to tackle the hard work of creating one—fast.

The new sources of competitive advantage

Mohanbir Sawhney
Kellogg School of Management at Northwestern University
McCormick Tribune Professor of Electronic Commerce and Technology

- What are the leadership challenges facing CEOs today?

We are witnessing a migration in value from the resources that were once the basis of competitive advantage, which tended to be physical assets and physical resources, toward the new sources for competitive advantage, intangible assets. These intangibles assets include human capital, structural capital such as intellectual property and brands, and relationship capital—the value of the firm's relationships with customers, suppliers, and partners. Every business is becoming more information-intensive and more intellectual capital–intensive, so the leadership challenges today have to do with managing intangible assets. Business leaders are much better at managing the tangibles. There's an old saying in management that, if you can't measure it, you can't manage it. This has created a "tangibility bias" in management, but you can't equate intangible with unimportant any longer. You have to figure out how to manage something that you don't have good metrics on and you don't know how well you're doing because it doesn't show up on your balance sheet and there aren't any good management control systems for it. You can't draw up a balance scorecard for intangible assets, but, clearly, human capital management is becoming as important as, or even more important than, physical asset management. Leaders therefore need to be able to identify, attract, and retain human capital regardless of the market's situation. Another challenge that leaders face today—to a much greater extent than before—is managing relationship capital, which includes relationships with customers, business partners, suppliers, resellers, and any other relationships that complement your business. The success of a company will depend to a large degree on management's ability to leverage its partners and to manage partner relationships strategically so that the company doesn't own all the assets it uses, and instead leverages the assets of its partners. There is increased pressure now for businesses to outsource noncore activities so they can focus better on their core business. I see an interesting paradox in terms of the scope of the firm. The core of the firm—what it does within its four walls—will continue to shrink, but its periphery, the scope of activities it orchestrates through partners, will continue to expand. The leadership challenge that emerges in this partner-intensive world is to be able to coordinate the activities of partners without whom you can't succeed but over whom you do not have direct control. As independent entities, they don't work directly for you. Their interests are not necessarily aligned with yours.

- You often talk about object thinking versus relation thinking, which
  is necessary in a connected economy. What are the implications
  for leadership in this relational model?

Object thinking is another way of expressing the fact that managers traditionally have managed physical objects, that is, physical assets, while relation thinking means that managers will increasingly have become better at managing connections, that is, relationships. Firms need to do a much better job of understanding what capital or equity these relationships represent; and how relational equity is created, managed, measured, deployed, and leveraged. As you partition consider the different types of relationships that the firm needs to manage, the leadership challenge is to make sure that all of these relationships function synergistically, and that you create the appropriate metrics and accountability for relationship management. There are strong organizational implications. Are you organized correctly for relationship management, or is your organization product-centric, that is, organized around the things that you make? Changing from a product-centric organization to a relationship-centric organization requires you to not only change technologically but also to change organizationally, change business processes, change philosophically. It's a complicated migration, and it requires a lot of fortitude from the leadership team to make it happen.

- How can companies organize around relationships instead
  of being product-centric?

Through business synchronization, which involves designing or redesigning your business around your customers, in other words, "getting in synch" with your customers. The way that firms sell and go to market is not typically the way customers buy or the way customers think about their life and their work. Businesses tend to think in terms of products, business units, positions, functional areas, and market share. Customers think in terms of activities, work flow, life events, benefits, solutions, and experiences. There is often a big disconnect between what customers want and how they want to interact with firms, and how firms actually interact with customers. The concept of synchronization is to redesign the firm's offerings, technology infrastructure, and organizational structure, simultaneously working on all these dimensions, to build a business that is clearly customer focused. We have talked about customer focus for a long time, but actually making it happen requires a simultaneous redesign and alignment. The implications for organizations are automatic, because your organization will have to be restructured so that it isn't organized around product or business units but around key customer accounts and key customer relationships; this way, the front end of your organization, which faces the customers, brings together all of the products and solutions for the customers, and the back end of the organization becomes the product-oriented organization as well as the shared services organization. This sort of hybrid front-back organization is dramatically different from the traditional product-centric business organization that is still in place in many companies. Given the radical nature of the redesign, the challenge for leaders is to get beyond the deeply ingrained ways of thinking and make the transition to a customer-focused approach.

- What are the skill sets to be successful in this environment?

The important skill that people need to develop as leaders is the ability to deal with ambiguity and manage in uncertain times. There is no longer a clear distinction among collaborators and competitors. There was a time when it was clear what the difference was between them and us—there was a neat distinction. You were either a friend or a foe. You were a competitor or a partner. But now, we see the new and somewhat exotic phenomenon of "co-opetition," in which you're collaborating with competitors and competing with them at the same time. To quote F. Scott Fitzgerald, the true mark of intelligence is being able to keep two conflicting ideas in your mind at the same time and retain the ability to function. Building these complex webs of relationships with partners who may actually compete with you in another domain or another area is a very ambiguous undertaking, and you need to be a lot more open-minded and creative about arrangements that enhance the organization. Another skill that becomes important in this environment is negotiation—the ability to search for win-win outcomes and win-win scenarios, to create a larger pie as opposed to competing for a share of the pie. Lastly, the skill of CEOs and senior managers to create a vision that everyone in the company can identify with and be motivated and excited by is critically important. Leaders are evangelists more than anything else, and need to constantly align people's and business activities toward the larger goal. Infusing the organization with a sense of purpose and a mission that is larger than profits is very important, because it will motivate people, and that, in turn, will determine your ability to retain good people; thus, ultimately, it will determine your organization's success in the marketplace.

- Many students of management today espouse the notion that sustainable competitive advantage is dependent on a company's ability to innovate and change continuously. What is your view on the built-to-change model, and should companies move in that direction? If so, how do they do that?

There are no new ideas in management; they're just repackaged. The notion of continuous innovation and changing to survive is not new. In fact, one of the first students of management was Charles Darwin. We often say that Darwin posited the theory of "survival of the fittest," but that's not exactly correct. What Darwin recognized was the survival of the most adaptable species. Species that don't adapt and can't change become extinct. This principle also applies to companies, and most critically in terms of business strategy. I absolutely believe that organizations need to change to survive; but, often, size dictates adaptability. You need skill to successfully innovate, and often the way to get skill is to have size, or critical mass. Leaders then leverage size and skill through innovation. For example, a lot of the mergers and acquisitions activity in telecommunications, financial services, and car manufacturing has made some companies very large, yet bigger is certainly not more adaptable, as we know. But, at the same time, you need critical mass to attract and be able to replicate critical skills; and, certainly, some of these companies found a way to leverage size and skill with the ability to innovate. One of the ways companies can begin moving in this direction is to differentiate between the operations in which skills are critical and those in which adaptability is critical. Then, you are able to use the scale you have achieved to your advantage by simultaneously encouraging innovation at the grassroots level within an organization. You do this by giving people a lot of autonomy and resources and telling them innovation is expected and that they won't be killed for trying something different. The relevant leadership issue is to have a very clear understanding of who's responsible for innovation and how the innovation process is actually managed at all levels. Innovation and ideas can come from many different directions; they can be bottom-up, they can be top-down, they can be inward-out, they can be outward-in, they can be lateral, within different business units. There are lots of sources for new ideas. Leaders need to think about how to encourage not only idea flow but also to understand the process and life cycle of an idea. Where do you take good ideas? How do you build them in to a business? How do you get resources? Have you removed bottlenecks in the organization to actually capitalize on the idea flow inside your company, as well as a created process for drawing on and sourcing external ideas? Have you created a culture that promotes risk-taking? Do you advocate dissent and diversity of opinion and voices? New ideas get created into new businesses, and new businesses can produce competitive advantage.

- What is your perspective on leadership during a crisis?

One critical aspect of crisis leadership is being able to maintain one's balance, equanimity, and composure in the midst of chaos. In the aftermath of the terrorist attacks, one CEO who lost several employees in the World Trade Center explosions said to me, "One day, I wake up thinking that I'm spending too much time on the human issues and neglecting the business issues; another day, I wake up and say, 'I'm being too coldhearted by focusing squarely on getting back to business and ignoring the human issues.'" So, finding the strength to stay balanced and not to overreact one way or the other in the face of crisis is one essential skill. Another important aspect of crisis leadership is empathy—really feeling for people who are suffering and communicating to them that you care. Being out in front while tragedy unfolds is critical, too, because the absence of management is extremely noticeable. Also, it is vital not to lose your perspective even when a crisis is larger than life and may seem insurmountable. Others are looking to you to see how they should react. It is important to stay on course for the long run to maintain long-term viability and success, even though it is difficult because you are reacting to day-to-day, or even minute-to-minute, to events that seem, and may actually be, overwhelming.

A consumer-driven leadership model

A. G. Lafley
Procter & Gamble Company
President and Chief Executive Officer

- What is your management or leadership philosophy
  at Procter & Gamble?

We operate under the clear directive that the consumer is boss. We have institutionalized a consumer-driven leadership model here, and everyone in the company worldwide understands this is our priority. Our entire behavior is dictated by what we call the two consumer moments of truth. The first moment of truth occurs when a shopper makes a purchase decision and chooses either the P & G brand or an alternative. To win at that moment of truth, we make sure our leaders and our people have done everything they can do to influence that decision in our favor. The second moment of truth occurs once the product is consumed at home and the experience is either delightful or not. We want the consumer to be satisfied with the value of our product, because, after winning a purchase decision, if we win a usage occasion, then we hope we're into a *series* of winning moments of truth. We spend a great deal of energy strategizing about how our brands—branded products and services—are going to win those two consumer moments of truth. We also talk about a third moment of truth because of the way we can capture consumer feedback and reactions around the world. When our consumers call or write us with questions and comments, for example, it is a third moment of truth because it gives us a chance to understand what additional benefits, services, and attributes we need to offer to win the first two primary moments of truth. We believe we have more contacts with consumers than any other business in the world. This consumer-is-boss concept is the most powerful motivator for our leaders and every P & G associate.

- **How do P & G's performance management and reward systems reinforce this behavior in your workforce?**

You have to walk the talk. I require our presidents, the line leaders of our businesses, to spend time with the consumer every week and with the retailer who serves that consumer. Periodically, we bring in the 20 presidents who run the line business operations and 10 or so heads of the staff organization and we spend a few hours, every one of us, individually, in a consumer home. We do one-on-one interviews with consumers, and granted, it is not quantitative research, but we learn one heck of a lot by doing this. We gain remarkable insights into the attitudes, behaviors, and beliefs of at least some of our consumers. We did this shortly after the terrorist attacks of September 11, 2001, to gauge how consumer attitudes might have been changed by those events, what the new needs and attitudes are and how we can address them. It was a tremendous learning experience. During our annual meeting, we bring in 250 or so of our top business executives worldwide to set objectives and discuss key issues for the year ahead. Every one of them will take time to shop a couple of hours with a consumer—not because shopping in Cincinnati is directly relevant to shopping in a bazaar or an open market in Pakistan, but to keep them up-to-date on the latest techniques for eliciting responses from consumers. Regarding the recognition and reward system process at P & G, people will do what they have seen done that is successful. In our kind of business, we have a fairly high correlation between individuals who really understand their consumer and their market and business success as measured by market share growth, sales and profit growth, total shareholder return, and other predictable financial return measures. That linkage is key. When our best leaders go into a new geographic market, the first place they really go is into consumers' homes.

For example, several years ago in Asia, every time I went to China, our president running the Chinese business took me into homes at night because most of the women worked during the day. The next morning, we went into stores to be among shoppers and witness the consumer's first moment of truth. Only after that did we go to the office and begin to discuss strategy, choices we were making, operational plans, quality of execution, and results. The process starts with the consumer and ends with performance management and reward systems.

- **What skills and attributes are you looking for in your leaders to continually develop this consumer-driven leadership model?**

We're obviously looking for leadership qualities—brainpower, creativity, and a demonstrated track record of achievement, contribution, and success. But, at P & G, we also look for certain unique values and principles. Some, such as integrity, are very straightforward, but others are even more relevant to our consumer-driven leadership model. We look for respect for the individual. We look for people who are open and as good at listening as they are at talking. We look for people who have operated and succeeded in diverse environments. In that 30-person group of leaders, we have a dozen different countries and cultures represented. So we try to incorporate a high value on our male/female, racial, and cultural differences.

- **You mentioned P & G's presence in China. What have your experiences been in emerging markets?**

What we characterize as developing markets are markets that are incredibly important to us. Our business is driven by demographics, so where the population is, where households are larger and growing, where incomes are rising, that is where we have to be—because most of our branded products are everyday, consumable products. Being in these markets starts with a business need. Today, nearly $10 billion, or 25 percent, of our sales, are in high-growth, developing markets. Future growth is not going to come from Japan, western Europe, or the United States, which are advancing rapidly toward zero population growth. China and Russia are good examples of markets that opened up to the rest of the world at about the same time. Regarding China, we were there in the first few months, and the first two people we put on the ground were the general manager and a market research specialist who happens to be proficient in Mandarin Chinese. Half their time was spent in the marketplace talking to consumers and in homes, because we knew from the beginning that we would not be successful there unless we had a deep understanding of Chinese consumers. We knew from experience that we couldn't take brands and products from the developed world into a developing market and be automatically successful. We struggled mightily for over a decade in Japan, because when we entered the market in the seventies, we tried to import products directly from western Europe and America and it just didn't work. We had to modify our products in some meaningful way, and we had to dramatically modify the aesthetic packaging and create brands that were meaningful to the Japanese consumer. We're also in developing markets that will take longer for us to cultivate because of native or other competitors which have been doing business there for fifty or a hundred years. In India, for example, which was part of the British Empire, the Anglo-Dutch Unilever Company has been in business there since the nineteenth century. We are relative latecomers in markets in the southern cone of Latin America, Brazil and Argentina, having just entered those markets in the last 5 to 10 years.

- **What are the elements of competitive advantage today?**

A company such as ours has only two sustainable competitive advantages. One is our people and the culture we have created around our people. The other competitive advantage is our brands; but, realistically, any new product has a competitive life cycle of about 12 months maximum. It's pretty clear that technology life cycles are shortening, and that new technologies and new products can be copied fairly quickly around the world. It is truly the quality, the power, the inspiration, and the passion of the people who work for us that is critical. I don't worry about the brainpower. I don't worry about the leadership potential. I try to inspire the passion and the commitment and the desire to be the best. If we can get that, that's what'll make the difference.

- **Regarding leadership potential, P & G has a long history of developing its people. What is your approach to executive development, and how have you institutionalized it within the company?**

We have recently rekindled connections with P & G alumni, all the people who've worked at P & G and now work elsewhere in the world. We were pleased with the magnitude of people who started their careers here 5 to 25 years ago and are now CEOs, company presidents, and board members. We know we have a system that works, and it all begins with recruiting. We spend an incredible amount of time recruiting. At the fundamental level, we recruit at the best schools right alongside McKinsey & Company, Goldman Sachs, and Microsoft to get our fair share of the talent. We try to recruit the best and the brightest, even though they may believe initially that it's more lucrative to go to Wall Street and be an investment banker or more fun to run off to Silicon Valley and do a start-up. Our recruiting process is disciplined and rigorous, and it is proven to work. All our business leaders are actively involved in the process. I personally go to three or four schools a year and recruit. Second, we have a pretty active training program that focuses on functional training. Our P & G College—which will increasingly become more important as the "war for talent" wages on—teaches business skills along with strategic, operational, and organizational development. Similar to GE's Crotonville, P & G College's faculty consists of the staff and line leadership of the company. Finally, our executive development process is driven by the consumer-is-boss concept and then by our business strategy, principles, and values. We try to move continually toward a more rigorous leadership development program.

- Jack Welch believed that a good beta test for leadership was to put a high potential executive in charge of a business unit that would not directly affect the core. The executive could make mistakes in this "popcorn stand" because the best learning is through failure. Do you agree with this philosophy?

I'll give you a great example, because I agree this is a great way to test, measure, and develop a person's potential. We sent an individual to a popcorn stand called Australia. He struggled mightily in the market and lost a bunch of money by Australian and New Zealand standards. It wasn't going to break the company, of course, but it was an extremely beneficial learning experience to him to make mistakes there. We then moved him into a business category in Japan; he had a great success. We then moved him into China, where he had another success in another business. We then moved him back to run our marketing and media function, where he was successful yet again. He then decided to leave the company, and he's in the ministry studying to be a minister. How's that for leadership development?

Obtaining market leadership by valuing innovation, autonomy, and partnership internally

Lucien Alziari
PepsiCo
Vice President, Staffing and Executive Development

- In terms of PepsiCo's next generation of leaders, what will the performance benchmarks be?

We focus on a number of areas in developing well-rounded and high-impact executives. The first requirement is results—that's what gets you in the game here.

Then we look for the right mix of leadership capability, functional excellence, and business breadth, or "knowing the business cold," as we say here at PepsiCo. Finally, we look at the critical experiences an executive has had over the course of many years, both to see how well they have adapted to different challenges and to ensure that each new experience is additive, not a duplication of something they've already done. In return, we need to offer new opportunities for growth, which provide a runway to enhance these talents. We adjust these factors over time to get the optimal balance, but we have found that this is the combination that creates impactful, successful leaders.

- How important is it that these executives possess soft skills—that is, active listening, empathy, and the ability to negotiate and communicate well?

It is very important. Our leadership model for several years now has been based on three overarching imperatives: "Setting the Agenda," "Taking Others with You," and "Doing It the Right Way." The importance of Taking Others with You has increased over time. In previous years, the emphasis was on Setting the Agenda; quite often, there were leaders who were really good at this but did a less than stellar job of building people and bringing the organization with them. The ability to take others with you and mobilize all of the resources that you are accountable for is very important; otherwise, you're merely really a very bright individual contributor. In large, complex businesses, this becomes even more important because the business is beyond an individual leader's ability to do it by himself or herself.

- Can you predict which skills and abilities will work in PepsiCo's corporate culture?

Although our workforce constitutes a fairly broad cross-section of people, some of the core characteristics of PepsiCo people are shared; these include a passion for what we do, a drive for results, a need to make a difference, a focus on growth, and then, the ability to pull it all together and get buy-in from the organization. Ours is a highly competitive industry; it's not called the cola wars for nothing. There is a level of energy and passion that people bring to this company that is extraordinary. It is what gets that extra 50 percent out of people. They want to make an impact, and we're a business that probably puts more focus on growth than others because of the categories we're in and our market share in those categories. Category leaders need to grow the business; it doesn't grow itself. This puts a premium on innovation, new thinking, taking fresh perspectives on the market, and driving change.

- **PepsiCo has developed a culture that is built to change and built to innovate, something very important for competitive advantage today. How do you get people to thrive on change and innovation so that they view problems as opportunities rather than roadblocks?**

The categories we're in demand innovation. In the soft drink business, as a number two competitor in the market, you can't win by copying the other guy or by outspending him. You win by outflanking the competition with ideas that they would never think of or that they would shy away from if they did. Our innovation pipeline needs to be full for many years to come; that's a necessity with businesses as large and as visible as ours. For example, if our Frito-Lay North America business is about $9-plus billion and we figure a substantial fraction of its growth will need to come from new ideas, then our pipeline needs to have at least $3 billion worth of innovative products headed for the market. The numbers and opportunities are huge. There isn't any business we're in where innovation isn't critical, either to keep an edge on Coke or, as with Frito-Lay, to keep on growing the category, even though there isn't a very clear competitor of our size. It's the same in the Tropicana business, where we're redefining the not-from-concentrate juice market. If you look into why Gatorade succeeded, you'll discover that it was because of enormous innovation over the years. Innovation is a core part of our culture; our people expect it and feel good about it, and it lies at the heart of their approach to solving problems.

- **Does it promote a team-oriented culture as well?**

We are getting better at working across organizational boundaries. Our goal is to find the right balance between the sense of ownership that our businesses have and the realization that sharing ideas can be a faster route to market. We are working hard to ensure that our people can work across functional or divisional lines in their efforts to drive innovation.

- **Is it a challenge to create a boundaryless organization where people look across, up, and down to achieve results instead of only straight ahead?**

In any culture, what works for you and makes you strong 95 percent of the time can limit you the other 5 percent of the time. What makes PepsiCo strong is the autonomy of our business units and divisions. We've never had a very intrusive corporate center. What appeals to people about coming to PepsiCo is a tremendous accountability for results, the expectation that they can make a difference, and the autonomy to do that and live by their results. Our culture of ownership has really driven a lot of our success. Obviously, there are areas such as information technology and purchasing where it makes compelling business sense to come together as a corporation; the challenge for us has been to organize in a way that achieves this kind of leverage without undermining the autonomy of our divisions.

- People have always been instrumental to the success of an organization, but performance is even more critical in this autonomous, high-achiever environment. Has your culture required PepsiCo's HR operation to evolve from the traditional transactional orientation into a more strategic human capital management platform?

There are only a handful of companies in the world that really do HR very, very well. The defining differences aren't related to process; they start with a sense of partnership. HR people need to know they are business executives; they should understand the business as deeply as everyone else, and they must be an integral part of the business and how it works. Their job is to translate their knowledge of the business into people and organizational strategies. You can have the best processes in the world; but without the partnership and integration, you'll have an HR department that is conducting transactions disconnected from the business. That is why [CEO] Steve [Reinemund] chose Peggy Moore as our HR head. She is both a talented business executive and an HR strategist. She speaks as a business leader and therefore has the credibility that other line executives respect.

- That position was one of your CEO's first hires when he came on board, which speaks volumes about the growing importance of the HR role. In terms of skill and scope, how are HR executives' jobs different now from those of their counterparts 10 or 15 years ago?

They are compelled to be much, much stronger business executives and thought leaders, since they need to connect business strategy and people capability. Also, with so much competition for top talent, the HR executive needs to make the organization a compelling place to work. In our case, we have the draw of our brands and the experience of working in a growth environment—but in the end, it boils down to 130,000 people deciding one by one whether this is a place where they can make a difference, be appreciated, learn more, and grow more than anywhere else.

Growing companies in a turbulent environment

Donald H. Morrison
Research in Motion
Chief Operating Officer

- Research in Motion (RIM) weathered the turbulent technology storm quite well. To what do you attribute your growth during a tumultuous economic time?

We were early participants in a brand-new industry sector, the wireless data industry. The reason we continue to grow is because of the utility of our unique product, Blackberry. This isn't something that sells because of its image; it sells because of its value to those who become accustomed to its immediacy. Also, our success is based principally on enabling and enhancing the products and services of very large corporate partners such as IBM, Compaq, and Cingular.

- How are you taking your company and product to new markets—that is, Europe, South America, and Asia?

Despite being an early-stage, relatively young company headquartered in Canada, RIM has very talented people who have lived and worked in other parts of the world. We have a good appreciation for the functions and decisions that you want to make close to the market outside of Canada, as well as those things that you continue to drive and control from international headquarters here at Waterloo [Ontario]. Because there is such a high degree of interest in this phase of our growth, we haven't had an especially hard time recruiting talent; if anything, we've experienced the reverse—having to cipher through all the folks who have an interest in joining us. Up to this point, our challenges related to entering new markets and bridging the gaps with other countries have had more to do with the readiness of the network and technological infrastructure than with having to find the right people to put in place. Also fortunate for us is the fact that it will be much easier to transition those countries' cultures toward our product because the populations there are already well-accustomed to mobile phones, given the unstable wireline systems. There is more room for those countries to adapt new wireless data and voice technology, as opposed to markets that have a traditionally high penetration of wireline use, such as Canada and the United States.

- **How does RIM ensure that it has attracted the best talent available in the marketplace?**

We work closely with a select number of universities and, in fact, we will even locate our facilities to be within close proximity to those technical centers where we believe academic institutions produce high-quality, supercompetent talent. In Canada, that's why we are in Waterloo; it's why we have a smaller office in Toronto; and it's why we have an office in Ottawa. We put stakes in the ground where companies compete for the best talent. We also use executive search firms for key senior positions.

- **It is one thing to bring the best talent on board, but what about developing and retaining them?**

In a relatively infant-stage company such as ours, essentially everyone here is new. What keeps them here is that they recognize and respect that this is not a company that runs on the old paradigm of command and control. Ours is an organic organization, comparable to an egalitarian workplace. One of our mantras is "Everybody works." There are no overseers here, not even with [co-CEOs] Jim Balsillie and Mike Lazaridis. *Everybody* works. So, when you come into a company like ours, you don't necessarily earn respect based on the position that you are given, you earn respect based on your contribution in working with others. We continually try to improve the way we describe and chart out career options for people. Another contributing factor to retention is that we attract people who have an insatiable appetite for learning. They put a very high value on personal growth. Our industry has a high degree of technical complexity, and the business model is in a constant state of flux; therefore, there continues to be new stuff to learn even by staying in the same position over a period of time.

- **Why not just pay well to keep talent?**

We very much believe that what keeps people here isn't just a competitive salary. When you talk with people about why they stay or why they leave, particularly when you have an organization where the median age is relatively young, it's whether or not they feel challenged. Whether or not they feel this place is exciting. People like to be with a winner and feel that spark of electricity when they walk in the door in the morning. Then the first question they expect CEOs and senior managers to address is: "How do I fit into all this?" If you don't have the programs in place to help somebody grow, ultimately you'll see attrition.

- How does today's age of intangibles change the way companies do business?

Generally, we are shifting away from a leadership style that puts authority in the hands of a few, and shifting more toward an egalitarian model of empowerment. You can use whatever barometer you want to use to gauge whether or not companies are doing the right thing, one might be financial performance, another may be reacting to customer's needs. Many companies have a lot to learn in this area. This may sound a bit corny because it can be misconstrued as being rhetoric or the latest fad, but I believe there is something much deeper going on with today's customer. There is a huge backlash of people who are absolutely fed up with superficial advertising that attempts to distinguish companies by their image yet these companies never actually execute well. In a way, we all go to business school and learn the scientific methods of analyses and then we spend the rest of our life in the process of unlearning. What you really learn that works is that sometimes it is better to listen, and to intuit, rather than trying to be distant and mathematical. Our company believes strongly in the notion of servant leadership, which is: "What do I have to do in order to serve you better?" It is our stance, our mindset. We are less inclined to spend tons of money doing market research and more inclined to rely on intuitive incrementalism, which is perpetually talking and incrementing with the marketplace, with the customers, with your partners. Ideally, you make small changes, rather than change being an event. Change is a perpetual incremental process, and it is embedded in your value proposition and your culture. So, in a sense, RIM is in a perpetual stage of "becoming."

- How is this reflected in your human capital strategy?

As part of our due diligence process, we spend a lot of time up front interviewing people because we do not want people here who only see themselves and are blind about the changing identity around them. What you really want are comparatively more selfless people who have a healthy self-awareness. At the end of the day, you are really just trying to create an environment that breeds whole people.

William A. Haseltine
Human Genome Sciences
Chairman and Chief Executive Officer

- Human Genome Sciences (HGS) was born almost 10 years ago out of the Human Genome Project, the group credited with decoding human DNA. Can you briefly describe your organization's mission and your vision of a genomics company?

From the outset we defined our goal as being to create a fully integrated pharmaceutical corporation that discovers, manufactures, and sells its own protein therapeutics. We are now also an antibody therapeutic company. We view genomics as an efficient way of accomplishing our goal, in terms of discovery and financing. Genomics provides us with a large number of candidate therapeutic proteins and proprietary antibody targets. I do not believe that genomics uncoupled from a therapeutics business is a healthy basis for a company.

- In terms of growth areas, where do you see HGS moving?

We plan to develop, manufacture, and conduct clinical trials on an ever-expanding number of our own protein and antibody drugs. We also intend to sell our drugs ourselves. We have completed construction of 200,000 square feet of manufacturing space to supply therapeutic proteins and antibodies for clinical trials, and we will shortly break ground on a manufacturing facility to support the commercial launch of our products. We plan to grow organically, not by acquiring products. We believe that growth by acquisitions should be a secondary goal. Acquired growth, without intrinsic growth, can be demoralizing.

- In terms of technology and innovation shaping your industry, what is reality?

A virtually complete set of human genes available in usable form is a reality for us. By this I do not mean knowledge of genes in the stored form in which they exist in the genome. Rather, I refer to an almost complete collection of genes in a condensed, highly usable form—technically, a cDNA copy of the messenger RNA. From this form, we can make at least one functional protein per gene. Having a library of genes in this form allows us to index them by sequence. We have other tools that allow us to understand the activity of genes in the body, and to evaluate their medical value. These tools extend the scope of our collection of usable genes, but the collection itself is our principal asset. We believe that we are the only company that possesses such an asset.

- It seems that the genomics revolution has prompted many companies, especially the big pharmaceutical companies, to become horizontally integrated. Many companies are now partnering to foster innovation and speed products to market. Do you agree with this trend?

The pharmaceutical industry is always looking for increased efficiencies. The large companies have long recognized they have a productivity crisis that has the potential to seriously affect enterprise valuations. They place a high premium on methods that increase productivity. Yet in spite of significant investments both in external and internal technologies, large pharmaceutical companies still have to demonstrate productivity gains in pharmaceutical discovery and development.

- How do you see partnership alliances playing out in the genomics industry?

We are opportunistic with our alliances. We see our future as being driven primarily by our own discovery, development, and manufacturing—and eventually, our own sales. In the early days after our formation, alliances helped us get off to a quick start. They provided credibility and access to capital. In the future we may enter product-based alliances to gain larger market share and shorter development times.

- Are alliances a way to share in the risk/reward game?

Our pharmaceutical partners have been slower than us to convert knowledge of genes to drugs. This has been our biggest surprise so far.

- What about the role of intellectual property in genomics and pharmaceuticals? Is there a duality of thought such as in the software industry, where there is a public-versus-proprietary debate?

There is a very simple rule in the pharmaceutical industry: no patent, no drug. Patents are the lifeblood of our industry. The requirements for patentability are novelty, utility, and enablement. We believe our patent applications meet these requirements. It has been clear from the outset that genomic data by itself does not meet the utility requirement. That is why we did not invest in genomic sequencing. Patents can be issued on genes that make proteins useful for medical purposes. Patents on human gene-based inventions have been issued for almost 20 years.

- Obviously, we believe that competitive advantage in the twenty-first century boils down to one thing, which is how well a company leverages its human capital. What is HGS's strategy for attracting and retaining the very best talent?

I believe we must create a new reality in which the most creative and dynamic people can identify themselves. We try to create a working environment in which individual aspirations are realized. We strive to make sure that each person's contributions can be fully recognized. We try to create an interactive and positive work environment that allows ideas to be freely shared and in which there is an open and positive feeling among employees. Compensation is also important. Because we want the best people, we set our compensation goals above average. We also believe that all employees should be shareholders, and ours are.

- Would you say there is a shortage of qualified talent in the biotech and genomic space?

We are fortunate in that we have been able to attract and retain the people we want. Our retention rate last year was very good. We lost only 2.5 percent of our workforce. We have a very talented human resources staff that has made an enormous difference to morale by helping people define internal career paths for themselves. We have great flexibility that allows people hired for one career path to move to another.

- A lot of companies view human resources as a transactional group of people who administer pay and benefits, not a strategic group of people who look at human capital.

If you look at our annual report to shareholders, you will notice that following the chairman's letter is a description of our people and the human resources group. This placement underscores how much we value our people. Human capital is an absolute priority for us. It is a job no chief executive should delegate.

- Can you talk about your role in the human gene consortium? There is a lot of talk right now all over the space around consortiums. You have been a member of this consortium and it appears to be doing quite well.

Yes. The Consortium, which includes GlaxoSmithKline, Schering-Plough, Takeda Chemical Industries, Sanofi-Synthelabo, and Merck KgaA, is based on HGS technology. The Consortium has always been structured as a technology lease, not a sale. The lease expired June 30, 2001. It will then be for us to determine how the

remaining assets, which are the vast majority, are deployed. We are well capitalized and have no need to enter other transactions immediately.

- Many are arguing about the whole notion of the role of the board and
  governance of consortiums. Are there any "best practices" with
  managing a consortium?

We have been very fortunate. Our Consortium is fundamentally hands-off. We
provide information, and the Consortium members do their own work. So it is
about as simple and as straightforward as it could be. This arrangement has allowed us to focus all of our efforts on developing our own drugs.

- Your board is impressively well endowed, with some big hitters. What
  makes a great board in the biotech industry?

What makes a great genomics board is what makes any great board. First and foremost, we have people with knowledge of our industry and experience in others.
We also have board members with long-term ties to the academic community who
are well versed in the practical and ethical issues of drug development.

Leadership in the globalized marketplace

Klaus Zumwinkel
Deutsche Post World Net
Chairman of the Board of Management

- It has been said: "The future of communications technology is global."
  Particularly in the aftermath of September 11, 2001, what are the
  challenges for the world economy?

The terrible and inhumane attacks in September 2001 and their aftershocks have
created challenges in every aspect and sector of the global marketplace The stock
exchanges and financial markets reacted swiftly and predictably, but longer-term
implications are harder to assess, as nations and corporations struggle to redefine
the opportunities and boundaries created by the aftereffects of the attacks. Yet,
amid this uncertainty, one thing is certain: Despite everything, the world is becoming closer. We are continuing to remove physical and psychological barriers
between countries, regions, and people. Trade barriers are coming down, and in
Europe, the euro has become a reality. The world economy never sleeps. Even now,
it runs 24 hours a day, right around the clock. While Europe sleeps, America pro-

duces. Twelve hours later, it is the other way around. Thanks to all these factors, it is certain that free trade will continue to increase on a worldwide basis. And, fortunately for us, logistics service providers will reap the benefits, since ordered goods must reach the customer—worldwide. The globalization of the world we live in has not been halted by logistics—indeed, logistics promote globalization. Given all these factors, Deutsche Post World Net (DPWN) remains steadfastly focused on its vision and personal challenge for the future—to become the world's leading service provider of mail, parcels and express delivery, logistics, and financial services. Even in the face of the unthinkable, this vision continues to define the way we operate—tomorrow as well as today.

- **Given the uncertainties you mentioned, what leadership skills will be required to mobilize the organization in pursuit of this vision?**

Our successes going forward will more than ever depend on solid execution through talented management. All current and future challenges faced by a modern logistics service provider can only be tackled with strong and forward-looking management, and it is the unique challenge of the leaders of the organization to ensure that management is present, by means of strong recruitment, internal development, and retention programs. It is the job of the leaders to provide them with challenges and foster their capabilities; only in this way can a corporation's visible success continue to increase in the future. The training and development of employees is a critical investment, because good, motivated employees are an organization's most valuable asset and the sine qua non of sustainable competitive advantage.

- **What competitive pressures do logistics service providers face vis-à-vis the growing globalization of the marketplace?**

Today, customers of logistics service providers demand international and effective transport networks. There are no countries or places in the world to which deliveries from any other location do not have to be made in order to fulfill customers' needs—in an expedient manner, by road and rail, by sea and by air. The demands on capacity and speed are increasing exponentially as free trade continues to expand on a global basis. The logistics sector expects a higher-than-average growth in crossborder dispatches. In relation to this, experts are talking about an estimated midterm market volume of around 800 billion deutsche marks in logistics and related distribution revenues. Modern and globally active logistics corporations must bear this trend in mind. The success of international logistics corporations will be dependent on their ability to adapt effectively to these and successive challenges of globalization as the trend continues.

- What political barriers exist in this industry, and how should they
  be addressed?

If companies are allowed to operate globally, they will do so. We must continue
to lower the barriers to trade that postal markets, in particular, still face. The transformation of national agencies and state-owned corporations into private-sector
companies run on market economy principles is a lengthy process—particularly
in Europe. The European Union is making efforts to liberalize European postal
markets further. Deutsche Post World Net welcomes these efforts. Only free and
fair competition for the best concepts and initiatives will provide a further boost
to global logistics—and also, and most important, to the benefit of the customer.

- Going forward, what role will technology play in freeing up trade
  for logistics service firms?

The World Wide Web and digitization, while they present new challenges for world
trade, offer almost unimaginable opportunities. Internet-based business is generating
higher shipment volumes internationally, which in turn necessitates forward-looking
distribution concepts. Despite the fact that it is spawning online business initiatives
at a furious pace, the Internet's full potential in terms of purchasing and distribution
has hardly even begun to be realized. It is predicted that virtual markets, in particular, will experience high growth rates. As far as data and information transfer is concerned, we cannot imagine life without the Internet today. Let me give you an example
that relates to our organization. For a long time now, Danzas, our logistics subsid-
iary, has been using the Internet not only for tracking shipments but also to allow
customers to place their orders online, via electronic order entry. Customer-oriented
e-business solutions ranging from online shipment tracking to e-fulfillment constitute our day-to-day business. I am convinced that in the future, these kinds of online
operations and services will play an increasingly vital role for logistics companies.

- How can a company like DPWN differentiate itself from the competition,
  with Internet business solutions available to all?

Companies must become more dynamic and more attuned to the marketplace
through such initiatives as customer relations management, supply chain management, and other strategic affiliations. In just the past 10 years, the number of logistics
service providers in Europe has decreased by around 70 percent. The world's logistics markets have moved closer together. New and more elaborate production
processes are evolving. Customers' requirements and requests have become more
complex and more targeted. Customers will increasingly choose one single partner

or at least few carefully selected partners which can offer the most attractive "one-stop shopping"—a company that is in a position to take care of their every need in all areas of logistics. Hence every global logistics service provider must aim to be that chosen partner—for every dispatch, in every weight category, at every speed, and with the issues surrounding finance taken care of. In the area of supply chain management, more and more corporations are outsourcing their entire logistics operations in order to better concentrate on their core competencies. Today, modern logistics organizations offer their customers full service at every point along the supply chain. These range from ordering and warehousing services through order processing and dispatch preparation to transport, distribution, and financial services. In the future, only a broadly based and sophisticated logistics group will be capable of fulfilling customers' needs in terms of supply chain management.

- What is on the immediate horizon for DPWN?

Today, there is a daily dialogue between Deutsche Post World Net and the world. We connect 228 countries across five continents. We move the world, and the world moves us. We connect nations and regions, cultures and people—by road and rail, by sea, by air, and each in its appropriate time frame. Our service is called communication. Deutsche Post World Net, with its global mail, express, logistics, and financial services network, is a partner in the dialogue. We connect the world and its people. Our employees, customers, and partners speak different languages and have different religions and different cultural backgrounds, but we have one thing in common. We are all partners in the dialogue, now and going forward. As the twenty-first century unfolds, global logistics and distribution service providers face new challenges. We are taking on these challenges in the free and fair competition for the best ideas and the best concepts.

Leadership in burgeoning markets

Edward Tian
China Netcom Corporation
President and Chief Executive Officer

- What is your leadership philosophy?

Leadership has a lot to do with really believing in something, no matter what. Take the passion you have for whatever it is, and balance it with a sense of responsibility and mission, and make sure that others believe it's possible. On a very basic level, I believe it is extremely positive if the whole organization understands and appreciates the mission, so we make our mission very goal oriented, and we give our people the direction and resources to achieve the goals. The ability to motivate is very important, but that alone is not enough to lead your people to success. People not only want to see the larger picture, they also want to know what you're going to do to achieve that vision next week, next quarter, next year. Also, culture—the atmosphere, the environment, the way people come together—plays a huge role in my management and leadership style. We go to great lengths to keep our culture productive and positive. It is also very important to build and institutionalize key processes, such as budget and succession planning, evaluating talent, and performance reviews. Finally and most fundamentally, we evaluate our performance on a quarter-to-quarter basis, but more important to our success, we believe it is our responsibility to build a foundation for China. Taking a long-term approach is vital to success in China.

- **What have been some defining moments along your career that helped you to develop your leadership skills?**

Several truthful moments occurred during negotiations with a venture capital firm and our board. Learning the requirements of a potential new investor helped me gain an appreciation of what investors look for and how they measure success. It was challenging for me transitioning from being an entrepreneur to leading this large and complex organization. I was concerned about my capacity and ability going from a very entrepreneurial type to a much more process- and number-oriented leader. Fortunately, the skills that transferred well had to do with motivating people. Other moments were in the early days of starting China Netcom. It was very difficult in the beginning because no one had done something like this before. Our owners are essentially the ministries of the Chinese government, and many people wondered how we could build an entirely new communications company with modern corporate governance in a noncommercial environment. Doubts about our ability to build and grow this company mounted, especially with other quasi-private ventures failing in the market. But the experience of starting this company from scratch against the market's doubts gave me courage—courage to make commitments in the face of what we were doing, courage to move forward with our ideas. You cannot afford to show any weakness or vulnerability in a tough environment like this one. We have a saying in China and that is "Eat first crab," which means take risks to do new things and be prepared for whatever may happen.

- **What are the leadership challenges associated with running a company in China now?**

Building a strong management team. This is probably true in most countries and companies, but it is even more challenging in China because our generation had little exposure to corporate culture and private businesses ventures growing up. There was also very little management culture, so building a midlevel management base and finding qualified people to manage people is more difficult. Educating the generation before me about the business has been challenging. Finding the most efficient way of achieving our objectives with people who lack business culture experience has been the single most challenging task in running a company in China. We do not lack entrepreneurs here, but we have a huge lack of trained professionals. In the United States, the Industrial Revolution spawned the concept of management and of professional management teams. So, in addition to years and years of MBA experience and numerous role models, the United States also has a large pool of quality companies from which to draw good management and talent. In China, it is like building something from scratch—and that is a very, very challenging job.

- Would you say that, from a private-sector perspective,
  China is in the infancy of its own industrial revolution?

Definitely. And not only are we at the dawn of our industrial revolution, but we are simultaneously facing an information revolution as well. Management was really very simple in the Industrial Age of the West. You focused on fixed assets, and there were only a couple of key issues to concern yourself with. However, we are building a whole new economy and new industries as we build new companies here in China, and the leadership for the intangibles is entirely different. Human capital is what I am referring to, and there has been a significant hurdle in learning how to manage both the tangible and intangible assets at the same time. Our strategy has been to hire people from new venture companies, people from overseas, including Thailand, Hong Kong, Singapore, Taiwan, and even the States, and, in particular, people with 5 or 10 years' experience in a multinational firm. We have found exceptional talent in middle management from large U.S.-based companies that have operations in China. When you are hiring more than three hundred people a month, the size and competitiveness of the pool is immediately noticeable. This will continue to be a very, very serious challenge for us.

- What is the best strategy for management and leadership development
  or for recruiting and retention in such an environment?

Our strategy is to recruit the best talent we can get at the top and empower each successive layer of management to replicate the process throughout the organization. We developed an academy two years ago to do just this. The purpose of the academy is to facilitate knowledge transfers and skills transfers. We need to train hundreds of thousands of people in basic business knowledge and experience. Fortunately, we have plenty of brainpower in China, and many young, smart kids who want to be successful. The trick is turning smart, motivated people into professional managers and, ideally, into leaders who value the culture, processes, and goal-oriented methodologies I've mentioned. To be team- or member-oriented is simple in concept but difficult to implement. Our educational system is great at producing engineers but has a way to go before it produces leaders.

- **Has your American training influenced your leadership style? Are you applying any Western management techniques?**

My U.S. experience has been a tremendous influence, but I don't believe there is a Chinese or U.S. management style. Management is a science, and most good companies have similar management styles. People say that we created our own Chinese management system and style, and I just don't think that's true. We had to learn how to do certain things related to corporate governance, shareholder value, and the strong capital market influence, for example, and the best management practices are those developed in the States. The companies I truly admire are represented on my board, and we hire from those companies, too. These people are proven performers, and we try to apply some of their techniques to our own management teams. So, I really appreciate my American experience; it showed me that the situation here calls for very realistic approaches, such as purposely having a long-term focus on doing business in China, because we are creating a whole new economy and a new foundation for China.

- **What is your advice for American or European CEOs wanting to do business in China?**

Companies coming into China to do business will have to do their homework in order to understand the culture and the way business works here. For example, we are partially owned by state government, and many of our employees have had long working relationships with state-owned enterprises. Therefore, leadership must have a respect for those relationships and yet also push toward more progressive management styles. The fundamental evolution of our economy will be very strong, and China will emerge as a contending market. In the telecommunications and information technology sectors, China may become the world's largest buyer of technology within five years. Therefore, China will be a critical market for all multinational companies in communications, equipment, and technology. China will play an important role in the manufacturing sector as well. Companies should also think about strategically outsourcing manufacturing operations here, because China will become a very competitive manufacturing base. We also have huge reservoirs of R & D, engineering, sales, and marketing talent, and we have developed some applications that work well in this market. I would also advise CEOs to hire and train local talent, and make sure they become integrated in your company and part of your global management team. China has a long history of promoting particularly Mainland Chinese graduates and Western-trained people. It is a very important part of a human capital strategy. You can hire critical skills from Hong Kong, Taiwan, and other markets, but in terms of understanding cultural issues, you really need to hire and promote Mainland Chinese. Finally, China has the potential to develop a strong capital market over the next 5 to 10 years. China is also focusing on building a stock market so that we can offer new businesses and high-growth businesses an efficient way to access capital. Even more important, through the capital market you can totally integrate your operations in the local environment. It is very hard to do equity-based transactions now, but over the next five years, most mergers and acquisitions will be primarily cash- or asset-based until our capital market is better developed. And especially as part of the World Trade Organization (WTO), China will be viewed as a potential capital source. In light of the recent global slowdown, international firms should think about a strategy for China, because it could represent a great growth opportunity. Without a good strategy for entering China, it will be very hard to compete and win. In fact, your strategy for China should be as important as your strategy for Japan or other major foreign markets.

- Several companies have announced moving manufacturing operations to China now that China is in the WTO. What will the impact be of China being in the WTO?

I think it will be a good opportunity for us and for China. It gives us more flexibility to choose international partners, because—particularly in the network and communications business—you need partners to operate. The WTO is going to accumulate what both international and domestic firms are spending on the telecommunications and technology sector, so this will create a demand for us. It will also, however, create a lot of competition in China—and we'll have to grow fast and smart to meet the challenge.

- What attracts people to China Netcom, and what keeps them there?

This is just like any other company when it comes to attracting, retaining, and developing great people; it's a combination of things. First, you must give them a unique and exciting opportunity to develop themselves. Second, pay them what they are worth to you; if you can't do it on salary, stock options are a great alternative and incentive. I am very fortunate that my board is supportive of issuing options from our stock incentive plan so that we can offer a comprehensive compensation package. Finally, create a company culture where people feel they belong, as in a family, so they are more willing to give part of their life to growing the company. We celebrate victories here, and that is a big part of our culture, too. And never stop developing these three things. Attracting, recruiting, and retaining and developing people is not a one-time activity; it's a continual process of improvement.

Chapter 4

Strategic Change and Transformation

Implementing strategic change

Elspeth Murray and Peter Richardson
Queen's University
Professors of Strategic Management, School of Business

Stephen Miles
Heidrick & Struggles International, Inc.
Business Analyst

This chapter details the experiences of some of today's most respected leaders of strategic change and transformation. Despite significant differences among the various types of change they discuss—from turnarounds to mergers and acquisitions—there are a number of common themes. These themes differentiate these organizations from the more typical, which may be successful in certain instances, but perhaps more through luck or chance than by design. Just what is it that separates change-able organizations from others?

The components of change leadership are reasonably well known: crafting a vision, creating buy-in, making tough decisions, modeling successful behaviors, and the like. The stories of change leadership in the following pages go beyond the familiar, however. What's different about them is that these leaders have mastered the art of managing the steps of change management. They have succeeding in creating a whole that is larger than the sum of its parts, using tried-and-true formulas in new combinations with powerful results. They have known, perhaps intuitively, that change has both short-term and long-term components and must be approached with what the U.S. court system has termed "deliberate speed," moving as quickly as human nature will allow. One thing they all have in common is the recognition that building and maintaining momentum is the key to success and that it must be in sufficient quantities to sustain a complex organization and its culture.

Physics 101 teaches us that momentum is the product of speed and mass. These new change managers understand this equation, either intuitively or explicitly, and make it a priority to establish both speed and critical mass at the outset of any effort to create major organizational change in today's fast-paced world. As Craig Conway of PeopleSoft notes, "The stakes are higher now. There is a dimension of speed, too. Not only are there fewer survivors, the difference between winning and losing can happen in a very short window of time."

Speed in the execution of any new direction is critical, as Michael Dell of Dell Computer summarizes: "The emerging formula for organizational success is one that combines the customer focus and financial acumen of the Old Economy with the agility and drive of the New Economy. The true winners will be organizations built on fundamentals, with the ability to understand and take advantage of key trends."

In addition to speed and mass, a change initiative also requires careful guidance and unwavering focus in order to overcome the inevitable obstacles and issues that arise along the way. The guidance must be steadfast throughout the change process. It is not enough to articulate where the journey will end; it is also critical for all involved to know how the journey will unfold.

To create guidance initially, leaders need to understand fully the nature of the challenge involved in a massive organizational change. How do you get the "real goods" on what the change challenge is? You ask questions, and lots of them. Ray Lane, former COO of Oracle, recounts his experience at that firm: "Not knowing the software business . . . allowed me to ask the basic questions about why we do things the way we do and to question the [business] fundamentals. You can only do it once: when you go in. [After that point], you can't ask those questions any longer, so taking advantage of that nascency to ask those questions is instrumental to a successful turnaround."

There are four distinct levels of change—operational, strategic, cultural, and paradigmatic. Each requires a distinct combination of approaches, skill sets and techniques.

Creating Shared Understanding

Once the nature of the challenge is understood by the leaders, it is critical that they share that understanding within the organization. If key decision-makers and team members are in the dark as to the objective and means of accomplishing it, the activity will probably experience any number of challenges. Shared understanding is a multifaceted facilitator of change, too often ignored or incompletely mobilized as a tool for success. If only the leaders know the game, then they are the only ones who will be able to play. Successful change requires that all involved in making it happen understand the what, the why, and the how. That's not necessarily as easy as it sounds, as Conway reflects: "The two toughest challenges are defining a vision and implementing it to the exclusion of everything else. Once a company understands what it needs to become, the more difficult next step is to decide what it is not going to become. Tougher still is doing this within the culture of the company without harming the assets of the company. Shutting down or decommitting to projects, for example, often makes for very difficult acceptance issues with employees."

Enriching and Maintaining Shared Understanding

Just as important as shared understanding of where the change journey will end—the vision—is the enriching and maintaining of this understanding across and throughout the organization. An ongoing review process designed to work in rapidly changing environments is critical to this effort. There are several components. One is continuing assessment of changes in the context within which the company operates, including the overall business environment, markets, and competition. A second is continuing evaluation and tweaking of the action plans developed to effect the change. Gary Wendt of Conseco used the solid management skills he developed during his years at General Electric to drive such an initiative: "The reinvigoration process consisted of putting in place various management processes and techniques that I had learned so well at GE. These processes can be applied to any business, but in particular, some were very applicable to what was needed here. Quarterly reviews, strategic planning sessions, and a formal budget process—all driven by the business units—were what we needed to implement."

After the establishment of guidance, shared understanding, and an ongoing process for maintenance of these two items, speed is the next priority.

Establishing a Sense of Urgency

Whatever the nature of the change, anticipatory or reactive, a sense of urgency is essential to the generation of speed. Creating a sense of urgency requires a major communications effort to build awareness and understanding of the need for change, and also the modeling of the desired behaviors on the part of the leaders. The immediate goal is not to win everyone over but to get buy-in from a core group of influential managers; once that is done, it is possible to build momentum rapidly. Anticipatory change is the most difficult, as Geoff Unwin of Cap Gemini knows. "Don't fear making changes or transitioning to a public company in a volatile market," he advises. "It may seem perverse, but when a market is difficult, it is easier to get people to change behavior than when a market is sunny. When a market is sunny and people are doing well and you say, 'Well, I think we need to change to do this,' they say, 'Why do we need to change? We're doing all right.' Also, you can get cohesion through the very pressure of change."

It is also true, however, that change is difficult under the pressures of poor market performance. In either case, it is important to arm oneself with the facts, because the facts are not hostile, and are indisputable if collected properly. As Lane attests: "I needed to collect data, establish facts as opposed to personal beliefs, put rules in place, and throw out the bad apples. In order for our change plan to work, we first had to know exactly what our customers thought of us. I hired McKinsey & Company to ask our customers the hard questions so we could determine what our clients really thought of us, and why our competitors had gained market and mind share over us. We heard startling answers that put an end to the old behaviors and got us thinking about our future."

He further claims that this was one of "the triggers that positioned me with the authority to win, and gave me the support and longevity to make the turnaround successful."

Creating a Focused, Strategic Agenda

One of the worst mistakes organizations make while undertaking change initiatives is trying to change everything at once. This doesn't work and never has worked. Know what has to come first, get the job done, and move on to the next wave. What we know is that one needs to focus on two or three critical initiatives at any one time. Wendt recalls: "In the first one hundred days of our transformation, all our focus was on restructuring our finances and regaining our A rating. There was no point in improving management techniques if we weren't sure the company would survive. After our survival period, we then had to reinvigorate the business."

In addition to focusing the effort, it is advisable to ensure that the phases to a major change effort are discernible and have tangible outcomes at every step, According to Pat Mitchell of PBS: "The secret is to make each step along the path of change have some recognizable value. You have to stand behind your risk and state your case for change in a very reasonable way. Then, you lead by doing and by setting the example. Building consensus is critical for a major strategic change to work."

Rapid Strategic Decision-Making and Deployment

To execute change rapidly requires that major decisions be made in a timely fashion. Too often in organizations, resource reallocations, whether financial or human in nature, take to long to make. They get mired in bureaucratic decision-making processes that just take too long. Worse, the "study and validate" approach gets used by the change "saboteurs" to slow down or stop change from happening. In addition to efficient decision-making processes, speed can be built by executing change-related activities in a parallel fashion, rather than the traditional linear, sequential approach. For example, while a major communications exercise is going on, pilot studies can already be underway. The leaders profiled in this book are virtually unanimous in their recognition that one must be prepared to work with imperfect information.

Focusing Resources for Each Key Initiative

Maintaining momentum requires that leaders make tough decisions about dedicating human resources and other resources to the process, dealing with nonperforming employees and the "sacred cows" that sometimes paralyze an organization. Larry Weinbach of Unisys, in discussing such tough choices, said: "[One of our best decisions was] getting out of the PC business, which is a commodity business. We weren't a large enough player. To make the transition, it was necessary to convince our manufacturing and engineering staffs that we could remain attractive to our customers and become more profitable by moving into the high end of technology, where we could add value."

Building a Flywheel of Support

In most organizations, relatively few employees are willing to engage in early-stage change activities, even when the change is perceived to be nonthreatening or even positive. A rule of thumb cited by some executives is that about 20 percent of the employee population can be motivated initially to drive change. Another 70 percent will remain neutral, "sitting on the fence" to see what happens. The remaining 10 percent will actively, even vocally, oppose the new direction. The real impact of the 20 percent who embrace it up front lies in their ability to convince the fence-sitters to become engaged. Here is the approach Conway used: "The first thing you have to do is stabilize the team and figure out who is with you and who isn't. A CEO coming into a company needs to co-opt the support of the current management team. It helps to understand on an individual basis what their concerns are, what their fears are, what their motivations and goals are, and see if you can convince them that they can meet those goals. Second, there has to be a compelling vision for the company, because people want to be on a winning team. If they believe that you have a vision that is going to result in the company's becoming a winner, they will stay; but without that sense of direction, they won't. The third thing is to face reality. The number one rule of business is to face reality."

Just how important is building the human flywheel? Mitchell concludes that it is critical: "If people feel they have been listened to, they are a lot more likely to become spokes in that flywheel than they are to stand outside and throw sticks in your way. Everybody needs to feel heard . . . that doesn't mean they're going to be served equally well by every risk you take, but they have to be willing to take the risks with you."

Conway agrees: "If you have a belief and a vision for the company and you optimize every factor you can, every single day, it is ultimately going to yield results. I remember thinking, in the middle of the turnaround at PeopleSoft, that I've been pushing on the company for a very long period of time and it hadn't moved an inch. But then it moved an inch. And then it moved a foot. And then it moved a yard. Pretty soon it was moving on its own momentum."

Identifying and Dealing with Resistance

Failure to deal adequately with opposition has derailed more than a few major change efforts. In many strategic change initiatives, executives spend far too much time dealing with the 10 percent of the workforce that will never get on the train— a complete waste of time. Tough decisions have to be made regarding those who don't or won't engage. Some CEOs may have an "I respect your decision to not come on this journey with us" conversation with such negative employees. Most important, however, senior executives need to spend time promoting and communicating the new direction, revising and modifying as needed along the way. Lane describes how he made the tough calls: "By the end of the second quarter, we had finished the McKinsey study and a best business practices study, and we had terminated about 30 managers and brought in some new senior people. Letting go of people who wouldn't be essential to the turnaround was important, especially of those who believed that they were untouchable and that the new management team was only temporary."

Effective Follow-Through

If you want to change strategy, change the performance measures and the corresponding recognition and rewards. This is the message we hear from senior executives time and time again. It's not quite as simple as that, but there's no doubt that many change initiatives fail because these two elements, as well as other key enablers, are not aligned with the new direction. Other key enablers include organizational structures, communication, policies, information reporting, and employee training. These are so badly misaligned in some cases that employees who are quick to embrace the new direction in fact risk being penalized by the old systems, formal and informal. If opponents of a new direction have the opportunity, they will often use an existing reward system to penalize the innovators. In addition, people who are opposed to change may use some of these enablers, especially policies and communications, as barriers and obstacles to progress. Conway continues: "I tied a great deal of incentives to the success of the company, but they were as much personal wealth creation as anything. Once everybody bought into the vision and the viability of the vision, I ensured that every key person had enough stock options so that if the vision came to be, that all of them would achieve their financial goals."

Using Demonstrated Leadership

Appropriate leadership styles are vital to successful change. Executives who fail as role models often do so because they don't know which leadership approach is appropriate or don't understand the key tasks. For example, failure to bring about change in a crisis situation may be traceable to senior executives abdicating their responsibility for tough decisions. By contrast, poor anticipatory change frequently results from a top-down, directive leadership style that fails to build broad commitment, as well as excessive secrecy about the new direction. Together, these result in a lack of awareness and understanding of the need for change on the part of the workforce and an inability to build a sense of urgency and momentum. Whatever the nature of the change, it is almost certain that the deeper it becomes, the more critical it is for an executive team to reflect on their leadership style, and demonstrate new behaviors and values appropriate to the future direction. As Unwin puts it: "Leadership is more than having people follow you out of curiosity or fear. The ability to persuade and communicate is absolutely crucial. The key requirement is to be clear and simple. The world is full of people who will try to complicate issues. The world is a complicated place, but the people who really succeed are those who can take complicated issues and express them in a way in which people can understand, follow, and act. Not ducking the issues and being decisive are qualities of good leaders."

Leadership is truly about demonstrating passion and commitment to the new future. Weinbach recalls: "My first day on the job, I went on our closed-circuit television system and shared with the employees my vision for the transformation: customers, employees, and reputation—simple, clear, and understandable. Then I went to the news media and stated that Unisys was committed to repaying a billion dollars in debt within two years. That was Day One. For the next 99 days, I visited 20,000 employees and communicated the vision and solicited their buy-in."

Achieving these *hows* establishes what we call the *winning conditions* for any organizational change process. Simply creating the winning conditions—developing a shared understanding, generating speed, and building momentum—won't guarantee success, but without them, failure is much more likely.

Leadership for mergers and acquisitions

Geoff Unwin
Cap Gemini SA
Chairman

- You took the U.S.-centric private partnership consultancy Ernst & Young and married it with a large, primarily European, publicly traded consulting services company. What challenges and opportunities did the integration present?

The dominant factor in any major acquisition or merger in the services sector is the issue of culture. There are all sorts of transactions that may make financial, market, or geographical sense in terms of being a good fit, but if the cultures are not compatible, you are just absolutely destroying value. Regarding the merger with E & Y, we had looked at hundreds of companies as potential merger partners before focusing in on this organization. We then spent nine months really getting to know each other prior to making the decision to go ahead with the transaction. The majority of the up-front due diligence was concerning cultural compatibility. We asked questions such as "Do we share the same values?" "Do we have the same way of behaving?" "Will we get along with each other?" "Do we trust each other?" We came to the conclusion that our cultures did fit. Contrasted to the other merger opportunities we considered, many were excellent companies, but our cultures were significantly different and we knew that a marriage wouldn't work. It wasn't a question of good culture over bad culture, it was a difference in organizational style, and you can't underestimate the importance of culture fit. In terms of the integration itself, we were impressed with the realistic way in which E & Y approached the issues, including their concerns about moving from a partnership culture into a public company environment.

- What other factors were considered in the merger? How long did it take?

There was other premerger planning from an operational point of view, having to do with our corporate structures, technological infrastructure, the services we would be selling, the clients and sectors we would focus on. You are required to do financial and operational due diligence, but it's the cultural due diligence that increases the likelihood of success. This was the largest merger in our industry and a very complex transaction in terms of merging a partnership—which by definition makes no money—and adjusting and redefining compensation and other financial benchmarks so that there is an "E" to which to apply a "P." We had to do this 27 times simultaneously because there were that many different partnerships involved. I likened the merger to giving birth to triplets sequentially. We spent nine months on evaluating whether the transaction made sense. We spent nine months making it happen from a legal and financial point of view. Then roughly nine months in postmerger integration. The whole process was emotional, tough, and painful, but worth every moment. After all, we viewed it as a "once in a lifetime" opportunity.

- **What are the dos and don'ts when two service-based organizations transition into a new culture?**

Particularly in the early stages of integration, it is important to find a balance, so that it is clear one side isn't dominating the other. Balancing is not as rigid as matching people one-on-one; it's more that when you look at the overall mix of things, there should be a fair mix of legacy company with new perspective, and a fair mix of nationality and geography so that everyone has appropriate representation. In the early stages, people need to feel comfortable and excited about the integration—because if their new environment is alien to them, it makes things more difficult. Beyond the early stages, capability drives decisions, so you have to know how to assess capability and react to strengths and weaknesses of both parties.

- **How do you assess the capabilities within an acquired company?**

The first step is to make an assessment of the talent at the top levels of both firms so that when the transaction is final, you know exactly what to do in terms of top line governance and identifying major positions within the merged entity. You can take a few months to assess talent in positions deeper down, because you will have the right senior person in place to assist in evaluating that talent. There is no quick solution; it is a matter of spending time with people and getting to know them and how they behave.

- **Do you take an active role in the talent assessment process?**

Sixty percent of my time is not spent with clients, surprisingly, but with our workforce. I spend a high proportion of my time on people issues such as spotting talent, succession planning, and staffing. Again, there's no shortcut; it's a matter of just spending time with people and talking to a lot of different people.

- Would you characterize your leadership style as "management by walking around?"

Yes, absolutely, and at all levels. I don't just spend my time with our top producers, I spend a lot of time with recent graduates, for example, so that I have a reasonable understanding of what their needs and requirements are, which are different from the way it was in my day!

- What is your leadership philosophy?

My leadership philosophy revolves almost entirely around people and teams. Geoff Unwin is virtually incapable of doing anything by himself. Teams generally produce better results than individuals, but the makeup of the individual members of those teams is very important. Again, you strive for the right mix. You want different personality types in a team, because you don't want a team of think-alikes. I try to concentrate very much on the capabilities of people around me. Some leaders are frightened by the notion that you should hire people who are better and smarter than yourself. I learned this from one of my mentors who strongly believed in recruiting people with better qualifications and credentials than he possessed. A client once remarked to him, "You know, John, the further down in your company we go, the better it gets," and my boss was immensely proud of that.

- Other than being people-centric, are there specific skills that leaders should have to be more effective?

Leadership is more than having people follow you out of curiosity or fear. The ability to persuade and communicate is absolutely crucial. The key requirement is to be clear and simple. The world is full of people who will try to complicate issues. The world is a complicated place, but the people who really succeed are those who can take complicated issues and express them in a way in which people can understand, follow, and act. Not ducking the issues and being decisive are qualities of good leaders. That doesn't necessarily mean leaders should be instantly decisive, but the worst managers are those who waver too much, too long.

- So, the best leaders have well-developed social skills,
  or a high emotional quotient (EQ)?

It's spot on. The first test for senior management candidates is for intelligence. The second test is social acceptability. There are a number of very intelligent people who are also abrasive and would not be ideal at interacting with clients, for instance. The social skills, social ability, the emotional quotient are undoubtedly crucial factors in leadership success.

- Your first position in your career was professional chocolate taster for
  Cadbury Schweppes. You eventually held various management positions
  with Cadbury, Hoskyns, and Cap Gemini. How have your past
  experiences prepared you for a CEO role?

I joined Cadbury fresh out of university in its graduate management trainee program. The training I received from Cadbury was superb, and it made a tremendous impact on me in terms of an introduction to finance, marketing, production techniques, distribution, advertising, and quality control. Even now, 35 years later, I can still remember a session we had with the CEO, Sir Adrian Cadbury. He went through accounting and financial statements and told us what was important and why it was important. I remember asking him what "goodwill" was, because, at the time, I had no concept of what on earth goodwill meant. At the time, it didn't feel like it was valuable training, and I didn't really appreciate what was happening. Only with the passage of time and reflecting back on the experience do I realize what a tremendous foundation that training was. Hoskyns was extremely people-oriented and developmental-oriented, and I was given a variety of roles within that company. Even though I spent a long career there, I was never in one job for any length of time. I never fought to move upward; I just tried to do the best job I could, always making sure succession was in place so that it was easier for me to be moved on if I was judged capable.

- What advice do you have for newly minted leaders in public companies
  or leaders thinking about taking their companies public?

Realize that we live in a goldfish bowl, so there's no hiding place. Be aware that investors have long memories. Don't fear making changes or transitioning to a public company in a volatile market. It may seem perverse, but when a market is difficult, it is easier to get people to change behavior than when a market is sunny. When a market is sunny and people are doing well and you say, "Well, I think we need to change to do this," they say, "Well, why do we need to change?

We're doing all right." Also, you can get cohesion through the very pressure of change. It becomes a common enemy, in a sense. The issue becomes responding to the market to protect our interests, and people realize their historical factions have become irrelevant and they will unite around the burning platform for change.

Leading a transformation

Ray Lane
Kleiner Perkins Caufield & Byers
General Partner

- Before we get into the strategic transformation at Oracle, can you reflect a bit on your transitions throughout your career—for example, moving from a nonoperating role at a partnership structured services company (Booz-Allen) to an operational role with P & L responsibility for a publicly held software company?

I've been fortunate to have diverse roles throughout my career. Since I try not to be one-dimensional and simply rely on analytical, operational or sales skills only, I had to combine the skills and experiences from Electronic Data Systems (EDS) and IBM to be successful at Booz-Allen. Then, at Oracle, my consulting skills and executive relationships gained at Booz-Allen served me well. This diversity is especially helpful in recruiting and communicating with others. Senior executives have to be able to relate to others, understand their points of view, and be able to leverage this knowledge for their own companies. This simple lesson escapes so many CEOs today, who continue to rely on the single talent that made them successful in the first place.

- There are few leaders who have led a transformation as successfully as you did at Oracle. Can you share with us how it all started?

Oracle, as you know, faced a financial crisis in the year before I came on board in June of 1992. In terms of day-to-day operations, it was basically out of control. People felt that they didn't have to pay attention to any rules, either internally or with customers. There were no established business practices, and the culture was one of "Win at any cost, the end always justifies the means." Rewards were based solely on bringing in business in the immediate time frame; no thought was given to the structure of deals or to building relationships. I was overwhelmed with very compelling, very smart salespeople trying to convince me of their individual points of view. I didn't have time to be a consultant; I needed data to be armed with the "truth" to fight this mindset and common behavior, which demonstrated that you can do anything you want for personal advantage, as long as you can convince your boss it's okay. The problem was that the boss often had the same self-serving objectives. So, I needed to collect data, establish facts as opposed to personal beliefs, put rules in place, and throw out the bad apples. In order for our change plan to work, we first had to know exactly what our customers thought of us. I hired McKinsey & Company to ask our customers the hard questions so we could determine what our clients really thought of us and why our competitors had gained market and mind share over us. We heard startling answers that put an end to the old behaviors and got us thinking about our future. The company was very much like a dysfunctional family in need of an authority figure who could lay down rules and enforce them.

- **Did you have a 100- or 250-day change process plan to execute against? Please outline your change plan. What were the priorities?**

My first quarter, following Oracle's fiscal year-end in May, I had to figure out who on the management team was going to focus on the company rather than on themselves and their personal expediency. I had to collect an enormous amount of data to separate truth from fiction, and start teams focusing on the areas that needed fixing. By the second quarter, I hoped to have a new organizational structure in place to implement the short-term fixes that were obvious. By the end of the second quarter, we had finished the McKinsey study and a best business practices study, and we had terminated about 30 managers and brought in some new senior people. Letting go of people who wouldn't be essential to the turnaround was important, especially of those who believed that they were untouchable and that the new management team was only temporary. Then, I chose the third quarter as the first time to test our strategy and new business practices. We wanted to test ourselves under strained conditions, and the third quarter is our toughest quarter. We knew that in the fourth quarter, any misstep would resolve itself because that was when we sold the most. Also, I wanted to use the fourth quarter to make all the changes we had identified along the way, because that would set us up for the new, first full year with the new plan. We produced, we beat expectations, and our stock rose 50 percent the day after we announced results. Seeing these results right away gave us confidence to launch the major reorganization the following quarter. These were big changes; we turned the place upside down. I did away with all the vertical industry organizations—ironically, I brought them back later—but only after we had started to focus on applications and services, in addition to the database business. I separated out consulting and support and made them global businesses. I put a big focus on the applications sales force, separating it from the database sales group. It was essential that we reorganize both structurally and process-wise by the end of that fiscal year to prepare for the next year. So, the focus was on getting the right market approach for the long term, as opposed to getting the next "deal." I knew in time this would bring in the business we needed in each quarter. By getting the sales force trained on the right products—the database business is very different from the applications business—and focusing on delivering real value to the customer, and sticking by our claims, by repeating this in front of customers over a long time frame rather than selling a deal in one quarter or one year, I felt the business had great prospects for growth.

- Were there any defining moments in this transformation?

There are a couple I can think of that now don't seem so big to me, but at the time they were huge. When I first came on board I found myself right in the middle of a political quagmire. The reason that [the CEO and founder] Larry Ellison had brought me in had not been fully communicated to everyone in the organization, so I had some senior people questioning whether they worked for me or I worked for them, and what my actual role was. Fortunately, I was able to realign some of the senior management and, in doing so, clarified my role right away. Having Larry support my efforts in this regard and not intervene in the process showed his trust and, to some degree, that I was the new sheriff in town. It allowed me to establish credibility and authority, and have the whole organization recognize that I would be making decisions and making them quickly, and that Larry would back me. That this happened early on was key. The other critical event was a two-day meeting in late September in which, having identified and taken the initial direction that I wanted the organization to go in, I brought in all the teams to hear my program for the turnaround. To get their buy-in, I drew on every skill I had, including selling, operational skills, and consulting skills. I rolled out the results of the surveys and internal studies we had done, and the action plans for the transformation. These defining moments were the triggers that positioned me with the authority to win, and gave me the support and longevity to make the turnaround successful.

- What was the most rewarding part of the transformation?

My first day on the job was the day we launched Oracle 7. We met with analysts to brief them on the competitive strengths of the product, and of course, they were curious about who the new guy was, and they were determined to test me. Just coming on board, I had no idea what we were doing. The analysts asked a lot of questions and I finally said, "Give me a break! I need at least 30 or 60 days under my belt before I can know how to answer your questions." So rather than answering them on the spot, I promised them answers in 60 days. Going from that point to hosting the analyst call after third quarter earnings were announced, which took us from a stock price of $15 to $24 the next day, was very rewarding because they were convinced there was a turnaround in progress. They saw that there was momentum—momentum not just related to our stock price but in acknowledgment of a viable, long-term plan. However, seeing the results of the work was absolutely the most rewarding.

- How does today's market environment affect the way a CEO would lead a transformation? Is leading a transformation during the current economic climate any different from the same process during the past 8 to 10 years?

The timing does not matter. There is still the process of assessing all aspects of what it takes to do the turnaround. Are the products competitive? What really contributes to the financial structure? What does the organization look like? What do our customers think of us? All those things are important, as well as the touchy-feely issues, such as "Do I think this person could do this job? Is each team the right team?" The fundamental elements for transformation do not change over the years.

- Many companies are facing a similar need to transform. What advice would you give CEOs who are contemplating or embarking on a major strategic transformation today?

Trust your gut. In my situation, it was very helpful to me not to know the software business. I understood the basics from an outside perspective, but I had never run a software company. This allowed me to ask the basic questions about why we do things the way we do and to question the fundamentals. This is very important. You can only do it once: when you go in. Being new on the scene allows you to ask the fundamental questions, but very quickly you become integrated into the culture and become "one of them." At that point, though, you can't ask those questions any longer, so taking advantage of that nascency to ask those questions is instrumental to a successful turnaround. The turnaround doesn't happen by just moving a few things around—that's like moving chairs on the Titanic. The little things you can move, you move quickly, but the major transformation happens by going down to the basement and examining the infrastructure and how things are done fundamentally. It took Lou Gerstner, for example, a long time to turn IBM around because it's a huge place. He questioned the foundation, how the place is built from the ground up. So, trust your gut to map out what you think you can do with no boundaries and no restrictions—then ask the bold questions that people who are typically consumed in the business do not ask. Then, execute, making adjustments along the way.

- A transformation can be quite disruptive to a company's culture. How did you balance your company's needs with that of its culture?

I do not believe you can change a culture. At the heart of every company, there is a culture, and once it exists, it is extremely hard to change. It is set by the founder and the early management, especially if the founder remains on as CEO, as in Oracle's case. It is very hard to change this, so what I tried to do is use the best part of the culture, because there's good and bad to every culture. It's interesting how most people talk about culture in a pejorative way. New people come in to change a company and culture is regarded as something that gets in the way, something to blame, and something that needs to be changed. I think it is Mission Impossible to change a culture. You should instead take the good aspects about the culture—whatever it was that made that company successful based on its culture in the past—and you repurpose those toward your new mission. Oracle, for example, had a culture of winning. Winning was highly rewarded. I took that piece of the culture and wrapped it around some of the values and philosophy I knew were necessary to mature the company. I didn't dare ruin the culture of winning. A mistake often made by incoming CEOs is to go in and start blaming and changing the culture, instead of using the good parts of it to achieve their goals.

- Generally speaking, what has changed in the past 10 years with respect to leadership?

In the past, leadership was done unilaterally. In other words, you sit at the top of an organization where there's a bit of the ivory tower mentality, you map out strategy, you map out the growth through acquisitions or organically, and you basically do this with a small team at the top. It is very hierarchical in nature. Today, though, it is very much a team effort. Basically, it's a process influencing each person on the team to move in a certain direction. Leadership through influence and ideas is more successful today than the top-down leadership we saw 10 years ago or more because it's more permanent. People tend to buy in and embrace the changes as their own, rather than gripe about the direction the boss wants to take. Second, communication has become much more important, especially in large companies where everybody needs to know a lot of information to keep focused on the mission at hand. Communication from the company's leadership is essential. I underestimated this many times in my career, especially at Oracle, where we went from 8,000 to 45,000 people and keeping all those people on the same page required a great deal of communication. If you don't continually tell them your vision or your strategy, they make up what they think the company is all about, and if you let that go too long, you end up with a disaster. I also think the need to have a real focus on competitive positioning is a significant change in leadership. If the leadership doesn't have a competitive mindset—how to position products, services, marketing, market share, what your competitor's weaknesses are, and so on—this could be disastrous as well.

• Many of the CEOs we've talked with believe that a fundamental attribute of leadership today is emotional quotient, or EQ—in other words, the softer skills such as being able to communicate with employees, doing alliances with partners, and building the brand. This attribute is viewed as that of managing intangible assets, as opposed to the tangible asset management of yesterday's CEO skill set. Would you agree?

Absolutely. The best thing that ever happened to me was not being formally trained as a manager. As I think back over the last 30 years, I left IBM too soon to be trained in its notorious management training program. EDS had no management training at the time I was there. Booz-Allen was a partnership structure. So, when I went into Oracle, I basically relied on my general work ethic, my gut beliefs, my personality, what my mother taught me, and my natural tendency to be a walk-around, hands-on leader.

• Are there any "must-have" skills for leaders today?

Any CEO I would endorse for a portfolio company has to have team-building skills. They have to know how to recruit and how to motivate people to execute for them. They have to be intensely focused on whatever creates value in that company. Being a CEO is not about managing, it's about producing a direction for a group of people that results in a desired outcome. Understanding the fundamental value that is produced by your company is essential. A CEO has to understand and direct that value into something simple and clear that customers, lots of customers, want to buy. Also, having a proficient skill around the numbers, being very numbers oriented, having immediate recall of the numbers in their heads, is essential. Do they need the CFO to tell me the revenue, margin, and balance sheet dynamics, or do they understand how the numbers work themselves? This, for me, is the acid test for a good CEO.

- Today it seems that R & D has evolved into a portfolio of options that incorporates traditional R & D, mergers and acquisitions, and corporate venture capital. Rather than developing innovation in-house, many companies are acquiring R & D through M & A initiatives. What are your thoughts on this?

I actually think we'll head back in the other direction. I'm not a big believer in acquiring your way to growth. Growth should be organically driven, with mergers and acquisitions to supplement. The core value of a company comes from its organic R & D, branding, and new product introduction, for example—with few exceptions.

- At Oracle, was there a program for developing and retaining "best of breed" talent?

We started a program called the Leaders Forum in 1994, and every month we would take 30 to 35 leaders from around the world, representing all different functions from R & D to sales and services, and put them together in a week-long workshop on leadership development. Each group was given a real business problem to solve, and what one group didn't finish was passed along to the next group to solve. It is a very effective training format. You have the benefit of walking in each other's shoes, getting to know each other, and working together to solve a current business issue. It reinforced the team concept well. My view is that, instead of someone coming in to my office and trying to sell me on how important he or she is to the firm, I am more impressed by a person who tells me he or she has just solved a problem with his or her peers without involving senior management. That kind of horizontal communication is impressive. You can't scale a company unless you have managers several layers down who are not afraid to approach each other to work through an issue and who are willing to work with each other toward a common good.

- As a reflection of how essential human capital is for competitive advantage, some companies are moving away from transactional HR departments structured around pay and benefits and the like to a more strategic human capital management approach. Is this the wave of the future? Would you agree that this is a significant strategic change?

Absolutely. In fact, software is helping this to happen because line managers are being surrounded by a lot of automated processes, so it's no longer necessary to have departments to conduct transactions. I think this extends beyond the HR department to department such as finance and purchasing as well. Many of the transactional, mundane jobs are being transformed by software automation. You can turn these departments into higher-value, more analytical operations that produce a great deal more value at a lower cost. Plus, I'd rather have line managers who are skilled and spending their time hiring, recruiting, training, and developing talent.

Leading a turnaround

Gary Wendt
Conseco
Chairman and Chief Executive Officer

- What is your management philosophy?

My management philosophy starts with the basics: thoroughly understand the environment in which you're managing. That means knowing the strengths and weaknesses of the company, its competitive position, its competitors, and where the markets for the products you're offering are heading. With that thorough understanding, you have to decide on the strategy that you intend to pursue. In each of my appointments at General Electric and in both of my CEO roles, I found that every situation is unique, so different strategies were required. I'm a reasonably loose manager when it comes to people. I believe that probably the most important single task of the CEO is to select the right people for the key jobs in the company and then let them go in the direction that you agree they should go. I am a firm believer in having a top tier of people who are very high quality and then letting them develop the teams below them.

- What is the culture at Conseco, and what were your biggest challenges in creating an effective, productive environment?

Conseco is both an insurance company and a finance company, and the cultures of these two businesses are quite separate and quite different from each other. The finance business had basically been the same company for 25 years, so the culture was quite ingrained, and it was a good culture. The insurance business, on the other hand, had been through 17 different acquisitions over a 15-year period, and the culture was in a state of shock. In essence, it had no culture of its own. Because of the way all the acquisitions had been integrated—or, rather, not integrated—there was a total lack of process in the insurance businesses, and with that, a total lack of culture. There was no process in place for people to exchange ideas; no formal, effective way to communicate; no quarterly review process so that the heads of various businesses could come in and explain their issues to senior management; and no budget process. The budget was actually determined by the corporate office and then sent down to the businesses to execute, as opposed to having it driven from the business units. These strategic business units are just that—strategic. The people running them are in the marketplace every day and therefore know their businesses and their capabilities better than corporate. Having the budgets handed down from corporate was an ineffective way to allocate resources. Basically, the business unit heads were told what they had to do as opposed to being asked what they could do. It's ironic how, when I came on board, I was looking forward to the experience of changing the culture. Then I discovered there wasn't any culture to change, and it really gave me a different perspective. I knew we had to build something new that would be sustainable over a very long time, and it would be something that we had to pay very close attention to because we are a small business without a lot of excess funds lying around. That was a big challenge, creating a culture that allowed us to move forward.

- Can you take us through the transformation process
  that you led at Conseco?

We had a six-month plan, and we needed to implement as much as possible in that six-month window because the company was in a severe debt crisis. Within 70 days of my coming on board, Conseco owed $1.2 billion, which would grow to $2.2 billion within the next year. We didn't have nearly that much cash in the bank, and A. M. Best had downgraded our claims-paying rating. We lost our A rating, which is usually a death knell for an insurance company. Not many companies recover from that. It was really a triage situation: very quickly, we had to sell a good many assets that we didn't think were important to the future of the company, and we had to totally change the business model of the finance company from a cash user to a cash producer. With those two things in place, we were able to put together a plan that showed how we could repay our debt, not just over the short term but over the longer term as well. So, in the first one hundred days of our transformation, all our focus was on restructuring our finances and regaining our A rating. There was no point in improving management techniques if we weren't sure the company would survive. After our survival period, we then had to reinvigorate the business. The reinvigoration process consisted of putting in place various management processes and techniques that I had learned so well at GE. These processes can be applied to any business, but in particular, some were very applicable to what was needed here. Quarterly reviews, strategic planning sessions, and a formal budget process—all driven by the business units—were what we needed to implement. In the quarterly reviews, the management of each of the businesses tells us how it is doing financially, makes projections for the near term, assesses what the market conditions are, and identifies which products are selling, which products aren't; it is basically a full and intense review of the activities of the business on a quarterly basis. In the strategic planning sessions, the businesses come up with a three-year plan for what they think they can do and what they have to do to accomplish that. In the budget process that takes place toward the end of the year, the businesses tell us what they can do and then we negotiate any stretch targets. Finally, but most important for our transformation to be successful, we had to begin evaluating the quality of our workforce. There had never been communication and feedback between manager and subordinate on virtually any level in this company. So, with the new year, we began a quarterly review process in which every supervisor and every subordinate sat down, filled out a fairly simple evaluation form, and talked about strengths and areas where improvements could be made, and then identified development needs the employee. It was very basic, but also very critical. We now have a company wide capability assessment review process for at least the top two layers of management at each business unit.

- You're developing a performance management–based culture that is a meritocracy, where people are evaluated and rewarded on their performance?

Before we went through the whole series of quality reviews, we initiated a bonus program that is based on performance for the top 250 people in the organization. It was the first time that Conseco had a program based on performance. So now, 25 percent of everyone's bonus in this top 250 rank comes from companywide financial performance; 50 percent comes from their business unit's financial performance; and 25 percent comes from specific criteria established for individual performance and individual goals that are negotiated between the manager and the employee, unrelated to earnings per share, sales growth, or asset returns. As a personal development plan, it is much more subjective than the other 75 percent.

- What is your perspective on Six Sigma, which you have instituted at Conseco?

I obviously learned this while at GE. Jack Welch was fanatical about it and brought it in for the purpose of improving productivity in the manufacturing businesses. And when one part of the company did something good, all parts of the company replicated it. Even NBC executives had to have black belts and master black belts in their organization to do Six Sigma projects. The good news about the Six Sigma approach, which came out of Motorola and was designed for manufacturing businesses, was that we learned it had aspects that were applicable to a good number of things in financial services. The basic concept, the "DMAIC" concept, helped us get a lot closer to our customers here at Conseco. DMAIC stands for D, determining customer's needs, which was the part we spent more time on than any other; M, measure the current situation; A, analyze the data; I, innovate a new process; and C, control the new process. I brought in Ruth Fattori, who was in charge of the Six Sigma at GE, to run the program for us. She has a textbook approach: once you've trained your master black belts and black belts, you find appropriate projects and you execute utilizing DMAIC principles. We found that there was a real thirst in people here to have something like this available. We are very encouraged by the early, visible results from implementing this kind of quality program. It is improving the business, taking out a lot of costs, and making our customer service better. Some people claim that Six Sigma adds bureaucracy to a business. By including it as one of several management techniques we use, however, we are finding that it really facilitates our business. With all the other pieces of the transformation strategy in place, Six Sigma is helping us significantly improve productivity at Conseco across the board.

Leadership challenges during a turnaround

Craig Conway
PeopleSoft
President and Chief Executive Officer

- You have had a successful career, starting at TymShare, then Atari, then Digital Research. You then spent eight years at Oracle, eventually becoming the executive vice president of marketing. After that, you took TGV Software public and subsequently sold it to Cisco. Prior to taking the helm at PeopleSoft, you led a turnaround at OneTouch Systems. What attracted you to the PeopleSoft opportunity?

One attraction was the PeopleSoft brand name. The company had one of the most respected brand names in the information technology industry. That was a strong factor in my decision to come here. Second, the company had a history of technology leadership, and in this industry it's important to lead technically. The third factor was that the company had a very high customer satisfaction level. Finally, the company had a great deal of cash for me to work with, and I knew I had the support of the board and of the founder and chairman, Dave Duffield. That is about as good as it gets when you come into a company.

- **What have been the defining moments along your career path that helped to develop your leadership style?**

A major defining moment was my first CEO position at TGV Software. Defining a commercial business at a start-up consisting mostly of scientists was a real challenge. A second defining moment for me was when I faced my first turnaround— OneTouch Systems. Turning a company around is very difficult, and there is a high mortality rate. Facing the possibility of failure of was a very sobering experience and one that tested my leadership. The third defining moment was PeopleSoft, because of its scale. At the time, PeopleSoft was a $1.5 billion-dollar company with five thousand employees; doing things on that scale called for me to demonstrate a different and broader set of leadership skills.

- **When you took over at PeopleSoft, you had three compounding factors: You were facing a slowdown in consumer and business IT spending; you were replacing a legendary founder; and many of the company's top people had recently left. Any one of these factors is difficult, but three combined constitute a leadership crisis. What needs to happen early on to lead successfully in these conditions?**

The first thing you have to do is stabilize the team and figure out who is with you and who isn't. A CEO coming into a company needs to co-opt the support of the current management team. It helps to understand on a personal basis what their concerns are, what their fears are, and what their motivations and goals are and see if you can convince them that they can meet those goals. Second, there has to be a compelling vision for the company, because people want to be on a winning team. If they believe that you have a vision that is going to result in the company's becoming a winner, they will stay; but without that sense of direction, they won't. The third thing is to face reality. The number one rule of business is to face reality. Achieving your vision will probably not be possible through iterative improvements in the business. It usually calls for something very bold and risky.

- **What are the leadership challenges in a turnaround?**

The two toughest challenges are defining a vision and implementing it to the exclusion of everything else. Once a company understands what it needs to become, the more difficult next step is to decide what it is not going to become. Tougher still is doing this within the culture of the company without harming the assets of the company. Shutting down or decommitting to projects, for example, often makes for very difficult acceptance issues with employees. Using the analogy of an orthodontist, you can't straighten teeth overnight. You have to put constant pressure on them over a longer period of time in order for them to straighten. Capitalizing on the culture without harming it is a difficult challenge. You definitely want to apply pressure, you definitely have a clear view of where you want to go, but too many draconian moves can kill a culture, which is sometimes what holds the company together.

- **Are there certain ways to apply pressure without harming the culture?**

There wasn't anything formulaic in what I did. It's a case-by-case, event-by-event process that requires sensitivity, a lot of listening, and consulting with your senior management. It is constantly adjusting the tension for optimal movement without breakage.

- **Often, when CEOs want to transform a company, it involves a strategic change in the performance management and reward system. Was this your approach as well?**

I tied a great deal of incentives to the success of the company, but they were as much personal wealth creation as anything. Once everybody bought into the vision and the viability of the vision, I ensured that every key person had enough stock options so that if the vision came to be, that all of them would achieve their financial goals. I did this in a very deliberate manner by asking every senior executive in the company how much a 20-point increase in the value of the company stock should be worth to them. I found that people had a pretty clear goal in mind for what this increase in market value should be worth to them. So, in most cases, I gave them the amount of options to get them there.

- **When embarking on a strategic change or transformation, are there any defining elements that mean the difference between success and failure?**

Yes, and these elements might seem at odds with each other, but they work in tandem. Success is ultimately going to require a combination of contributors and events to occur. At the same time, though, the key characteristic of success that is most overlooked is personal persistence. If you have a belief and a vision for the company and you optimize every factor you can, every single day, it is ultimately going to yield results. I remember thinking, in the middle of the turnaround at PeopleSoft, I've been pushing on the company for a very long period of time and it hasn't moved an inch. But then it moved an inch. And then it moved a foot. And then it moved a yard. Pretty soon it was moving on its own momentum. Making a strategic change in a company is enormously heavy lifting. It makes you feel awfully tired and lonely.

- **Is there a difference leading a transformation today versus 10 or 15 years ago?**

Today, the downside for failure is much greater because all markets have significantly consolidated from 10 or 15 years ago. For example, there are three major U.S. airlines; three major U.S. car companies; three major retail chains; a couple of major operating systems, and so on, whereas 10 plus years ago the world tolerated more successes. The stakes are higher now. There is a dimension of speed, too. Not only are there fewer survivors, the difference between winning and losing can happen in a very short window of time. Companies that were regarded as the hottest plays in high technology 3 to 24 months ago could be downsizing or in reorganization or bankruptcy today.

- **Given the current environment, what are the "must-have" skills for transformation leaders today?**

The two that I am continually reminded of are creativity and communication. I am amazed to see people running companies who do not have the creativity to respond in a dynamic environment. In an unforgiving, fast-paced business climate, you are infinitely better prepared if you are a creative person. Good communicators have an enormous advantage over poor communicators because so much of running a company is inspirational, external and internal, that is, inspiring your employees, shareholders, industry analysts, and customers.

- **When your culture is based on innovation and creativity, the soft skills become even more important.**

If you go back to the premise that you will ultimately need to have an enormous number of highly talented people to execute well, you'll find the ability to communicate at the core. You just have to be able to persuade people that they are a part of something bigger. If you have a creative vision and you can communicate it in a compelling way to get people excited, you will recruit better people as a result. Then, it is easy to convince the world that you have a more dynamic company.

- And at the heart of these dynamic companies, we have found that they have evolved the human resources department into a strategic human capital group that is focused on leadership development, coaching, mentoring, stretch roles, executive education, talent acquisition and development, and retention. They have created a people operating system within the company.

HR has become ground zero in the war for business. Traditionally, HR has been a cost center, an administrative necessity, but not strategic to the business and certainly not viewed as a competitive advantage. The functions that it fulfilled were transactional in nature. Because HR was viewed in this way, it attracted people suited for that kind of function. Today, human capital management is being regarded as the competitive differentiation that ultimately will make your company successful. The recruitment, retention, and development of people is considered a company's core asset. With this heightened visibility, a new breed of people are working in HR. They are people who appreciate the value that human capital adds to a company, and they realize that they are part of the value proposition of the company. They need to think differently because it is more cost-effective to develop in-house talent than going to the market for talent.

- Do you use a trusted advisor?

I have an informal short list of CEO acquaintances I tap into for feedback on various issues. It is often thought that the CEO of a company gets that feedback from the board, but I don't think that's the case at very many companies. Certainly, some of your trusted advisors could be on your board, but I have found that it depends very much on the challenge that I face. If I am facing a challenge having to do with scaling a company, I will seek out a CEO acquaintance who is running a much larger company than PeopleSoft. When I joined PeopleSoft and I was trying to understand how to run a company of this size and circumstance, I called [Chairman and former CEO] Eric Benhamou at 3Com because he was running a large company that was facing adversity. Maybe some CEOs have formalized the process by using either their boards or a CEO mentor or advisor, but if there was a single person who had all the skills for every question, that person should probably have my job.

Strategies for implementing a large-scale, rapid transformation

Lawrence A. Weinbach
Unisys Corporation
Chairman, President, and Chief Executive Officer

- You were brought in to lead Unisys through a transformation from a hardware and software company to a services company. What initially attracted you to the opportunity?

When I was approached about the Unisys opportunity, I did a lot of homework. I reviewed everything I could get my hands on that had been written about the company in the prior 12 months and made some interesting discoveries. The first was that, by all rights, the company should have been bankrupt back in the midnineties, but it was able to sustain itself; the question was, How? When I looked a little closer I found the answer: Unisys had customer relationship capital. There were companies still choosing to do business with Unisys even though its financial health was critical. This meant that there were employees inside the company looking after these customers by delivering critical products and services, which kept the company alive. I made my decision to join on the basis of customer capital that was still in the company. Business is really all about winning customer loyalty, so I had that advantage going in as CEO.

- What differences between a partnership and a public company played a role in the transformation?

A partnership is all about people, and in a service partnership, you quickly learn that the customer views whoever is working on his or her account as "the company." Customers don't think of the company as being the CEO or chairman; they look at who's servicing the account. So I learned pretty quickly that in a partnership, you have to have motivated people because they are your sales force and your interface with the customer. They have to represent the company to the customer, and if they do it well, the company can be successful even if there are other problems. Coming to a public company, I brought the knowledge of what is required to be successful in a service company. As we moved Unisys into the services arena, my background helped me to understand where we were and where we had to go from a cultural perspective.

- **What have been the defining moments of the transformation?**

The first was the financial turnaround. At the outset, we had $2.4 billion in debt. We had $1.4 billion in preferred stock that had an annual dividend requirement making it similar to debt, and we basically had no tangible net worth. The annual pretax cost of interest and preferred dividends was about $370 million. The company just wasn't competitive. Today, about four years later, our preferred stock is gone, our debt is down to about $700 million, and the annual cost has been reduced from $370 million to approximately $70 million dollars. We have a debt-to-equity ratio of 25 percent, and we're competitive. The second defining accomplishment was getting employees to believe in the company again. We did that by first creating a performance management system and a 401K match. We began to take diversity seriously, making sure we were hiring people with varied backgrounds. We resumed our recruiting program at colleges and universities so that we could go after the best and brightest right out of college and thus could refresh our organizational culture. We began Unisys University so we could train our employees in the ever-changing technology environment. The third defining point was restructuring our entire go-to-market proposition so that we could be more responsive to the needs of the customers and the marketplace. And fourth was making the company profitable again. We have now had 16 straight profitable quarters from operations. We've done that by eliminating the low-margin commodity business and going after services businesses where we could add value. And, finally, we developed an advertising and branding program to begin letting the world know about our improvements.

- **What has to happen in the first one hundred days**
  of a strategic transformation?

Let's talk about the first day and the first one hundred days. My first day on the job, I went on our closed-circuit television system and shared with the employees my vision for the transformation: customers, employees, and reputation—simple, clear, and understandable. Then I went to the news media and stated that Unisys was committed to repaying a billion dollars in debt within two years. That was Day One. For the next 99 days, I visited 20,000 employees and communicated the vision and solicited their buy-in. At the end of four months, we had paid off $800 million of debt—80 percent of our goal in 15 percent of the time frame. The lesson there is that the first hundred days are important, but the most important of them is Day One, because that's when you have to win people's confidence that you have a plan and that you are personally engaged.

- **What has been the toughest challenge to date?**

Getting out of the PC business, which is a commodity business. We weren't a large enough player. To make the transition, it was necessary to convince our manufacturing and engineering staffs that we could remain attractive to our customers and become more profitable by moving into the high end of technology, where we could add value. This was a very difficult proposition because it involved getting people to change their mental models of Unisys. In other words, we had to change the culture of the organization in order to change our niche, and we did it. Today, Unisys is over 70 percent in the service business.

- **What sort of things does Unisys do to foster leadership development?**

We have Unisys University, where we deliver our entire employee training and leadership programs. One of them is a leadership school, which is open to all levels of management. All my direct reports have been through the one-week school, and we are now putting their direct reports through. Our goal is to have everyone in management complete the program. That represents about 2,000 of our 40,000 employees. It took us awhile to develop the curriculum, but it was worth the time investment. Now, we are very methodically getting the message out, getting people to understand our new culture—not a command-and-control culture, but one in which employees are given authority and responsibility, and they're held accountable. Because it is markedly different from the way things used to be done at Unisys, we are taking every opportunity to communicate and reinforce the message with our people.

- **Do you teach at the university?**

Typically, I attend at least one day of a week-long course. I spend some time teaching and answering questions and the rest of the time getting to know the people.

- **What is your leadership philosophy, and, bottom line, what does it mean to be a leader today?**

My philosophy is hire the brightest people that you can hire, give them a vision of where you would like the company to go, and get out of the way. What it means being a leader today is simply the desire to find and hire people who are smarter than you. Then, you have to place them in an environment—for example, a performance management system—where they can flourish. Leadership is all about people wanting to follow you. It isn't about your being a dictator. If people want to follow you, you're a leader. If people don't want to follow you, you're in trouble.

Leading change in a nonprofit organization

Pat Mitchell
PBS Corporation
President and Chief Executive Officer

• Can you share some your experiences in leading the transformation of PBS?

The transformation began and continues under a framework that I describe as "keeping the best and reinventing the rest." Public broadcasting is an institution with a proud and worthy legacy. Approaching a transformation of PBS, we wanted to keep intact all the good attributes that many people had built into the organization's foundation, attributes such as trust and goodwill, and rethink, reshape, and redesign the parts of the organization that were not working as well. We needed to take those elements that we do well, build them into a sustainable model, and incorporate it into a system of hundreds of independently managed businesses. Change is not easy in any organization, but it's particularly challenging in nonprofit organizations because nonprofits always work with fewer resources than are needed to actually do anything. That situation tends to support the status quo, because it's harder to take risks when you don't have resources. In a membership organization such as ours, there is a huge diversity of need. We have to accommodate the audience and programming needs of 347 different American communities that are as diverse as this nation is diverse. These are all factors that work against change, and I've therefore had to do a little bulldozing to rebuild this organization into one that is built to change. I characterize it as pushing a rock up a hill every morning. You push it up and some days it slides back a couple of inches, generally due to the lack of resources and the risk aversion that arises from that lack of resources.

• How did you overcome these challenges?

The secret is to make each step along the path of change have some recognizable value. You have to stand behind your risk and state your case for change in a very reasonable way. Then, you lead by doing and by setting the example. Building consensus is critical for a major strategic change to work. In my case here, I visited over a hundred of our stations in the first six months, listened to their staffs' concerns, and worked with them to come up with some new plans. That face time was absolutely essential to the success of our transformation. Because of the bold steps we would have to take for the transformation to succeed, that is, changing programing schedules, canceling programs, reorganizing staff, it was critical that I spent quality time up front with our constituencies to reinforce the message that we were keeping the best and reinventing the rest.

- Is it like building the flywheel—the more people you get behind the initiative, the quicker it starts to move, and then people start to buy in on why it's a good thing?

Sure, and if people feel they have been listened to, they are a lot more likely to become spokes in that flywheel than they are to stand outside and throw sticks in your way. Everybody needs to feel heard, especially in a membership organization. That doesn't mean they're going to be served equally well by every risk you take, but they have to be willing to take the risks with you.

- Does your organization operate in a competitive environment?

We're not competitive with our commercial colleagues because we're in a completely different business. They're in the business of being competitive for eyeballs to deliver to advertisers or competitive for profits that they return to stockholders. We're not in either one of those businesses. We're in the business of public service, and we're the only one in this business. We are a singular, noncommercial license in a media landscape, providing public service content to hundreds of commercial broadcasters that have to run their businesses based on other principles. We are not competitive, but we need to be more collegial and work more carefully and closely with our commercial colleagues to make sure that we're not offering the same services that they offer. The way to ensure that the public will continue to value us, and therefore continue to watch us, and therefore continue to support us, is to be singular and unique, and distinct and distinguished from our commercial colleagues.

- Many businesses are facing the need to transform. Were there any lessons you learned through your transformation that other businesses can adopt?

One lesson that we're all learning is how dramatically the world around us has changed. We can't simply sit here and do exactly the same thing we've been doing since 1968. It's even hard to justify doing the same things we were doing as recently as September 10, 2001. The PBS mission has to stay unconditionally intact because that's the reason we exist, but we have to continually redefine our goals and business in light of current needs. Otherwise, there'd be little reason for our supporters to continue supporting us. Perpetually redefining a business is easy to forget to do because it is difficult to do, and often the need to change happens at the moment you are fulfilling your customer's every wish. We're not changing for change's sake; we're changing in anticipation of a changing market so that we are always accountable and impactful on delivering.

- **What keeps you awake at night now, posttransformation?**

Public broadcasting is at a very critical intersection. Given the rapid changes in both technology and distribution, and every other way that the media landscape around us is changing, we're going to have to redefine everything, from the foundation to the services we offer. We need to find new funding mechanisms. Economic downturns don't create weaknesses; they only point out what your weaknesses have always been. It puts everything on the edge. There is no contingency or comfort level anywhere. There was never much of one in public broadcasting anyway, but it diminishes even more when your resources get stretched and your revenues go down. We are already at work on developing a new and more sustainable financial model.

- **With limited resources being stretched even further, how do you attract, develop, and retain the talent necessary to take your organization to the next level?**

I was very concerned about that when I first came to this job, because I knew that in the economic environment of 2000, it was going to be very difficult to be competitive—in terms of salary and benefits—with the cable companies and networks. We were still competing to some degree with Internet salaries, since a lot of Internet-related and new media companies had lured the top talent away and the figures had escalated to the point that all media companies were raising salaries at almost every level. I was surprised, though, when I started recruiting for senior staff at how many people in those high-paying jobs were attracted to the opportunity of doing good and working in a mission-based organization. That is still a major plus for us, even though when the economy takes a dive and major layoffs occur, our recruiting efforts are much easier.

- If it's not all about money, what are other things that attract people to your organization?

It's the feeling in this organization that you are contributing to something worthy, something that makes a positive difference in the lives of individuals and communities. There are people in the media business who believe we really do educate and we really do have an impact, and frankly, they got a little tired of having everything judged by only one measurement: profits. "How high is your EBITDA?" was the question of the day, and this narrow focus on short-term profits and short-term evaluations was not fulfilling to many top people. There are still a significant number of very talented people who do not want their work only judged by one measurement, and who are attracted to a place where there are other things that figure in to what your responsibilities are and what your accountability is. We really do look at impact and accountability, even though we do not have that pressure on us to grow profits. For example, if you are head of promotion, or head of online, are you running the department, or selling videotapes, or whatever is necessary in such a way that it brings value to each and every one of our 347 members? Does it increase the individual support in their communities? Are you reaching the people you need to reach? Are you satisfying the "stakeholders"— that is, everyone from Congress to every American citizen? That's how we have to evaluate. We measure long-term impact at the local community level because that is whom we are serving.

- Do those measurements tie back into a variable component or some part of compensation?

Absolutely. Our bonus plans are based on evaluating. For example, if you're head of promotion and we have very few promotion dollars, have you targeted those dollars toward programing so that it delivered well and significantly impacted this market or that market? We have a point system that is based on how well you manage your resources, your budget, and your people. Drawing from my commercial experience, I've strengthened accountability so that every dollar spent has to be accounted for in ways that we have targeted and can measure.

- Are there any "must-have" skills to be an effective nonprofit leader?

The number one thing is to have faith in yourself. You are going to be challenged constantly by those who are not sure, so you have to believe you're doing the right thing. You have to be willing to take risks and to put a personal stake in the ground and stand behind it. You have to be a consensus builder. You need to be able to listen to others and be willing to take other opinions into account, and then try to make the most consensus-based decision you can.

- What have been some defining moments in your personal and professional life that helped you to develop your leadership style?

My leadership style and many personal goals have been shaped out of failures. My grandpa always used to say that falling on your face is the first step forward. My first unemployment experience in New York in the early seventies really forced me to re-evaluate my career plans. I discovered I needed to adapt some new skills and take some big risks because, ultimately, I was going to have to jump into something new. So, even though things hadn't worked out as I had planned, there was an opportunity to go through another door. Another defining moment occurred in Boston, where I was one of the first senior-level women executives in a media company—and that was true across the country—and I realized that men and women manage differently, lead differently, contribute differently. Finding a voice that felt authentic, that was truly based on my own experiences as a woman, a mother, a wife, a citizen, all of those things rolled in together was part of what I felt I could contribute to an industry that did not have very many of those voices. During this time, along with my male and female colleagues, I tried to figure out what women brought to the table in business. Years later, running my own company gave me an avenue to apply many of the discoveries I made regarding this. Overall, it has really been a matter of developing a management philosophy that was based on personal principles and values, and then knowing that my style not only defined what I wanted to do but also could ultimately define a business.

New lessons for the new economy

Michael Dell
Dell Computer Corporation
Chairman and Chief Executive Officer

The New Economy and the Old Economy have much to learn from each other. As the New Economy struggles through its adolescence, it's learning some new lessons about old fundamentals. Due to the often fruitless cycle of raising capital and spending it to build a brand, many start-ups . . . didn't. Business basics like customers, cash flow, and earnings have reemerged as the building blocks of a successful enterprise. However, a solid business foundation is no longer enough to guarantee continued success. Many venerable Old Economy companies have learned harsh lessons about the need for speed and adaptability in the new business environment.

The emerging formula for organizational success is one that combines the customer focus and financial acumen of the Old Economy with the agility and drive of the New Economy. The true winners will be organizations built on fundamentals, with the ability to understand and take advantage of key trends.

The most essential trend, indeed the trend that spawned the New Economy, is the transition from atoms to electrons and now photons as a medium for information. With each of these transitions, the vehicles upon which information rides have become lighter. Thoughts, ideas, and productivity now flow with less friction than ever before, decreasing transaction costs and removing barriers to communication. As a result, it's now as simple and inexpensive to communicate a world away as it is to send a message across a room.

The Internet is the infrastructure through which organizations, both Old and New Economy, will thrive. The reduction of friction and transaction costs facilitates collaboration on a worldwide basis—with customers, suppliers, and partners. This collaboration, and the efficiencies associated with it, creates competitive advantages that can't be ignored by any company that wishes to survive in the marketplace. And collaboration through the Internet will continue to evolve, fading the lines that previously marked where one organization ended and the other began.

In the continuing evolution of Internet-based collaboration, the most important issue, and often the most contentious, is standards. Proprietary hardware architectures and software environments are stumbling blocks on the pathways of progress. The high costs and low innovation associated with nonstandard, single-source infrastructures eventually come under considerable pressure and conform to popular will. But in the meantime, the march of progress is slowed. With industry and open standards governing the Internet and the airwaves, a community will thrive.

The issue of standards is central to the burgeoning growth of wireless technology at the edge of the Internet. A maelstrom of wireless client systems, from notebook computers to handheld devices, is accessing the Internet over a variety of protocols. The market will eventually sort out a clear winner, but until that time, the lack of a uniform platform standard is the missing covenant of universal collaboration.

Dell is a proud steward of technological progress and we look forward to a continuing tradition of cooperation among the leaders of the global digital economy. Through the coordinated efforts of all stakeholders—governments, organizations, and communities—we can build the systemic infrastructure that is essential for the growth of a digital infrastructure. With a single vision, we'll all succeed.

Chapter 5

The Stakeholder's View

Aligning stakeholders' interests with long-term value

J. Stuart Francis
Lehman Brothers
Managing Director and Head of Global Technology Investment Banking

In nearly all successful companies today, whether they are global organizations or emerging companies with exciting new technology, there is an increasing recognition among leaders that building and integrating commitment among all stakeholders maximizes the long-term success of an organization. With information so universally accessible, consistency of communication has become essential, and thanks to the instant flow of information via the Internet, all stakeholders, including investors, employees, customers, and communities, now receive a consistent message from corporate leaders. This integrated view has become a virtually universal principle of organizations, but having been implicit in the leadership style of effective managers throughout the industrial age, it is now accelerating in importance during the current information and technological revolution. As a result of the impact of technological advances, integration is now mandatory for success. Thus, a new challenge for leaders is driving the organization to effectively integrate all of these perspectives into the organization's strategic direction and operations while maintaining the speed and focus needed to compete effectively in the global marketplace.

In the following pages, the authors examine the implications of varying stakeholder perspectives as they relate to leading a complex organization. All of the contributors have solid credentials for their viewpoints, having been very successful business leaders by creating, analyzing, or guiding some of the world's most successful and innovative companies over the past 25 years. While their perspectives on the topic vary slightly, a broad common theme emerges: for a company to provide the greatest long-term returns, all the stakeholders' perspectives need to be effectively integrated in an organization—one that is, in the words of Jim Breyer and his colleagues at Accel Partners, "a hub for innovation that has the appropriate 'spokes' to reach outside its borders."

One of the most effective ways to ensure that the interests of all stakeholders are aligned toward building long-term value is to have the leaders of the organization also be owners, that is, shareholders of stock, of the organization. As David Rubenstein of the Carlyle Group notes: "By making a manager an owner, you empower that manager to do things that he or she might not otherwise have wanted to do or thought of doing."

Building long-term value by integrating all the stakeholder interests is obviously a difficult task, but as one contributor points out in this chapter, it is also critical. Each contributor in his or her own way notes that it is necessary to foster innovation, inspire the team, be responsive to customers, understand the differences in global cultures, and add value to the communities in which the company operates. It takes great leadership to do all of these things in an integrated manner. However, it is also increasingly important in the current global environment to build and maintain a long-term capital base as an instrument for enabling the company to integrate all of these interests and ensure the ability to build long-term value. Capital has been readily available for most successful companies over the past two decades, with attractive, liquid stock and bond markets around the globe for the majority of that period. Many companies took advantage of the enormous liquidity in the world markets to raise either equity or debt capital when they needed it because it was nearly always available. In addition, many companies operated with a greater degree of debt leverage than in the past, since the ability to reduce leverage and finance on a long-term basis has essentially always been available for over 20 years. This consistent availability of long-term capital has been a huge factor in the enormous growth in global economic activity during the past decade.

For now, those days are gone. Celtic House's Andrew Waitman observes: "Even some great technology firms with good brands will have difficulty raising money, and there will continue to be lower valuations across the board." The days of instantly available long-term capital are certainly over, at least for the short term and possibly longer. We are entering a period when, in order to build long-term value, companies need to raise long-term capital prudently, when the markets allow them to raise it, rather than only after capital needs have become apparent.

The companies that have a well-thought-out, long-term capital structure and those that raise long-term equity and debt capital when the markets allow it will have increasingly strong advantages over companies that have not provided that balance sheet strength to underlie their business. In addition, there is a widening valuation and cost-of-capital gap between the competitors with the strongest capital base in an industry and those that may have comparable organizational and product strengths but a less strong capital base. Constantly evaluating the appropriate capital base of a company is now a critical factor in ensuring that the resources are available for a company to excel. Stakeholders, particularly equity holders and executive management, often debate the merits of raising additional capital. However, volatility in capital markets enables companies that have already raised capital to deploy that capital at times when competitors are unable to do so. In raising capital when it is available, rather than when it is required, companies demonstrate a strategic understanding of the importance of readiness in the marketplace, an understanding that can achieve a competitive edge and produce returns for their stakeholders.

Even in a company with a solid capital base, all stakeholder interests are incorporated, and long-term value is being maintained, it is still challenging to maintain that position over time, and that, these contributors all agree, is where aligning stakeholder interests is critical. It is critically important, as William Crist of CalPERS, writes, "the twenty-first century must become the century of the long run." Even a great innovation or product with the most rapid path to customers will not succeed solely on the basis of short-term decisions. What works is a long-range approach with a depth of management ability and consistent communication to all stakeholders of the organization, internal and external. As noted by Dana Ardi of JPMorgan Partners, "The next generation of leaders will have to be able to manage through chaos." There must be continual alignment between the company's operations and the long-term interests of customers, shareholders, employees, and other key groups.

In the stock market environment of the past 10 years, it has become increasingly difficult to manage for the longer term, given the narrow focus on short-term results. It takes courage to make strategic decisions that may have a negative short-term impact. That courage comes from the top—from an organization's leadership—and is reinforced only over time, as companies like GE have proven.

In many instances, that courage and guidance can be most effectively augmented by the board of directors and key shareholders, rather than emanating solely from senior management. Elspeth Murray of Queen's University identifies the importance of boards "who understand some of the finer aspects of competing in today's environment." Integrated corporate governance is critical to the global financial system and, as John Biggs of TIAA-CREF notes, is important as leadership for emerging economies as well. The increasingly important role of an involved, knowledgeable board that has the courage to challenge management decisions could have been hugely important in preventing some of the major negative surprises that confronted companies such as Enron in 2001. As Ken West, the chairman of the National Association of Corporate Directors, pens: "No matter what else a director brings to the boardroom table, it takes courage to be a fully competent, effective board member."

In summary, the current environment has global opportunities that have never been greater, but the risks in achieving those opportunities have never been higher. Great companies are led by management and boards that effectively integrate the interests of all stakeholders to build long-term value. In all cases, these companies will also have planned for their success by having a strong long-term capital base that is equal to or superior to that of their competitors.

A cultural anthropologic approach to leadership

Dana Beth Ardi
JPMorgan Partners
Human Capital Partner

- What is your role as Human Capital Partner at JPMorgan Partners?

I am a corporate anthropologist. I study organizations, their cultures, the way they grow and develop, and the people who are responsible for forming their communities. Just as an anthropologist would study cultures or tribes or individuals in the cultures around them, analytically and for the purpose of enhanced understanding—that's the way I study companies. I'm responsible for finding, developing, and retaining talent throughout our portfolio, which consists of six hundred companies operating in every major industry sector around the world. We believe in a holistic approach to investing in which all the resources—financial and human—come together in a synchronistic fashion to grow a world-class company.

- How does your role fit with those of the other partners there? What competitive advantages does your role provide in the marketplace?

As an investment professional, I sit at the table as a peer to the investment teams and we evaluate potential investments together. As they look at the business model, the strategy, the financial capital that's required, I look at exactly the same issues but with the people piece in mind. While they are brainstorming about industries and industry sectors, about trends and where we might want to invest, I'm brainstorming about the talent pool, the industry sector, where the viable talent is, and what kind of talent we need to execute the business strategy. We are talent scouting before we even put down our money in any particular opportunity. Human capital has always been a part of the equation, but often it was an afterthought.

We've tried to innovate in this regard to make our deal process unique. This diverse approach to coordinating strategic information allows us to offer better services to the marketplace.

- **Assuming your talent needs vary depending on the business, what competencies are you looking for to execute strategies in a start-up versus an established company?**

Just as you go from an idea, a seed, an embryo, to an infant, a toddler, to pre-adolescence, all the way through the different stages of development, that is how we look at companies. Because of the diverse nature of our investment portfolio, the first thing we do when a company is introduced is evaluate the stage it is at and the kind of leadership it needs to grow to the next level. My background is in child development and psychology, and this layered approach to assessing a company's growth needs very much parallels the life cycle of an individual. Different leadership attributes are called for at different stages of a company's development. Some people are really good at early stage companies because they love the growing and nurturing aspect of leading. Some people are better executors and operators, so they excel at leading companies out of adolescence into adulthood. There are really charismatic leaders who are able to carry mature companies into the next generation. The communal qualities among all these types of leaders tend to be strong character, strong communication skills, and the ability to function as builders in some way. People who can manage transitions well, for example, have what I call the ability to put a stake in the stream, rather than a stake in the ground. People who can put a stake in the stream are collaborative and can manage diverse organizations; they understand the nature of business as an evolving process, not a stationary object. They can lead futuristically, and they can invent, then reinvent, by continually innovating. We look for these kinds of people.

- **Are you applying these criteria to the entire management teams of the portfolio companies or just to their CEOs?**

I do not believe that one individual can take an organization where it needs to go. That's why I describe myself as a corporate anthropologist, because it's really about mining the community. What you need in that community is a sense of having the core values that you all hold dear, but also the ability to challenge each other to stretch. If you are a good tennis player and you play with someone who is at your level or slightly better, then you have a great workout. If you play with someone who has a different game, however—who takes the ball to the net, who hits the ball long, who just has a different game—not only do you work harder, but your game goes to a new level. A lot of companies miss out by expecting one person to lead when, really, you need to evaluate the capabilities and the competencies of the whole team—because it's the team that creates the opportunity for its members to stretch. A distributed model of leadership is how most companies will lead going forward.

- **What is the future of the human resources function?**

Just as all CEOs are not created equal, all individuals who are dealing with the people side of the business are not created equal, and that's okay. The traditional human resource functions, developing effective compensation and benefits systems, identifying training and development needs of employees, and similar functions, will always be very critical. At some point, though, companies will have to appoint an advocate for their human capital, and it may be the top HR executive or it may not. In some companies, that responsibility may be divided between the CEO and the chief knowledge officer. In others, it could be a dedicated human capital executive with the title of chief of strategy, chief people officer, or something along those lines. Every organization will probably have a knowledge management executive to identify, collect, and propagate best practices. This role should amalgamate with the human capital function so that it extends to training, leadership development, and mentoring. Regarding performance review and reward systems, a human capital–focused approach will encapsulate the whole opportunity to retain talent by crafting programs specific to the individual—programs that take into account their goals for personal development, their lifestyles, their life stages, their motivations, their critical competencies, and their motivated skills.

- **How have the events of the past two years, including the dotcom surge and bust, affected the available pool of talent in the marketplace?**

The New Economy wasn't a new economy at all. It was a revolution of the knowledge worker. It was a revolution of talent. In hindsight, when we try to get a perspective on what happened during the dotcom era, it will be that, for the first time, talent flexed. Executives said, "We are talent. We want to be treated like that. We want to be respected. We want to be developed and nurtured. We want to set some of the rules. We want you to know how we like to work, what hours we like to work, the ways in which we work, how we like to dress, how we think about benefits. Give me the ability to choose what's in my own interest." One of the things that will have changed American business forever is that the New Economy was really a worker's movement; it was a form of labor movement. It had much more long-term impact than the short-term bubble of investors supporting business models that held no sustainable competitive advantage.

- In an economy in which many companies have to downsize, how does a company continue to nurture and develop human capital?

The organizations trying to grow strong foundations of talent recognize that there is more opportunity to do this in a downturn. When the market rebounds, it's your people, not your physical assets, that will repair and rebuild and be able to respond to heightened demand. It's not about downsizing in a tough economic period; it's about rightsizing so that you have the right people in the right slots. You know who these people are because you've already identified the skills you need to go to the next level, and you've talent-scouted for them, recruited them, and nurtured them. In many instances, the survivors of downsizing feel relief and new optimism by recognizing that their company is now poised for re-growth.

- To do this, is it necessary to top-grade your talent?

This is where I would differ with many very successful leaders. It is important for you to know your teams. Yes, you have to know the people in the organization and who your high performers are, but an all-star team is usually more productive than individual stars. Glorifying the top 20 percent doesn't ensure that you get the job done. Some people are good at sales and marketing, some are great executors, some are loyal soldiers, some are really good customer relations types. It's not about the top; it's about finding the right combination of people to accomplish the mission. Some of the underperformers may be the jewels in the rock that you have to mine and develop. Clearly, there's a top tier of talent and leadership, and you have to find and develop those people and hold them close to you. But it's also your responsibility as a leader to continually mine and develop in the substrata. Some of those people who fall in the middle ranges of top-grading can turn out to be your breakaway "A" players once you put them in the right seats.

- How do you get the most out of your team?

The secret is to build an emotional network between people. It's about making connections and building a community. It doesn't happen overnight. And a lot of organizations don't value connectivity as much as they should, so they may not create opportunities to build an emotional network. But you really have to bring people together on a variety of levels and allow for genuine dialogue and interaction to make the whole team effective. If you look at the reasons people leave companies, it usually has more to do with a cultural incompatibility than with going to another organization to make more money. When cultural incompatibility is the reason, it means that they were never comfortable in the community that took them in; they didn't value the same things or have the same sense of purpose. I always ask my partners and CEOs, If you have two candidates who are equal, which of them would you want to go to a baseball game with, or be stranded in an airport with? In other words, which one are you most interested in talking with about something other than the business? Identifying people of this caliber involves a different approach; instead of asking "Where did you work during this time?" it's about asking "What did you learn about yourself while working for that company?" This is a fabulous beginning for getting to know someone. Leaders must continually encourage creativity. Creativity is bad ideas filtering to good ideas. True effectiveness begins by mining for the good ideas and pushing the envelope of creativity, that is, your thoughts triggering my thoughts. People respond best when they feel safe being creative. Sometimes narcissism in leadership inhibits a free flow of thought and creativity, making it harder for people to let down their guard and make an emotional connection. To be productive and perform optimally in the business environment, people have to feel safe and believe that the community they're in will value their opinions and respect them. To foster this, you create mentoring opportunities, social occasions, whatever activities demonstrate the value of the individual and their contributions at all levels. The worst thing a leader can do is stifle people's sense of safety by shutting down ideas and creativity.

- **What are the skills that young executives should develop in order to be an effective leader?**

Listening skills are key, and this doesn't mean listening for a pause to make your next point or comment. It's the whole process of active listening, aggregating information, processing information, and communicating it back. This is the same as developing your knowledge management skills, a matter of gathering input from a lot of different places, aggregating it, and then communicating it back in a way that makes it clear what the mission is and how we'll drive to it. The ability to negotiate decisions so that everyone is happy is important, too. The next generation of leaders will have to be able to manage through chaos. In the chaos we are inventing, reinventing, innovating, inventing, reinventing, and innovating. That's the cycle. That's the challenge.

The importance of leadership focusing on the long run

William Dale Crist
California Public Employees' Retirement System (CalPERS)
President and Chairman of the Board of Administration

There is an old saying that "if the admiral dies, the navy sails on." Likewise, if individual sailors die, the navy will sail on. The fact that none of us is indispensable does not change the fact that all of us are, in some way, important. The capitalized market value of many of the world's great corporations now stands at a fraction of what it was two years ago. Bubbles have burst and economies have changed. And yet business goes on. And people must continue to eat and be sheltered to survive. And each one of these people is, in some way, important.

During the past 10 years, much has been made of the importance of improving the governance of corporations as a way to make them more efficient and more competitive as global business enterprises. Shareowner pleas for more independent directors, more transparency, and increased accountability have resonated with many leaders and have resulted in change. A new generation of corporate board members will admit that these changes have been changes for the good and have resulted in more serious, more critical evaluation of management and of each other.

The information revolution, with its giant strides in communication technology, has put us in closer touch with one another than ever before. New discoveries in medicine and the exponential growth of knowledge in the biological sciences promise to keep humans alive longer and longer. The limitless horizons of computer technology have afforded humankind mathematical solutions and an understanding of physics that great minds of the past barely imagined. The technological achievements of the twentieth century have been grand.

But it is now the twenty-first century, and better corporate governance for greater efficiency and improved profit from quarter to quarter is not enough. Technology will continue to develop and lift us up, but relying on technological change will not be enough. The ability of advanced economies to produce more than their citizens can consume is not enough. The reduced probability of war between nations over ideological differences is not enough. As long as there are large numbers of people in the global economy who suffer from hunger and disease over a long period of time while others with access to abundance quarrel over short-run distributions, the possibility of seemingly irrational terrorist attacks will remain a constant threat to real peace.

The twenty-first century must become the century of the long run. Every three months during the latter part of the twentieth century, a business attempting to raise capital in the public market has been required by competition to report current operating results to the public. These quarterly reports are then "analyzed" by "experts" on a totally short-term basis, and the company's market value is thus influenced by very short-term performance. Such short-term reports and supposed objective analyses have often been counterproductive in the twentieth century. Such short-term thinking will become absolutely destructive in the twenty-first century unless business leaders and investors from every developed economy simultaneously focus on the longer term. More attention must be paid to the probable effects of a company's business policy decisions over a period of years, not months. Further, and more difficult, the company's long-term view must include more than just shareowners and stakeholders; it must encompass all people, everywhere.

The most common response to this twenty-first-century admonition from most twentieth-century managers, business policy makers, and investors will be "Nonsense." Balderdash, they will say. They will argue that, if they are themselves going to survive, the grindstone to which their noses must be applied can only be a short-term, results-oriented grindstone. They will say that not only is it implausible to suggest that they can be held responsible for anything that happens more than a few quarters into the future, it is foolish idealism to suggest that they can impact the welfare of people in other economies. In fact, they will insist that the welfare of people immediately within their sphere of control is about all they can hope to influence. Even this is almost impossible, they will argue, because of competing market forces and intervention from the outside by rule.

This response is justified. It is an essentially accurate, realistic response. But it is a response that will be unacceptable in a century characterized by shrinking distances and clashing cultures. Sustainability should be the business objective of the twenty-first century. Philanthropy and good deeds will not get the job done. Positive change in the long run will only endure when such change is good for business in a free-enterprise world. But who will take the risk in a free-enterprise world to move competition out of the short term? Politicians and philosophers can help or hinder, but only those persons with authority in the business world have the power to bring about such change.

Today's business leaders have more than a business responsibility to be competitive in the short run. There must be a new focus on helping the market find a way to evaluate and reward long-term performance—to be accepting of sustainability. Somehow, the effect of business policy on people around the world must be analyzed and factored in when determining value. The importance of people other than shareowners, customers, and employees has to be taken into consideration. And, perhaps most important of all, the shareowners themselves must learn to trust in the market over the longer term. But none of this happens without leadership.

The notion of planned, centrally controlled economic activity has nearly disappeared from the face of the earth. The notion of free enterprise, with increased reliance on private property and competition, seems to have taken over the imagination of people from every economic level. Intellectual property and the need to invest in human capital become increasingly important with every new technological breakthrough. Nevertheless, all of humankind still lives in the very short run because life is short. Individual freedom and initiative must be taken advantage of and exercised quickly.

So the dilemma of the twenty-first century becomes clear. Individuals protecting themselves, as we have learned is the way of things, cannot be expected to move out of the short run. But individual leaders, with the power to effect change by establishing institutions that will last beyond a lifetime, can guide the decision-making process in the direction of such change. The individual leaders with the most power in today's world are the leaders of big business. The terms "global" and "multinational" are now used as commonly as the terms local, regional, national, and international. The potential importance of this new common language is lost on many, but not on most of the world's business leadership. The responsibility for bringing a short-term world into a long-term focus must lie somewhere. It clearly lies within the reach of some business leaders. Perhaps it lies within their grasp.

All of which brings us once again to the circular truth that no one person is indispensable, but all people are important. Those people with the ability to bring about change are the lucky ones. John Maynard Keynes was wrong; in the long run we are *not* all dead, because "we" must include those not yet born. It is those who live entirely in the short term who are in the most danger, even though such a practice seems to carry less risk at the time. But our time must begin to stretch into the future with meaning. It must.

Leadership characteristics for venture-backed portfolio companies

Andrew Waitman
Celtic House International
Managing General Partner

- What is the worldwide venture capital marketplace for 2002?

The shift in power from general partners to limited partners will continue, given that the interests of the two continue to be misaligned. With the benefit of hindsight, these two groups will point the finger at each other for "irrationally exuberant" deals done during the dotcom and telecom boom, and we'll see some infighting, due to claw-backs, and excessive fees, due to a dramatic investment slowdown. The focus will continue to be protecting the existing portfolio. Committed capital will slow the pace of new investment for three to four years. The amateur venture capital investor will disappear. Even some great technology firms with good brands will have difficulty raising money, and there will continue to be lower valuations across the board. Everyone is concerned about the increased uncertainties in today's fear-driven, global environment. Cash and cash flow will continue to be emphasized in every business, with funding going to those companies that attract two years of capital or to those with convincing strategies for cash-flow-positive business models.

- Some of today's younger managers are what recruiters call "upside managers" because, having become managers during an economic heyday, they are unproven leaders in tough economic times or through naturally occurring business cycles. How do you compensate for this lack of experience in your selection process for start-up company talent?

Experienced managers may inspire more confidence in employees and investors than the youthful enthusiasm of dotcom leaders; however, even experience can prove to be as much a mirage as the dotcom customers. We look for people who are uncommonly well qualified to lead a business, period. Economic downturns, competitive threats, and channel growth challenges are all part of building a business, and we seek individuals who can lead through many conditions. The ability to communicate, to creatively solve problems, to partner, and to execute efficiently and effectively are skills required by leaders in any environment. Younger managers may not have the experience of working through the recessions of the seventies or eighties; however, the macroeconomic conditions at these times were very different: inflation, small-scale global trade, and developing Internet. The world has changed so much that even the old movie script provides few clues on appropriate decisions today. If experience is the only gauge of business leadership, then you may as well be driving using the rear-view mirror.

- Why not just hire smart people, regardless of experience or track records?

Nothing is so static as to allow a simplistic solution such as hiring the "best" or right people as a guarantee for success. Even smart people cannot predict the future of a complex economic environment. Most Global 2000 companies make the attempt to hire the best and brightest yet rarely demonstrate an unbroken history of success. Why? Unanticipated economic shocks such as inflation, the introduction of disruptive technology such as the PC, disruptive business models such as Dell's, and the interdependent dynamics of human relationships affect the long-term sustainability of any model. It is important to hire and hold on to smart people, however, luck and timing also play roles in sustained success.

- Many companies are moving away from transactional-oriented human resources departments to a more strategic human capital management approach that includes the transactional component but also leadership development, coaching, mentoring, learning, executive education, career planning, talent acquisition, and retention. Is this the future of the HR function, and, if so, why?

Yes. The HR function is now viewed as a strategic and critical early-hire. Four years ago, that was not the case. Now it's all-important to hire the right first-in people—the recruiting role is viewed as a top priority. Regardless of industry, the intellectual contribution of employees is the single greatest builder of value and profits. It is the key asset of any substantial enterprise. As such, it must be developed, nurtured, and maintained in a healthy, rewarding manner. Without sufficient attention to maintenance, the machinery in the factories of the Industrial Revolution would have ground to a halt, and in today's Information Age, the loss of a key architect, a creative brand builder, or a dedicated customer support representative can erode market share and competitive position. Human capital management is the oil that keeps the machinery running smoothly.

- How would you describe the human capital environment in the various industries in which Celtic House invests?

We continue to invest aggressively in the telecom, Internet infrastructure, storage and networking spaces. However, regardless of the industry, the success of a start-up is largely due to the quality, experience, and capability of the people. There were dramatic layoffs at some of the largest telecom companies in the past year of so—Nortel, 45,000 layoffs; JDS, 30,000—and almost every high-technology firm pared back headcount to improve the cash burn–rate or profitability. Although there are more people available now than in the past five years, the competition for the best people remains intense since they are still in great demand.

- Is it a global marketplace for recruiting people?

There is more migration of talent today than historically, but is the net flow dramatically different? My sense is that it is not. There are many examples in our portfolio where C-level talent—CIO, CEO, CFO—has moved from one country to another without too much struggle in the transition. What has changed most is the desire to find the right opportunities. There is more willingness to relocate to places that might not have been previously considered. Another trend is the multiple-headquartered company. Good products are being built everywhere, and companies realize that they cannot just invest in or acquire companies located next door. Can I find quality people in each country? Yes, but certain skills can be generalized by region. For example, some of the best technical people we work with are based in the United Kingdom and Canada. We have also found that the strongest business leadership, sales, and marketing skills can be found in the United States—culturally the Americans tend to be more aggressive. However, both the United Kingdom and Canada are evolving into more aggressive corporate cultures, as is the rest of the world.

- Is the war for talent all about money?

In these times, with significant job losses and corporate restructuring, people are just pleased to avoid the pink slip. At the upper tier of recruiting for talent, money is important, but so are other aspects such as job satisfaction, working environment, peer recognition, and advancement. Stock options continue to have their ephemeral appeal, although less so than historically.

- In the eyes of a financier, how has governance changed
  for start-up companies?

The fundamental issues have not changed. The board still represents the shareholders, and, to that extent, it has the fiduciary duty to advise senior management and make decisions on behalf of shareholders to ensure a company's success. However, today, a board member's connections (including those of the venture capital firm) are much more critical. In our time-short world, you can cut through the traditional processes and build channels with a well-placed phone call to a well-known name. We filter according to the credibility of who is making the introduction. That is a big issue now for boards. Boards traditionally are made up of people who have lived through the wars and can offer advice because of prior experience. But today, the landscape changes so rapidly that that advice may not be as valuable or as relevant.

- What advice would you give legacy companies in terms
  of filling board seats?

I would bias toward the younger set, because they tend to be more immersed in the ebbs and flows of today's business and Internet climate. Balance your board membership between directors who have 20, 30 or 40-plus years of experience and people with relevant experience in a specific area that has received a lot of attention over the past few years, such as e-commerce or customer relationship management. Another approach would be to seek out board members who have expertise in a particular subject that is both relevant to the business and is missing on the board. The final consideration is the person's network into the ecosystems of the new world.

- What are characteristics you look for in leaders
  for your portfolio companies?

The traits of good leaders include demonstrated competence and success in a specific area. That is the intelligence test. Also, do they bring some sort of situational credibility in certain areas? Persistence is a virtue in today's tough build-up environment. Demonstrated decision-making ability is critical. Leaders not only inspire, they have to make tough decisions daily. One of the key characteristics you see in people who have been given leadership roles and failed is an inability to give clear messages and to make decisions. For the purpose of inspiration, leaders need to be good storytellers. They need to be able to give people a sense of what they are doing, why they are doing it, and where they are going. Leaders have to be likable, but tough and bold, too. Finally, but most important, high integrity and strong principles define a good leader, and that is what ultimately attracts the collective body of talent you need.

- How can leaders make decisions at the fast pace of business today,
  when often they have less-than-perfect information?

One of the big problems today is that there is too much information, and everybody makes claims. The issue of credibility is important. There are all kinds of deceptions, either maliciously or ignorantly motivated. Time is really the only solvent to wash away the deception. When you lack time, you must go to people you trust. It is important to use your networks of people to establish the credibility of partners. This is why a well-connected network is critical, because the proliferation of information and noise makes it difficult to discern what is real and valuable to the business and what is not.

- How do you see the role of venture capital evolving?

Venture capital or private equity capital, in general, will continue to grow in size and relevance in the global economy. It will continue to play a crucial role as a business-building and wealth-creation asset. With improvements in standards, market efficiency, and professionalism, this asset class will extend its lead in financial returns over other asset classes.

The private equity investor's role in developing management teams

David M. Rubenstein
Carlyle Group
Cofounder, Managing Director, and Partner

- Can you give us a snapshot of the private equity industry,
  both historically and into the future?

The private equity industry began in the United States in the early 1960s with venture capital investments. Today, the size of the global private equity industry is more than $500 billion, with participation from investors all over the world. As a result, it touches many parts of the domestic and global economy, and in the last five years the private equity industry has become accepted by most institutional and high-net-worth investors. Twenty years ago, few people understood private equity. Now, many investment professionals actively seek to invest in this area. Virtually every investment organization has some allocation to private equity, from 1 percent to as high as 10 percent. Private equity is recognized as a serious investment category that is likely to produce attractive rates of return over a sustained period. Projecting five years down the road, I believe the private equity industry will consolidate substantially. There will be fewer small firms, many more large firms, and probably five to eight global firms.

- What changes have occurred in terms of the type of people
  who are attracted to work in the private equity industry?

Private equity now attracts highly talented people across the board. In years past, business school students would look quizzical when asked of their interest in the private equity field. Now, private equity firms compete with leading consulting firms to attract the most talented business school graduates. In addition, these days Wall Street advisors are much more receptive about joining the private equity world than in 1987, for instance, when Carlyle was founded. The same is the case around the world: investment bankers, financial professionals, lawyers, and business executives all seem interested in being in the industry. The result is a high-quality talent pool. Clearly, the economics are attractive, but equally attractive is the opportunity to do something exciting and challenging, and to participate in building great companies.

- Regarding your investments, how do you assess the management team
  of your portfolio companies?

Management is critical to any investment in the venture world or the buyout world. In the venture world, Carlyle invests only in companies with strong management teams that we believe are able to grow young companies. The same is true in the buyout world. If the management team were weak and incapable of running a company in a leveraged environment, Carlyle probably wouldn't make the investment. Carlyle is known for working with management, not replacing them, and generally likes to keep the management teams already in place. However, sometimes changes are needed. When Carlyle changes management it does so after a careful assessment that the management team in place wasn't able to deliver the expected results.

- When you look at the management teams both on the buyout side and
  the venture side, are there any common sets of skills you're looking for?

The principal objective of all management teams must be to grow and run the company in a way that achieves the financial results its investors seek. Management teams also need to be sensitive to the needs of employees in the local community and sensitive to various customer or client needs. There are many different skills that are required for a good executive in the venture capital or buyout industry. Intelligence, experience, and the ability to lead people are important in both environments.

- Is there a shortage of talent, or is the pool pretty large?

There are many talented people around the world who could do the jobs that are needed; but, as investment professionals, we don't have the time, inclination, or skill set to find them by ourselves. The search industry has become a beneficiary to some extent of the growth in the private equity industry.

- What does great leadership look like to you?

A great business leader is somebody who can move an organization forward in a direction that's positive for all parties involved. A classic example is Jack Welch. When he took the helm of General Electric 20 years ago, it was a well-respected company. At the time, no one thought that GE had any significant problems, yet Welch, in a mere two decades, transformed it into a completely different organization by building on existing strengths. Now, had he just *presided* during this period and not *led*, GE would probably still be a reasonably successful electrical appliances company. But by dramatically expanding its mission and turning it toward a path it would never otherwise have taken, he set the gold standard for business leadership. Welch will be remembered for asking questions that others hadn't asked, motivating people, asking employees to dig a little deeper and work a little bit harder, and giving them a sense of why that was important to them, to their families, and to their communities.

- Following up on that point, how do you attract, retain, and develop key talent for your portfolio companies?

Typically, in a buyout situation, the company is led by managers who have not been owners. Carlyle aligns their interests with those of our investors by giving managers a piece of the equity of the company. We encourage them to buy additional equity and provide opportunities to earn equity down the road. It is a three-pronged approach: the first equity awards are in good faith, essentially free. Then, early on, managers earn equity by virtue of their skills, and eventually we enable them to invest even more capital by lending them funds. By making managers owners, they are empowered to do things that might not otherwise get done. Over the past 25 years, the buyout industry has demonstrated that when managers become owners, they find economic value and create value for shareholders and investors. It is important to make our portfolio teams feel a part of the Carlyle family, to reinforce that they're not just managing a company for themselves. They are encouraged to draw on the assets and the resources that Carlyle has throughout the world. In our case, many of our CEOs have come back to run other companies for Carlyle after we sold the companies they were leading, and many of our CEOs serve on other boards that we have. Significantly, many of our CEOs have become investors with Carlyle outside of the company in which they were involved. It is a family. So when we're trying to buy a company we encourage the people we're working with to talk to our CEOs, existing and former.

- In this way, you are creating your own talent pool.

It does feed on itself. Remember, the buyout industry didn't have a wonderful reputation in the 1980s. The phrase then was not "management buyout," it was "leveraged buyout," with the emphasis on leveraged. Generally, at that time, because of the way the tax laws were structured and for other reasons, there was great incentive to break up companies, to close down plants, and to really focus on things that were not in the best interests of the communities these companies served. That has changed, and the buyout industry now recognizes that some excesses occur.

Carlyle strives to make sure that management understands that our role is to increase the value of the company and increase the value of the whole organization for themselves, their families, and their communities.

- When you are making an investment in a company, what emphasis do you put on leadership versus other elements such as marketing, finance, and proprietary technology?

All those elements play key roles, but clearly, to move toward building growing and profitable companies, we have to place a high value on the people running the show. We seek a management team with intelligence and integrity—we want people who are honest and open about what they do and what they're thinking. We also want people who share the same high ethical standards we've instilled throughout our organization. We maintain an environment that is conducive to a team approach, continuously monitoring the team's collective experience and how it all fits together.

- Compared with the talent in your portfolio companies, what about the leaders and professionals you seek for the Carlyle Group? What skills do you need and how do you acquire them?

Because Carlyle is a growing organization, we use search firms to help us acquire talent at the senior and middle management levels. At the junior level, we tend to hire people right out of business schools or Wall Street training programs. For our investment professionals, we seek some of the same qualities as we do for our portfolio investments: a high degree of intelligence and integrity, a strong work ethic, the ability to get along with other people, a desire to be part of a growing and global organization, and a desire to make the firm their career. Carlyle generally is not interested in recruiting people who want to come here for one or two years and then go elsewhere. Whenever you have an organization that brings in people laterally, you have to balance that by showing your newer people that they can be promoted.

- How do you attract and retain your professionals?

To some extent, Carlyle has forged new ground as the first private equity firm to establish a family of funds that operates all over the world. First, we have instilled in our team a culture that we call "One Carlyle," emphasizing that we are one firm and not a group of individual organizations. We are not in the franchise business and don't lend our name to other groups looking to raise money just by using our name. We are a better firm if everybody pulls together. Second, we incentivize our professionals in a unique way. Most private equity firms compensate their deals teams with carried interest only from the funds they manage, and that is largely the case at Carlyle. However our structure ensures that every professional in our firm gets a piece of the carried interest off every deal, every year, in every part of the firm. Third, we strongly encourage employees to invest in all of our funds and we lend money to them to do so. This gives them their own personal investments in addition to the funds they might receive as part of the carried interest. Fourth, we've set up a capital account for most of the professionals in the firm that takes firm capital and invests it on behalf of the employees throughout all of our funds. Therefore, an employee may reap the benefits from personal investments, carried interest, and a capital pool. This all reinforces our culture, in which people are motivated to work together. We work every day to make our system better, but we believe ours is generous and innovative and we are proud of what we can offer. The result is that people rarely leave the firm on a voluntary basis, and rarely leave Carlyle to go to a competing firm.

•   **What is your development program for MBA and Wall Street hires?**

Carlyle has an active recruiting program at business schools. Historically, we have preferred to not be in a training position. We preferred to hire people who went to college, went to Wall Street, were trained in Wall Street for a few years, went to business school, and then came to us. We felt that we could not provide a great training ground because we were too small and too focused on growing the business. As we've grown, we have developed training programs and retreats that fit our unique culture and approach. We try to hire people with traditional educational backgrounds, but also look for people who are different from one another. As an example, let's say you hire everybody who is a graduate of Wharton, then spent two years at Morgan Stanley, then went to Harvard Business School; you'd have a very homogeneous group, and everybody would like everybody and get along; but that's not necessarily the best thing to do. In addition, we frequently try to find somebody who is brilliant but has not yet gone to business school or may never go to business school. Or, somebody who has expertise in a given area or experiences that have nothing to do with our business but who seems to be able to make a significant contribution in terms of perspective.

•   **Diversity truly brings a creative rub to an organization.**

It happens often enough that somebody has the best education, the best pedigree, and on paper is perfect for the job, but just doesn't have what it takes to really be a great professional in our field. Ironically, the three founders of this firm probably could not get hired here today, because none of us really has had the training that Carlyle traditionally seeks in people. One of the founders was an officer at Marriott Corporation, no Wall Street training. Another had worked in a telecommunications company, no Wall Street training. I was a lawyer and former government official, no Wall Street training. I honestly doubt that, if our resumes landed on the desks of our hiring managers today, any of us would even get an interview. Now that we are an organization of critical mass, we don't have to restrict our requirements for education and experience, and we provide training to cover any missing talents and skills. You need to have openness to different perspectives, different grounds of intelligence, and you also always want people to have that certain spark. Sometimes, people just have a knack for the business.

The institutional investor's role in leadership and globalization

John H. Biggs
Teachers Insurance & Annuity Association—College Retirement
Equities Fund (TIAA-CREF)
Chairman, President, and Chief Executive Officer

I was in the middle of Thomas Friedman's excellent book on globalization, *The Lexus and the Olive Tree*, when the horrible events of September 11 occurred. The Lexus represents, through the image of the high-tech car, the rapid development of democratized and highly technological societies and their extraordinary progress—particularly through globalization. The olive tree symbolizes the rooted culture of people who do not wish or are not able to enjoy the fruits of globalization. The olive tree, in a desperate and awful sense, showed its continuing power in destroying the ultimate symbol of globalization, the World Trade Towers.

Corporate governance is clearly another fascinating and important battleground as we cope with the conflicts between the two symbols. American leadership is important in encouraging improvement in governance, but, as Friedman argues in other spheres, American leadership is both respected worldwide while also resented deeply by many. How can American institutional investors play an effective, useful, and sensitive role in this important aspect of globalization? And how can we avoid unproductive backlash? Several initiatives seem important to us at TIAA-CREF.

The first is to appreciate the significant and legitimate differences that exist in different countries and cultures. One example, from many, is the differences that exist in the underlying legal systems. Among developed countries, the most striking differences are those rooted in the Anglo-Saxon system of equity and judicially derived law, which can effectively respond to changing circumstances compared to those of many European countries whose systems evolve from the civil law of rules and statutes that spread across much of Europe by the Napoleonic codes. Asian, Muslim, and African countries have even more striking differences. American and other Anglo-Saxon advocates need to understand such basic differences.

Second, we must focus on improving the capital markets in underdeveloped countries. Patient discussion of differences must take place. The international economic institutions foster such exchanges. TIAA-CREF has been very active in the International Corporate Governance Network, and has seen some significant victories. For example, Brazil has welcomed recommendations on corporate governance that would lead to greater likelihood of "patient money" investments in their markets by establishing the Novo Mercado, a segment of the main stock exchange which would be reserved for companies with good corporate governance practices.

Third, we must focus on the essential issues—fair treatment of all investors; opposition to expropriation by governments or majority investors; open and comprehensive financial reporting; and vigorous government actions against corrupt practices. Much useful work needs to be done on global accounting and auditing standards, at least minimal protections for investors, better shareholder communications, and other areas falling under the rubric of global corporate governance.

Clearly, the private corporation is the vehicle for worldwide progress in the physical well-being of our populations. If investment funds are not deployed in the "olive tree" countries, the "Lexus" will continue to create intense opposition—but hopefully never again like the apocalypse of September 11, 2001.

Leadership in diversified businesses

Gerald Schwartz
Onex Corporation
Founder, Chairman and Chief Executive Officer

- What is your leadership philosophy?

It's simple: I find people who are better than me at doing everything that comes across my desk and I make sure that they become responsible for it.

- What were some defining moments in your professional and personal life that shaped this straightforward leadership style?

My father was a small businessman and an entrepreneur. From the time I was a very little kid, he would come home every night and talk about his business, what was happening, what he was doing to grow the business, what was going well and what was going terribly. I worked at his business nights and weekends, so I grew up in an entrepreneurial environment. That was probably the most shaping thing because I was so impressionable. Later, as a young man, I went to work in an environment where many different business leaders across America came in to try to do business with us, and that was a huge influence, too. I learned early on that we all put our pants on one leg at a time, and this simple lesson helped to put things in perspective and to make those leaders more real to me. Eventually, Izzy Asper and I founded CanWest Global. He was chairman; I was president. In this experience, I learned a lot about discipline, hard work, and determination.

- **What are the leadership skills you look for in senior managers of your various industrial businesses?**

The qualities we look for in the CEOs include high intellect, high intelligence, high energy, an ability to see a very broad picture; we look for people who like people, people who want to help other people grow and build their careers, and people who are good listeners as well as good communicators. Then, we like to have people who have a deep knowledge of the business, who have been in the industry for some time, and we particularly like to have people who have run a large organization. Good leaders must be good salespeople; they are selling a point of view, a set of ideals, a set of values. An appreciation for people is key, though; because, ultimately, if you have great assets but bad people, you end up with bad assets.

- **We hear a lot about the war for talent and the shortage of true, high quality leadership talent. What is your view?**

I don't agree that there is a shortage of talent. I think there are enormous reservoirs of leadership talent; you just have to tap into them. Every business we own is filled with leadership talent at various levels in the company. The challenge is to create an environment in which people can come forward and do things that would come out of that definition of leadership. I don't think there's a shortage of people at all; I think there's a deficit in our ability to find them and nurture them into good leaders.

- **Do people learn more by success or by failure?**

Typically, good people don't fail. There are mistakes, yes—those are inevitable in a learning situation—but very few outright failures. Usually, it's that they may be modestly successful instead of blazingly successful, or that they are successful but have some challenges left to overcome. One of the things that we always try to inculcate in our people is to do things with speed. Don't take forever. The invasion on Normandy was designed, created, and executed in a year, so don't tell me that it takes two years to do something major. When you move with speed, you're going to make some mistakes, but that's okay because the good things will work and the bad things will surface soon enough and we'll fix them.

- **You also insist that management invest alongside Onex?**

We think that people who have the opportunity to reap rewards for their endeavors should also take the risk. When we're buying a business and we can get the management of that business to view themselves as owners, then it is more likely they will show us all the potholes, problems, and issues in a company and make sure we buy it at the right price. That is a big plus, because we can go in and study a business for months, hire all kinds of consultants, and look at it backwards and forwards, but we'll never understand it as well as the people who've been running the business for 20 years. Getting them on our side of the table as part of the buying process is important. Secondarily, it forms a partnership in which we are all working toward the same goals and vision for the business.

- **When you buy a company, is there a process in place for assessing the talent?**

Our focus is to assess the most senior talent, the chief executive and his or her direct reports. Then, when appropriate, we dig deeper down, and eventually end up evaluating the loading dock, how it operates, the disciplines, the capability, and the productivity. We're not assessing the people at that level, but rather, the process. We almost always keep the senior management in place. We sometimes request that they supplement the team with a particularly strong marketing person, or maybe a change of the chief financial officer, or another area if there is a perceived gap of strength.

- **Many of your businesses are involved with outsourcing. Do you see this as a long-term trend?**

For sure, for sure, for sure. Let me give you the proposition for outsourcing. It is very straightforward: We say to a company, "Sell off the tangible assets that you use to produce your products and services for your own consumption. Sell them to us. Then we'll give you all your capital back. We'll sign a long-term contract to supply you with those products and services, and we will make a complete quality commitment and do this at a lower price than you can manufacture for your company today." How can anybody turn that proposition down? It makes good business sense. Plus, it is a lot easier for most companies to demand a high bar of standards from an external vendor than it is to be demanding on an internal department.

- **Your turnover rate in your corporate office is zero.
  To what do you attribute this?**

Every professional who joined us at our corporate office since the day we started the business is still here, and most of our support staff is, too. We treat everybody as partners in the same enterprise. There are few hierarchical relationships; the organization is very flat. People have something they're responsible for, and it's their job to take care of it and come see me if they need to; but people have a responsibility as well as an opportunity. We've tried to wipe out the bureaucratic structure found in so many organizations and, as a result, we have created a great, collegial environment. For example, we won't hire a new person even at the youngest level unless everybody else on the team interviews that person. We take chemistry and fit very seriously. It's all about teamwork. We even have our compensation all tied into one pool; that way, we are not only motivated to genuinely care about the person coming in, but once they are here, we all benefit from their success, so it's to our advantage to do what we can to ensure that they perform well in this culture and within our performance reward system.

- **Does your culture value and encourage innovation?**

Yes, and particularly in relation to digital technology. We insist that our people have a working knowledge of technology. For instance, there is almost no paper floating around Onex. Everything comes in through our network and is managed there. The same is true at our subsidiaries. We got an early start on this when we bought SkyChefs in the mideighties. It had a new chief executive, Jim O'Neill, who was the former head of information technology at American Airlines. He had a predilection to technology, and really opened my eyes to the wonders of technology and how it can change businesses. We really changed that business over the next four years so that it was information driven, and it was the only caterer that *was* information-driven. However, doing that meant that we had to change the type of people we hired. Before that, few of the people who were running the place had university degrees or a knack for growing a business digitally. We needed people with technical sophistication and who could apply it to operations. I was an early convert of technological innovation and I am a complete convert, because now we drive it everywhere, through all our businesses.

Corporate venture capital's role in innovation

James Breyer, Bruce Golden, and Eli Cohen
Accel Partners
Partners

Over the past few years, every chief executive and business leader has been hammered with exhortations to "get digital or get dead," and to squeeze the best returns out of technology investments.

In this quest to become lean and mean, large corporations have tried to become "intrapreneurial," to become "innovation factories," and to "ideate." While corporate venture capital programs have achieved some success in boosting innovation within large companies, most corporate venture capital programs would be more effective if companies thought creatively about where and how to use them.

Corporate Venture Capital: An Untapped Weapon

Corporate venture capital is the practice of making investments in start-up companies, especially those that are a strategic fit with the established company's business. Too often, corporate venture programs have become separated from corporations' core businesses and have focused on returns. While the public market initially rewarded this behavior, the party is now over, and a hangover has set in for many. The knee-jerk reaction may be to drastically reduce or eliminate the programs.

This is exactly the wrong thing to do. Instead, companies should reexamine their venture programs to ensure they are getting the most out of them. Venture investing, done correctly, is an important way for a company to increase its leadership role in its respective industry. Further, as technological change continues to accelerate, corporations will need to use technology to unlock the considerable assets they already possess. In this article, we'll explore best practices in corporate venture programs, and we'll explore how and why companies can expand their focus to valuable internal projects.

Best Practices in Traditional Corporate Venture Capital

We believe that being successful in this new era has less to do with what you do—whether you make potato chips or computer chips, or whether you express output in megawatts or megabytes—and more to do with how you do it. The most common characteristic of companies that are defining excellent financial performance, many of which were already thriving when the first Web browser was downloaded, is their primal need to be at the center of innovation in their industries.

To satisfy this need, a company must become a hub for innovation, and that requires that it have the appropriate "spokes" to reach outside its borders. Corporate venture capital is one of the most important spokes available. Through connecting the resources of a big company with innovative start-ups, a great corporate venture unit can foster industry trends and help create significant new products.

To reach these levels of performance, we recommend benchmarking the best. Some important practices we've observed include the following:

Create a Balanced Scorecard.   A corporate venture unit should be evaluated on a balanced set of criteria that measures financial returns, discovery of innovative technologies, creation of relationships with entrepreneurs, and expansion of markets for existing products. Such a dashboard encourages the leaders of a corporate venture fund to engage in the right long-term behaviors and diminishes the impact of market swings.

Role Model Involvement.   Through direct and visible involvement, senior corporate executives can turbocharge their companies' impact on venture investments. Specifically, senior executives should identify the appropriate business teams within their companies that should be working with start-ups. Then, they should facilitate cooperation between the teams and the start-ups. This does not mean that senior executives ought to mandate that their companies become customers of specific start-ups. The value is in ensuring the start-ups have the opportunity to win business on their own merit.

Integrate the Venture Team.   The corporate venture group must have frequent access to and credibility with the CEO and CFO of the company. Most important, the venture unit must be able to communicate areas of interest to outside venture firms and to start-ups. This leads to a very important characteristic of corporate venture units: They must have the ability to make decisions quickly. Some corporations have sought speed for their venture units not through integration but rather through extremely high levels of autonomy. This approach can lead to skewed objectives and a lack of cooperation between the unit and the rest of the company.

Focus on Being a Great Partner.   Corporate investors learn the most, and start-ups gain the most, when a corporate investor is active in the development of the start-up company. Importantly, corporate investors can start by ensuring that they have a streamlined process for making business arrangements with their portfolio companies. The longer it takes to negotiate a distribution or licensing deal or the more onerous the terms (such as unreasonable exclusivity), the less valuable a corporate investor is.

Finding Good Investments Where You Don't Expect Them

The vast majority of corporate venture activity is aimed at early-stage businesses outside a company. This is important, and best practices such as the foregoing are worthy of study and emulation. But, it's amazing to us that so many companies focus exclusively on external start-ups for their venture activity and ignore some of the most compelling opportunities to create new businesses. These businesses lie in the considerable assets—brand, scale, people, technology and patents, and financial strength—that would greatly benefit any start-up. Further, within a company sit the very people and ideas to reinvent the way the company does business.

For the most visionary companies, corporate venture programs have expanded to creative investments that started inside their companies. Specifically, we are talking about technology and Internet-related carve-outs. By a carve-out, we mean more than a tracking stock. A carve-out is an independent company, created and capitalized by a parent corporation and outside investors. Unlike a spinout, in a carve-out situation the parent company remains the most significant investor and maintains tight operational links with the carve-out.

Carve-outs are not for everyone, particularly those who wish to rush through key issues or attempt a "quick flip." In fact, the public markets have shown a disdain for technology assets that are spun out carelessly.

A carve-out is a serious investment that requires significant work upfront and a great deal more to make it successful. By constructing a carve-out, a company is in effect exposing its assets (human, financial, technological) to the marketplace in which all venture-backed companies operate. Here, the carve-out will have to find investors, win customers, and recruit talent. It will do so with a transparent P & L and a requisite focus on cash flow.

For those willing to subject their ideas to these mortal tests, carve-outs can offer an opportunity for a company to capture value. The following examples show the advantages of this approach.

McDonald's has assembled some of the world's most impressive skills in purchasing and logistics. In the early part of 2000, the management of McDonald's saw the opportunity to apply those skills to reshape the company's operations using the Internet. It also felt that its clout and market power could dramatically impact any business-to-business (B2B) exchange in the food service industry.

The company faced a range of choices, from simply buying Internet-based software for supply chain management to investing in start-ups in the field, to going it alone. In the end, McDonald's chose to carve out its Internet operations and several staff members into a company capitalized by itself and Accel-KKR. The new company, eMac Digital, quickly made its mark on the industry. Together with Cargill, Sysco, and Tyson Foods, it created the Electronic Foodservice Network (eFS) to automate and improve the supply chain in its industry. With the McDonald's volume flowing through the eFS, the eFS will bypass the illiquidity that has plagued many such exchanges.

The creation of eMac Digital enabled the speedy creation of the eFS. McDonald's felt that in order to use its expertise and its size, it had to find a way to work with other restaurant companies and service providers on a neutral platform. The presence of outside investors and the intent to keep eMac independent convinced Sysco, Cargill, and Tyson that they were working with a company (eMac) intently focused on the success of the eFS.

For eFS and for other initiatives in the food service industry, eMac Digital is going to be the technology and operations leader. So McDonald's needed a way to attract people (both from inside and outside McDonald's) who could run a technology company. The creation of eMac Digital gave the company a currency to do so, and partnering with Accel-KKR gave the company access to rich networks of executives.

Because a carve-out requires the same nurturing and coaching as any start-up, experienced and relevant outside investors are critical. While the fit is clear, the agreements must be considered carefully, and great trust is required. The financial investor generally allows the parent company to maintain more control than founders generally enjoy in a venture deal. Likewise, the parent company gives the financial investor more operational control than its ownership stake would normally indicate.

The parent company and financial investors must anticipate and address important issues before the company is created. What access will the carve-out have to brand names and intellectual property? How far will the carve-out go in working with the parent company's competitors? How active will the parent company be in financing the carveout? How will this affect employees at all levels who remain with the parent? For example, when Wal-Mart created Wal-Mart.com, it knew that a key to Wal-Mart.com's success would be leveraging the one hundred million customer interactions that take place each week in Wal-Mart stores. Therefore, it made sure to give store managers a share of the upside of Wal-Mart.com's success so that they did not see Wal-Mart.com as competitive.

Partners in Transformation: Venture Firms and Corporations

Those who pick up the challenge to lead the new era of corporate venture investing will reap incredible rewards to accompany significant work. As capital has become a commodity, being a hub for innovation will be a clear differentiator.

The forward-thinking members of the venture capital community realize that there is a great deal of power in cooperating. Venture capital is facing many challenges—scaling a heretofore "cottage industry," mixing specialization with flexibility, and globalizing—that were met by world-class companies over the last decade. Venture firms and corporations can learn a great deal about critical topics from one another.

Governance requires courage

B. Kenneth West
National Association of Corporate Directors
Chairman

TIAA-CREF
Senior Consultant for Corporate Governance

Millions of words have been written and spoken on various aspects of corporate governance in recent years. Perhaps no single topic has generated more rhetoric than how to create an effective board, including which personal and professional characteristics its directors should possess to make the board a genuine strategic asset.

Most specifications for board composition start with the functional skill sets a company needs in its directors—finance, marketing, and international experience, for example. Other desirable attributes might fall in a broad category termed "general business savvy" and include descriptions such as "knows the business," "understands the competition," and "sound strategic thinker." Finally, and in many ways more important, are hard-to-measure qualities, such as independence, collegiality, and integrity.

A vital characteristic seldom cited is courage. No matter how many other requisite skills and values corporate directors possess, if they do not have courage, the board will fall short of making the level of contribution that shareholders expect.

Directors do, indeed, have a difficult job. Sometimes, the job appears almost beyond fulfillment, given realistic constraints on the time most board members can devote to the task. Board members must select and evaluate current top management of the company and ensure an adequate supply of future leadership. They must review and approve the strategic plans of the enterprise. They must monitor performance against specific objectives and establish appropriate reward systems and incentives to meet these objectives. They must attest to the integrity of the internal controls and accounting systems. They have oversight responsibilities for corporate behavior, compliance with laws and regulations, external and internal audits, and a seeming myriad of other matters. One board member recently commented that being a director at times makes him feel like a mental contortionist, being pulled in numerous directions simultaneously. It may not be that tricky, but it isn't easy.

There is no question that it takes a lot for a director to fully discharge her or his duties to shareholders. But without courage to speak out openly and forthrightly—sometimes in the face of strongly opposing points of view—board members are not fulfilling the full measure of their obligations to investors and other constituencies of the corporation, no matter how competent they may be in other respects.

Perhaps the most vivid example of how important courage is to board effectiveness involves evaluating performance of the company's leadership. Most observers contend that this ranks among the most important of the board's responsibilities. Evaluation requires an honest assessment of how well management is constructing winning strategies and how well it is executing those plans. The task sometimes requires the board to challenge—or even reject—recommendations submitted by company management. To do less means the board is merely a rubber stamp, adding little or nothing to shareholder value beyond its perfunctory duties. Yet, as Warren Buffett observed in Berkshire Hathaway's 1988 annual report to shareholders, criticism of the CEO's performance [at board meetings] is often viewed as the social equivalent of belching. It may be unseemly, but it certainly should not be viewed as out of place to objectively criticize management. That takes *courage*.

It takes even more courage to replace top management, especially when performance is mediocre, as opposed to downright unacceptable. A prominent investor once said that the three main impetuses to make a change of management are: (1) the personal investments board members have made in the company relative to their personal wealth; (2) fear of personal liability; and/or (3) embarrassment. It takes real courage to take action when one or more of those motives is not present or is less than compelling.

Expressing one's views, especially in the face of opposition, is, indeed, challenging. After all, it is important to maintain collegiality and decorum in the boardroom, otherwise, the board may become dysfunctional. Disagreeing gracefully involves striking a delicate balance between being critical in a constructive way and being obstinate and disruptive. It is difficult, but it can be done. I know of one situation in which a board member repeatedly pointed out—over a period of years—that a particular segment of the company was consistently yielding insufficient returns to cover its cost of capital. The segment was essentially wasting capital instead of creating value for shareowners. The board understood this point of view, and, perhaps, even a majority agreed. However, management consistently resisted restructuring the business unit. The board went along with management, even though the numbers became increasingly convincing that remedial action was needed. Eventually, the situation demanded a complete repositioning of that area for the reasons originally put forth. The repositioning resulted in very substantial charges to the income statement—charges that could have been minimized had action been taken sooner. That dissenting board member had courage and the diplomacy to present the issue in a manner that was forceful but not disruptive. It is unfortunate that other nonmanagement board members were not more supportive (courageous?) themselves, at least to the extent of insisting that management present more tangible support of their position. They could have saved that company's shareholders a lot of money.

My guess is that almost every businessperson has their own examples of where courage has made a difference—or where a lack of courage has failed to confront and correct critical issues. No matter what else a director brings to the boardroom table, it takes courage to be a fully competent, effective board member. Maybe my board colleague was right. Perhaps one does have to be a mental gymnast to be a good director after all. It surely takes courage!

The twenty-first-century board of directors

Elspeth Murray
Queen's University
Professor of Strategic Management, School of Business

The business world is already proving vastly different in the twenty-first century. The old rules of competition—differentiate your products or services, be a low-cost producer, focus on core competencies—are giving way to new rules centering on speed, innovation, and flexibility.

The rapid evolution of technologies—biotechnologies and information technologies—combined with an unprecedented availability of and access to venture capital, has served to create a very uncomfortable competitive environment in many industries. It is interesting to follow the dramatic changes afoot in such corporate behemoths as General Motors. The success of General Motors' OnStar System begs the question, "Why not give the cars away for free, and charge for the services provided to the driver?" Such questions as these can dramatically change corporate strategies and are already doing so. Thus, it is incumbent upon boards of directors not only to fully understand the implications of their answers but also to raise the questions in the first place. To do so suggests that today's boards need to be vastly different from their counterparts of the past.

Numerous studies and articles have been written on the roles and characteristics of the CEOs who are successful in leading firms into the future. Relatively little has been written, however, on the changing role of the board of directors. The fundamental question is whether corporate governance needs to be different in order for companies to be successful in the current marketplace. If so, how must it be different? These two questions have been the focus of a long-range study under way in Canada and the United States, initiated by Queen's University. Following are preliminary results of the study and summaries of the key findings to date.

In order to better understand if and how today's effective boards differ from yesterday's, and to understand how successful boards operate, we surveyed a number of directors whose experience spans the immediate past and current economy. We asked them these questions:

- Who are the most successful directors and what characteristics do they share?
- Why are they attracted to certain businesses?
- What roles do they play in the governance of their companies today, and how do those roles differ from in the past?
- How do the best boards function?

Who Are the Best Directors?

Our respondents told us that the best new-style directors have, in the words of Andrew Waitman, the CEO of the Canadian venture capital firm Celtic House International, "seen the movie before." In this time of seemingly endless technological turbulence, it is critical to have directors who have had direct experience with firms that successfully address these challenges. According to Waitman, this experience base is critical because one doesn't "have time to wait for directors to learn the business before they're useful." Equally critical is that the "movie" had better be current. One seasoned director in the telecommunications industry noted: "I've seen more change take place in this industry in the last three years than in the previous 30. Much of the knowledge I've carried forward from my days as an executive is irrelevant, if not downright dangerous. Much as I try to avoid it, I am somewhat blinded by my previous perspective on the nature of the industry."

Closely tied to the requirement of in-depth knowledge of the industry is the need for directors to have a relevant network of contacts they can leverage on behalf of the firm in its search for capital, customers, and partners. By relevant, we mean current, active involvement in a most productive and value-adding way, so that contacts are current and dynamic as well. We have found that the best directors individually spend more time assisting the firm in a number of different respects, from establishing critical contacts with strategic partners to assisting in complex acquisition negotiations. The emerging importance of so-called economic webs is another critical component of a firm's ability to compete, and directors can play a central role in enabling a firm to tap into the best network. In short, although the relevance of directors' expertise and experience is important, whom they know and how much they are willing to leverage their contacts on behalf of the firm is paramount as well.

The best directors appear to spend more time with the board and on company-related activities than their counterparts in the past. It is imperative that today's firm operate in Internet time, and so must its board if it is to add any value at all. And, since speed is of the essence, directors are called on more frequently to participate in key decisions. We have found that not only do the best boards meet more frequently, but traditional face-to-face meetings are augmented with conference calls and videoconferenced meetings.

Great boards appear to have directors who think big and think fast and who understand some of the finer aspects of competing in today's environment. For many emerging ventures, unlike the classic message of the fabled tortoise and hare, not only does "slow and steady" *lose* the race, but it may even kill the runner. Microsoft won the battle for dominance of the desktop PC category not because its software was superior but because it created a huge installed base almost overnight.

Lotus 1-2-3 and WordPerfect never had a chance. In many instances, gaining market dominance and gaining it quickly is all that matters; without it, you risk the future. Success is not about return on investment, it is about staking potentially profitable territory. As one interviewee noted: "Board members who don't understand the need for rapid scaling can kill the company by denying it resources that are needed for rapid growth."

Another interesting finding thus far has been that more emphasis is placed on good chemistry among the members. One director we interviewed said: "Chemistry on the board is critical. We don't have time for egos or grandstanding. We have to make decisions based on fact and experience, not on who wants the most air time."

At the same time, there was a general view that too much "fit" could lead to "group-think:" "We are all successful people. We check our egos at the door, but this doesn't mean that we don't have vigorous discussions. It is not a club. We are there to ensure that tough decisions get made when necessary."

Consequently, while an ability to work together as a group is critical for making timely decisions, a lack of diversity often limits the board's ability to think outside the proverbial box. The landscape is littered with the vestiges of once-successful firms—Digital Equipment (DEC) and Wang come to mind—that missed identifying the impact of disruptive technologies such as the personal computer on the nature of competition in their industries. In such cases, an interesting question remains: Where were the boards?

Expectations of Directors

In the twentieth century, the rule of thumb for effective corporate governance was "Stick your nose in, but keep your fingers out." In reality, this was much more difficult in practice than in theory. Executives sometimes feed board members selective information, and with a board that meets only four times a year, it is difficult for directors to understand what's really going on with the company. In many cases, reams of financial statements are all the board sees. Hence board meetings may become sessions about demonstrating financial prowess, with the tiniest inconsistency on the income statement capable of generating hours of discussion. In an attempt to remedy this situation and to reduce the filtering of information, the most forward-thinking boards of the recent past had already begun conducting annual strategic audits in addition to the traditional financial audits.

This is no longer the case. Our research indicates that directors are expected to know and do a lot more today. Because they are often called on to leverage their personal networks, they tend to have a more intimate knowledge not only of the company's strategy but also of operational matters—which was basically unheard of in the past. Today's boards, consequently, are functioning as mentors and advisors for the executive team on a diverse set of strategic and operational issues—so much so that strategic audits are conducted on an ongoing, albeit more informal, basis. It is no longer just about early warning of lower-than-expected quarterly results, it is about early warning of if and when a firm's core business is about to become history.

In addition to the role of strategic advisors, more and more directors are being called on to provide continuity for the organization as management changes. There are increased levels of churn within North American companies, as executives move in and out of organizations to the new rhythms of corporate growth and change. In emerging firms, as founders are being replaced by more experienced executives during periods of rapid growth, the board is often a primary repository of organizational history and culture. The board's role, as opposed to that of the senior executive team, as "keeper of the culture" is signaling an additional, and as yet relatively unknown, role for new-style directors.

Who Are the Twenty-First-Century Directors?

Today's directors are typically geographically closer to the firms on whose boards they serve. We believe there are several reasons for this. First, a greater number of meetings and deeper involvement with the firms they govern necessitate closer proximity for logistical reasons. Second, many of the directors we surveyed reside in a significant economic and geographical cluster such as Silicon Valley, Route 128, Silicon Valley North, or Silicon Alley. The concentration of firms in such areas, as well as the number of experienced directors, often means that no director has to travel very far to find worthwhile firms to work with.

There is a risk in this situation, however, as illustrated by the comments of one Canadian CEO we surveyed who lamented about the number of qualified directors available in Canada. Because of the country's relatively small population, many of the same people sit on the boards of its major corporations. Some would argue, in fact, that inbreeding is a problem. The CEO said: "With longtime friendships at stake, the likelihood that tough and/or risky decisions will be taken at the board level is remote. We need a larger pool of qualified directors to draw from, or we're going to have trouble."

New Incentives for Corporate Governance

Why, in this age of increased director responsibility, would anyone want to be a director? There is a significant increase the time commitment as well as the need to leverage personal networks and gain a deeper understanding of the organization and its industry. Yet, in some ways, the reasons are not so different from before, and may even be intensified by the new demands: the opportunity to contribute to an important effort, ego gratification, and interaction with other influential people.

In other ways, however, there appear to be significantly different motivations. On the negative side, some are driven almost solely by financial considerations and are involved primarily for share price appreciation. These are questionable candidates for directors, since the strategic decisions associated with driving up valuation are often counter to those associated with building long-term value. More positively, the current changes in corporate governance attract a new group of potential directors who are genuinely interested in giving back to the business community, having realized significant financial gains elsewhere. Most encouraging is the fact that there are more and more successful entrepreneurs who have the time, experience, and motivation to serve on boards. They have "seen the movie before" and want to give their reviews.

Whereas yesterday's boards were sometimes constituted with little thought as to the value members could add beyond name recognition and prestige, successful firms of today spend more time identifying and recruiting for specific skill sets in directors. Several of the firms we are studying have stated that they deliberately appoint certain members to serve as devil's advocates. One CEO commented: "We all see the world through our own set of lenses. These glasses we wear provide a slightly different view of reality. We wanted to make sure that everyone at the table had a slightly different prescription."

How Does the Nature of the Board's Focus Change?

One of the last areas in our study of governance is whether the function of a successful board has changed. Thus far, we have found that the leading boards have been given orientation and training to ensure they understand the company and its history very quickly and can be effective right away.

In one firm, the directors went through a team-building exercise to ensure that they understood each others' experience bases and value-adds right from the start. In addition, a number of interviewees commented on the importance of the chairman's role, not only in running good meetings but also in interfacing with the management team. One chairman told us: "I don't want to spend time at a board meeting reviewing endless reams of paper. I ask the CEO to come to each meeting with a focused list of things he or she wants from the board, and we go from there."

The last finding relates to the substance of board-level discussions: There is more discussion of the "soft" skills, and intangible assets such as relationships, employee motivation, knowledge management, and intellectual capital. These are the currencies today, and the best boards know it. Net income is an outcome. Boards that focus solely on net income have already missed the point. It's all about speed, momentum, and execution. Dividends and net income are lag indicators of success. The most effective boards choose instead to focus on inputs and leading indicators such as culture, creativity, and the formation of core competencies and customer relationships. By the time the financial statements take a turn for the worse, it is often too late to effect meaningful change.

Building a Great Board for the Future

In summary, our preliminary results suggest that boards of successful twenty-first-century firms are significantly different from the boards of the past. While today's boards still have to retain a degree of objectivity, they require a different stance:

- Proactive rather than reactive
- Active rather than passive
- Future-oriented rather than current or historic
- Intimate rather than distant
- Mentors and advisors rather than governors

In addition to this change of perspective, successful boards differ on a number of dimensions—from the types of individuals that are needed to the nature of the board level discussions themselves to the frequency of meetings and the nature of how they operate. In the twenty-first century, directors have to be more intimately involved with and knowledgeable about the firms they govern—it's new-age governance for twenty-first-century firms.

Optimizing Human Capital with a "People Operating System" Approach

Jay A. Conger, Stephen A. Miles, and Meredith D. Ashby

From these leadership vignettes, and Heidrick & Struggles' longstanding recognition of the centrality of human capital to corporate success, we see an evolving framework, a fresh and responsive approach to institutionalizing the management of this century's greatest asset—talent. Solutions to the challenges corporate leaders now face could be greatly facilitated, we believe, by a new method of managing talent—a systematic, holistic approach that leverages upside potential in the day-to-day workplace by translating it into sustainable value. It is based on the most current thought leadership and best practices in business today. We call this approach a People Operating System (POS), in which the term "people" represents the collective talent and "operating system" denotes the fundamental system that an organization engages to manage, motivate, recruit, and retain its workforce. Therefore, a POS is a human capital management system.

A company's POS should stem from the underlying talent philosophy of the organization. It should clearly lay out the expectations and responsibilities that the company has toward its employees and toward their development. It should also set out what the organization expects in return—specifically, a proactive stance regarding their individual development, along with understanding and acceptance of a set of performance expectations. In essence, an effective POS is not simply a philosophy; it is a contract of mutual obligations. If done effectively, the POS not only attracts the best and brightest but also develops them to realize their highest potential. At the same time, everyone understands the levels of performance that are expected of "talented individuals" within the organization. Thus, instead of trying to fit people into preconceived molds, as if they were masses of aluminum or copper to be shaped into widgets, a POS assesses strengths, weaknesses, and the potential of individuals and of operating teams, and then creates a series of support and development mechanisms around them.

Equally important, an effective POS ensures an adaptive organization. With the need for companies to continuously change, one of the central purposes of a POS is to provide a method for managing and developing a company's workforce in a way that fosters continuous innovation and optimizes the organization's capacity for targeted change. As such, the best POS has built-in mechanisms that allow flexibility in responding to emerging needs or to radical shifts inside or outside an organization.

Finally, an effective POS should reinforce the values of the organization's culture and its performance management and development systems. Part of the process of formulating a POS is to examine the cultural dimensions that have predicated the company's success and then to match these with strategies for identifying and attracting talent. The simple process of reflecting on and identifying cultural influences forces the organization to be clear about what it expects from its talent in terms of values and behaviors. To measure the effectiveness of the POS, the organization must also devise both developmental-based and performance-based measurement systems. Similar to a cultural assessment, this process forces the organization to reflect deeply on its choice of development experiences and on what it defines as "performance" at each level.

Getting started

A successful POS begins with and is framed by the company's articulation of its strategy, vision, and core values. These should drive the talent-acquisition, retention, promotion, and development activities of the organization. As we see it, a comprehensive POS sets out the firm's philosophy and beliefs about human capital as well as company-specific programs for performance management, succession, and leadership development. Therefore, the responsibility for its design and day-to-day operation rests with influential individuals in the management ranks and in human resources and, ultimately, with everyone in the organization.

Each POS needs to be proprietary and customized to the unique profile and culture of the organization. The idea of an "off-the-shelf POS" is counterproductive—one size does not fit all. We say this for several reasons. Talent requirements vary widely between companies, even between companies in the same industry. For example, different organizational cultures call for different attraction and retention strategies. Rapid growth in one area of a company could create a serious talent shortage. A marketplace shift may demand the infusion of completely new skill sets and competencies. A customized POS would not only identify these demands but also establish the appropriate attraction and development interventions. A tailored POS also provides competitive advantage. Because it is customized, it reflects the unique cultural and strategic demands of an organization. In some ways, this is its greatest advantage: because each one is unique, it is very difficult to emulate.

The exercise of crafting a POS forces a senior team to be disciplined in their approaches to human capital. In addition to creating a consciousness about the criticality of talent, it provides a model for acting on this value in the everyday activities and decisions of the organization. Drawing on the company's core values and ethical principles, the best POS architects build a foundation of shared beliefs that serve as a basis for the tough day-to-day decisions employees are called on to make in regard to others. This foundation is also the backbone of the performance management, compensation, succession, and training and development programs of the company.

Moreover, the discipline of crafting and nurturing a POS serves as a powerful reminder to senior management that talent development is more than just promotions and rewards. In other words, a great company doesn't do just one or two things well in the arena of human capital management, and it doesn't do them sporadically. It manages most of the components well each and every day. In its highest use, the POS can serve as the anchor for a company's values and a symbol of its commitment to its employees and their development.

McKinsey & Company, in its oft-cited "War for Talent" study, advocates the need for everyone in an organization to continuously and relentlessly think about people in order to build an attractive value proposition for talent. Formalizing a world-class POS takes this concept to new levels. Spanning the human capital value chain—from hiring, motivating, developing, and retaining to putting special emphasis on creating programs and opportunities for leadership talent and to the most difficult, which is managing out "C" talent who could otherwise be an "A" or "B" elsewhere—the POS is a continuous, dynamic process that involves every person in the company every day.

The POS development team

The governing, executive, managing, and operating bodies of an organization play pivotal roles in crafting a human capital strategy. Developing a workable POS starts with an initiative from the board, the CEO, and the senior management team. This initiative represents a major commitment, because a POS, once in operation, becomes both the fabric of the company and a daily priority. The people leading a company need to be sure they understand the magnitude of this endeavor at the outset.

The development team members begin with the CEO and include the person charged with leading the company's workforce, traditionally known as the officer in charge of human resources. Whatever title is assigned to this role, it should reflect the heightened emphasis on human capital management. The chief of human capital no longer merely presides over pay and benefits transactions; rather, he or she has a seat on the executive committee and advises the CEO and board of directors on human capital issues as they relate to the company's strategic direction. This expanded role for HR officers calls for new, critical competencies as well: primarily, a multifaceted understanding of business strategy and operations, as well as of HR and management development. Most important, this person must possess the ability to connect these areas most effectively.

As we learned in interviewing Steve Reinemund, for example, one of his first steps as CEO at PepsiCo was the appointment of a strategically qualified executive to the position of head of worldwide human resources. His appointee, Peggy Moore, was extremely well qualified, with a background that included investor relations and finance as well as HR. This variety of experiences qualified Moore for the critical role that Reinemund needed her to play: assessing and incorporating the long-term strategic objectives of the company as part of its human capital plan. Similarly, Microsoft's senior vice president of human resources, Deborah Willingham, has marketing, product manufacturing, and corporate development experience, which enhance her ability to develop human capital strategies that support Microsoft's innovative business initiatives.

The POS-building team should certainly include the chief learning officers of the organization and in many cases the chief information officer as well. Cases in point are GE's CIO, Gary Reiner, and Steven Kerr, the CLO for Goldman Sachs, both of whom sit at the operational table of their organizations.

In the final analysis, all traditional and nontraditional members of the senior executive team should play a role in this process, since the POS is a system to support the new corporate emphasis on human capital. In the emerging paradigm of the "boundary-less corporation," the name of the game is inclusion, not exclusion.

Responsibilities of the POS

As previously noted, the greatest single advantage of a POS is the way it is customized to the company's culture, mission, and operations. Rather than attempting to lay out a primer, therefore, for designing a generic POS, we will now offer some general principles derived from our interviews that reflect the ways a POS can improve a company's management of its employees. These include attracting, developing, recognizing/rewarding, and retaining talent.

Attracting Talent

A successful POS is a potent tool for attracting talented people. It comprises a value proposition that either entices a potential hire or sends a poorly fitting individual to your competitor. In other words, it sets expectations about the types of individuals who flourish in the organization's culture and performance demands.

According to our research, the most strategic companies understand that the very best people come into the market at different times, which may not correspond with the timing of job openings. For example, Microsoft has "strike teams" for recruiting. These teams travel to companies that are planning layoffs to pick the "best of the crop" or to countries where economic shifts have made talent more available. Companies with a strong POS view the acquisition of talent as a continuous process across multiple geographies. They typically use a multifaceted approach to search for talent; it might include recruiting from MBA programs, in-house recruiting, employee referrals, and the use of executive search consultants. They are always on the lookout for talented people and are willing to make a place for truly talented candidates even in cases where no formal vacancy exists. These companies are also adept at looking horizontally across multiple industries to import new competencies. For example, some major financial services firms have been hiring Six Sigma practitioners from the manufacturing sector and branding experts from the consumer goods sector. In other words, they are bringing in human capital in a strategic fashion to help take the organization to a new level. This approach recognizes the value of diversity—not only of cultures and gender but of thinking and ideas as well. A healthy creative rub between coworkers facilitates the process through which good ideas become "new lines" on the profit page. This process is less likely to occur when thinking and acting are homogeneous. A diversity of backgrounds also enriches the company's bench strength via the employee gene pool, which must be heterogeneous in order to promote innovation and creative thinking.

Developing Talent

The ability of an organization's workforce to learn continuously can make the difference between a great company and a merely good one. The companies that work to tear down boundaries and make learning and sharing of information integral within a horizontal system such as a POS enjoy a huge advantage over the competition. They are able to change and adapt to prevailing conditions faster, they are able to diffuse best practices faster, and they are able to innovate and create faster. The foregoing principle is aptly summed up by chief executive Lord John Browne of BP: "In order to generate extraordinary value for shareholders, a company has to learn better than its competitors, and apply that knowledge throughout its businesses faster and more widely than they do." Learning is not simply a company-centered event. Some of the best learning can come from interactions with partners, customers, suppliers, and even competitors. The best POS places a strong emphasis on talent development—in other words, continuous learning for everyone.

This emphasis on ongoing talent development manifests itself in the form of integrative education, training, and resourceful learning programs. The approach is very different from the traditional view of development as an administrative necessity, that is, something assigned mechanistically to modular compartments labeled "education" and "training" that do not incorporate real-world opportunities that exist within a company for teaching. For instance, at GE's John F. Welch Crotonville Leadership Center, the curriculum and classroom cases that executives tackle are the exact business issues that are facing the organization. Through this real-world learning process, GE's people essentially serve as internal consultants to solve its businesses challenges.

This kind of developmental orientation makes an effective POS the perfect environment for offering experiences that build confidence as well as ability. One method is the assignment of "stretch roles," in which people are given increased responsibilities at an earlier stage than might traditionally be judged appropriate, but with added support in order to help them grow into the new jobs. Cross-training is another means in which horizontal communication among colleagues expands their perspectives about the interaction among the company's lines of business. Similar to stretch roles and cross-training is the "popcorn stand" concept pioneered so successfully at GE. "Popcorn stands" are leadership development positions that aren't directly tied to the core business so that, when mistakes are made, there is no a material impact on the bottom line. This concept creates, on a relatively small scale and at little risk, opportunities for high-potential employees to assume expanded operational responsibilities. Assignment to a task force or committee tackling critical companywide challenges is yet another vehicle for broadening perspectives and expanding influence skills. The best POS forces an organization to be clear on which jobs, approaches, bosses, mentors, and educational experiences will maximize learning and development for talented employees. Then, the POS development team can create a process for successfully delivering these experiences.

Recognizing and Rewarding Talent

A performance management program in which senior management is actively involved is a critical component of a world-class POS. It must be equitable in content and execution, and everyone must be clear on its role in the corporation. A company that has no method for recognizing breakaway talent and discouraging mediocre performance is not likely to attract "A" players, let alone weed out "C" players.

To perform optimally, a company must identify its top performers and develop them holistically, incorporating compensation, stretch roles, bosses and mentors, early opportunities to lead, coaching and development plans, and education—both short- and long-term. It also must either transform or replace its weakest performers, a process that is most equitable and effective within the framework of a POS, where strengths and weaknesses are assessed and addressed in a constructive and consistent fashion.

Very few companies make full use of their reward and recognition programs. Often, the responsibility is delegated to an HR person who is oriented administratively rather than strategically. To be truly effective, the performance management program must align the organizational goals with those of its employees as closely as possible and with the successful execution of a company's strategy. A static performance management program that does not measure and reward appropriately will not produce the desired results. It should be a dynamic program that adapts to a company's objectives, which in turn are adjusted as the market ebbs and flows.

Spotting Leadership Talent: Key Attributes

Continuous Learning. One of the most important attributes of all leaders is their ability to learn continuously throughout their careers. Leadership, like most abilities, exists on a continuum, with one extreme housing the born leaders and the other extreme holding those who need remediation just to get to a low level of mastery. Most people fall somewhere in the middle of the extremes of innate ability and environmental nurturing. The CEO of PepsiCo, Steve Reinemund, remarks that when he moved from the company's Frito-Lay division to become corporate CEO, he had to change many of his operating methods in order to be successful. "Few people recognize that when their jobs change, their leadership styles often have to change as well," he says. It involves more than just learning new skills; it is also being able to function introspectively and to assess potential areas for development in an objective manner. It involves listening to feedback from others and making adjustments. Throughout careers, new roles and challenges arise, and the skills that led to success in a previous role may be detrimental in the next one. It is essential to be able to recognize the new realities and adapt accordingly.

(continued)

Courage. The courage to lead involves making the tough decisions and taking a risk when one needs to be taken, and keeping employee motivation and morale high even when the path is not clear or appears dangerous. It's relatively easy to take the high road and defer the tough decisions and not take any risk; and, in an environment of incremental change and evolution, this tactic worked over the short haul. In today's world, where incremental change is the norm, the courage to lead with a long-term perspective is a critical quality for all managers in an organization.

Passion for Creativity and Innovation. Traditional forms of competitive advantage have all but disappeared. Product quality, for example, is simply the price of entry into the game today, not an automatic guarantee of winning it altogether. The significance of workers being mobile and connected is that ideas diffuse at a pace never before experienced. Operating in such an atmosphere, companies must attract and retain passionate and creative managers who can generate and help develop ideas. It's not sufficient to have one pearl of wisdom on the table; it's much better to have a cornucopia of ideas, even if some of them are bad ideas, on the table. Perpetual innovation is a continuous process of creative idea generation among people who have perspectives that are different from one another.

Proper Selfishness. Charles Handy, a preeminent management scholar, believes that good leaders display "proper selfishness," and that, in fact, all successful people do. Simply put, if you don't believe in yourself, nobody else will. It is selfish in a positive way, instilling confidence and assertive-ness in your ability to lead others. It is proper because the role of a leader is to create other leaders by giving them a vision to follow and rewarding them along the way. Many leaders are capable of setting a direction but less comfortable giving the spotlight to the people who take them there. In an era of intangible assets, successful executives have figured out that the best way to ensure their own success is to promote the success of others.

Emotional Quotient (EQ). Some management scholars have used the term "emotional intelligence" to describe the "soft" skills associated with managing human capital. Emotionally intelligent people have a high degree of self-awareness, self-regard, and self-actualization. Self-awareness is comfort in one's own skin. It includes the ability to view one's own behavior objectively and regulate it in response to the prevailing environment or situation. It also involves understanding the impact of one's behavior on others and being able to see others' perspectives. In this age of intangible assets, empathy gives leaders the potential to turn adversarial relationships into collaborative alliances, which is vital, since intangible assets are built on multiple streams of relationships. Self-regard is simply knowing your strengths and weaknesses and feeling comfortable about both, keeping your "head in the game." Leaders who possess this have a passion for achievement for its own sake and not simply in response to whatever incentives a company might offer. People with high self-regard and self-actualization know when they need help or have made a mistake. On the other hand, they have the capacity to operate without knowing all the answers or pretending to. At times, leaders who lack these qualities feel threatened by "A" players—peers and subordinates alike—and as a defense mechanism they may surround themselves with "B"s and "C"s. Acting from insecurity, they prefer to have "yes people" around them who will artificially bolster their self-esteem while posing no threat. These social skills, representing the sum of the foregoing attributes in a "directed friendliness" fashion, enable leaders to succeed by building rapport and cooperation with others, inspiring them to move in the desired direction.

Communication. Success in managing intangible assets often requires that leaders communicate daily with partners, employees, suppliers, analysts, and other key stakeholder groups. We know from research that leaders are most powerful when they use stories to communicate their ideas and values. In addition, one of the most important aspects of great communication is the ability to listen actively. In this fast-paced world, true listening—not merely keeping silent while formulating your response, or selectively hearing—is a disappearing art. Further, effective communicators know the message inside-out and deliver it seamlessly and consistently to all audiences, in appropriate mediums.

Strategic Vision. Critical to leadership is the capacity to think strategically. Given today's fast-paced and complex marketplaces, senior leaders must be able to rethink their business models to capitalize to emerging demands. They must possess a keen sense of their competition in order to anticipate moves that may rewrite industry rules. They must also have a profound sense of customers and non-customers in order to craft strategic initiatives that capitalize on unarticulated needs that are gaining in importance or on fundamental shifts that are underway. Finally, government regulations and macroeconomic trends may reset the dynamics of an industry. Senior leaders must not only anticipate such forces but also use their position and skills of influence and persuasion to shape outcomes.

Retaining Leadership Talent

The best talent in an organization often get courted by other organizations. One aim of an effective POS is to create mechanisms that identify not only which employees may be at risk of departure but also ways to retain those people. A successful retention effort becomes, over time, a management succession plan. Ideally, the succession-planning dimension of the POS provides a thorough review of both the highest-potential managers and the people most at risk for leaving. The POS teaches managers to be vigilant for the signs that a key player is restless. Once a person is identified as at risk of departing, it facilitates the process of exploring ways that individual might become more engaged—finding new jobs and bosses that are attractive, for example. The POS creates many metrics, among them are ways to determine the rate of loss of talented individuals and to identify "hot spots" in the organization where turnover is higher than usual. (The really progressive POS tracks this at competitors, too!) Whenever there is turnover of talented people, investigations are conducted to identify the real sources of turnover and to provide effective remedies for them. The organization must also spell out serious penalties for bosses who have a track record of driving good employees away. Finally, assignments must come at a fast enough pace so that individuals are continually challenged and learning. At the same time, the pace must be tempered enough so that people learn the outcomes of their actions before departing for another assignment.

In conclusion, we believe that organizations must make their talent philosophies explicit. It is no longer enough to say "People are our greatest asset." Rather, senior leaders must spell out the premium that the organization places on its human capital, and then support that clearly articulated philosophy with an integrative approach to talent attraction, development, recognition and reward, and retention. Moreover, measurement systems must be in place to make certain that the promises of the POS are indeed delivered on. Ultimately, a wide range of activities and interventions are critical to ensure that a human capital strategy works well. The success will be evident in the competitive advantage and sustainable value that a company is able to maintain.

Does your company have a POS approach? Here are some things to consider.

- Does the CEO have a people-centric vision and strategy for the company?
- Does the person in charge of human resources report directly to the CEO? Does that person have a seat at the executive or management table of your organization? Does he or she counsel the board?
- Is the person in charge of HR able to relate your company's human capital strategy with its business strategy?

- Do your managers set high standards, hold others accountable, and reward appropriately for attracting and retaining good people? Are they themselves rewarded for developing others?
- Has your company developed a clear set of competencies for specific leadership positions?
- Does your company use a multidisciplinary approach to recruiting new talent?
- Does your company balance looking inward for talent with external recruits?
- Does your company have a leadership pipeline? Are there succession plans in place for the senior management team as well as for each business unit?
- Are succession systems weighted more heavily toward development than replacement?
- Are succession plans and systems successful at identifying key development assignments and do they have mechanisms for quick-reaction placements?
- Are the attributes and skills your company seek in people conceived for the long term or are they based on short-term, immediate needs?
- Does your company give people opportunities to lead early on in their careers? Are there P & L positions that are primarily developmental in nature, that is, heading up business units outside the core?
- Does your company provide job assignments that broaden perspectives early on in a person's career, that is, line-to-staff rotations, or project task force assignments?
- Are good mentors and executive coaches available at critical junctures in an individual's development?
- Are there specific systems and development opportunities for high potential talent?
- Are your executive education, training, and development programs customized to address current and emerging strategic demands? Do participants study actual business issues the company is facing or are the programs more "education in a box"?
- Are executives from your company involved in the training programs, that is, do they lecture, teach, present business cases, and help to develop the curriculum? Are they "taught" how to teach beforehand, and are they the appropriate company role models?
- How are poor performers handled in your organization? Are they moved into other roles or given new initiatives or mandates to develop them, or are they managed out altogether?
- Is your performance management system a strategic development tool that has clear objectives, rewards, and time frames?

(*continued*)

- Depending on the size of your company, do you have a Chief Learning Officer or a similar type of outsourced learning consultant?
- Is your CIO able to link the company's people strategy with a global human resource management information system?
- If an identified future leader leaves the company, is there an exit review process to understand the real reasons of the departure? And, if warranted, are those reasons rectified or otherwise contemplated?

About the Contributors

Accel Partners
James Breyer, Bruce Golden, and Eli Cohen, Partners

Founded in 1983, Accel has a history of partnering with outstanding management teams to build sustainable world-class companies. With over $3 billion under management, Accel maintains a sharp focus in the fundamentally important areas of communications, software, and the Internet. Within these sectors, Accel brings a solid base of domain knowledge, relevant experience, and industry contacts to its portfolio companies. Accel's investments include UUNet, RealNetworks, Veritas Software, and Foundry Networks, along with other successful companies. Golden and Cohen are partners at the venture capital firm; Breyer has been managing partner since 1990.

American Express Company
Kenneth Chenault, Chairman and Chief Executive Officer

American Express Company is a diversified worldwide travel, financial, and network services company founded in 1850. The company is a world leader in charge and credit cards, Travelers Cheques, travel, financial planning, business services, insurance, and international banking. Chenault has held various management positions with American Express since 1981, including being named president of travel related services in 1990. In 2001, the year he become chairman and chief executive officer, Chenault ranked twenty-third in *Worth* magazine's Best CEOs of the Year. He has been listed among the Top

Blacks in Corporate America ranking by *Black Enterprise* magazine, and he was named a Top 25 Manager of the Year by *BusinessWeek.*

Bain & Company
Orit Gadiesh, Chairman

A global management consulting firm, Bain was founded on the principle that consultants must measure their success in terms of their clients' financial results. Bain helps top management teams make critical decisions on strategy, operations, mergers and acquisitions, and organization. Bain's clients have historically outperformed the stock market by 3:1. Bain has more than two thousand employees in 25 offices worldwide. Gadiesh has repeatedly been honored as one of the 50 Most Powerful U.S. Businesswomen by *Fortune.*

Bank of America Corporation
Kenneth D. Lewis, Chairman, President, and Chief Executive Officer
Steele Alphin, Principal Personnel Executive

Bank of America, the nation's first coast-to-coast bank as a result of the 1998 merger of NationsBank and BankAmerica, has offices in nearly 40 other countries and an expanding Internet presence in its four key lines of business: consumer and commercial banking, international investment banking, asset management, and equity investments. Bank of America has more than 140,000 employees operating from 38 countries and has $600 billion in assets. Alphin has been with the bank since 1977. A 30-year veteran of the banking industry, Lewis has been in his current post since April 2001. In addition, he chairs the National Urban League.

BEA Systems
William Coleman, Chairman and Chief Strategy Officer

Since its founding in 1995, BEA Systems has become a leading provider in the highly competitive application server software sector through a combination of focused acquisition and strategic alliances. Its e-commerce platforms, WebLogic and Tuxedo, have set industry standards for quality, and the company and its cofounders have won numerous awards and accolades from technology and business publications, including *Forbes ASAP, Fortune, BusinessWeek, Software Business, and Investor Relations.* Coleman co-founded BEA Systems.

California Public Employees' Retirement System (CalPERS)
William Dale Crist, President and Chairman of the Board of Administration

CalPERS, with more than $150 billion in assets, is the largest public pension system in the United States, managing retirement and health plans for 1.2 million beneficiaries from more than 2,500 government agencies. Through its extensive investment program, which includes U.S. and foreign securities, real estate, venture capital, hedge funds, and private equity in financial services firms, CalPERS has become a leading voice in the dialogue on corporate governance issues in the international business community. Crist has served as president since 1992.

Cap Gemini SA
Geoff Unwin, Chairman

Cap Gemini focuses its information technology and consulting services around core sectors, including financial services, life sciences, manufacturing, health care, telecommunications, utilities, and the public sector. With the 2001 acquisition of Ernst & Young, the Paris-based firm created a strong U.S. presence. It continues to expand its range of products and services in areas such as supply chain management, enterprise resource planning, customer relationship management, and the creation of electronic marketplaces, often through alliances with such industry icons as Microsoft and Oracle. Unwin served as chief executive officer from May 2000 until being named chairman in early 2002.

Carlyle Group
David M. Rubenstein, Cofounder, Managing Director, and Partner

Carlyle Group, based in Washington, D.C., is a global private equity firm with more than $12.5 billion under management. Carlyle's mission is to generate extraordinary returns by employing a conservative, proven, and disciplined approach to investing. Carlyle invests in buy-outs, real estate, high-yield, and ventures in the United States, Europe, Japan, and Asia, focusing on aerospace and defense, consumer and industrial, energy, health care, technology, real estate, and telecommunications and media. Since 1987, the firm has invested $6.4 billion and achieved a realized internal rate of return of 36 percent. The Carlyle Group has more than five hundred employees in 24 offices in 13 countries. Rubenstein helped form the firm in 1987. Previously, he served for six years as a partner in the Washington, D.C., law firm of Shaw, Pittman, Potts & Trowbridge, where he was counsel on a number of major corporate acquisitions and mergers. At the age of 27, Rubenstein became deputy domestic policy assistant to the president of the United States, a position he held until 1981.

Celestica
Eugene V. Polistuk, Chairman and Chief Executive Officer

Celestica is a world leader in electronics manufacturing services for industry-leading original equipment manufacturers (OEMs). With facilities in North America, Europe, Asia and Latin America, Celestica provides a broad range of services, including design, prototyping, assembly, testing, product assurance, supply chain management, worldwide distribution, and after-sales service. Polistuk is a recipient of *Electronic Business* magazine's Outstanding CEO Award. Under his leadership, Celestica has been recognized as the number one–ranking company on *BusinessWeek*'s 2001 InfoTech 100 list and as *Canadian Business*'s Company of the Year in the publication's 2001 Tech 100 issue.

Celtic House International
Andrew Waitman, Managing General Partner

Celtic House, an early-stage technology venture capital firm established in 1994, has offices in Ottawa, Toronto, and London, England. Funded by the Mitel and Newbridge Networks founder Terence Matthews, it has more than 30 companies under management in its portfolio. A recent winner of the Canadian Venture Capital Association's Deal of the Year Award and the European Technology Forum's Seed Investor of the Year Award for 2001, Celtic House invests in companies that specialize in telecommunications, storage, networking, and Internet infrastructure. Waitman's corporate experience before joining Celtic House includes founding a high-tech investment boutique firm and a stint at CitiBank Canada.

China Netcom Corporation
Edward Tian, President and Chief Executive Officer

China Netcom Corporation (CNC) is the leading integrated facilities-based broadband telecommunications operator in China. In 2000, CNC launched its national fiber optic backbone network, CNCNet, with a 40 Gbps overall bandwidth covering 17 major cities throughout the nation. The network is also the first in the world to deploy IP over DWDM optimized optic fiber telecommunications technology on a large scale. Starting from international gateways, through CNC's national backbone, to local access networks, down to the very last mile, CNC's "end-to-end" network provides customers with revolutionary gateway into the world of broadband. CNC is focused on providing integrated telecom services, including bandwidth, managed network, Internet data, and satellite and voice products to business customers in China and the world. Tian was named "Star of Asia" by *BusinessWeek*, a "Global Leader for Tomorrow" by the World Economic Forum, and a Top 10 Entrepreneur by *Red Herring* magazine.

Conseco
Gary Wendt, Chairman and Chief Executive Officer

Conseco, with an array of insurance, investment, and lending products, has approximately $93.5 billion in managed assets and a strong middle-American franchise, reaching out to more than 50 million potential customer households. The company was incorporated in 1979 and went public in 1985. Its three-pronged mission: to be more efficient than other insurance companies; to actively manage its investments to generate greater returns with no additional risk; and to develop products that meet real market needs and find more effective channels for distributing them. Its distinctive "Step Up" brand reflects its dedication to consistently seeking the next highest level of accomplishment and performance. After 24 years at GE, Wendt was tapped to be Conseco's chairman and chief executive officer in June 2000.

Dell Computer Corporation
Michael Dell, Chairman and Chief Executive Officer

Dell is the world's number one computer systems company. The company ranks number 48 on the *Fortune* 500, number 122 on the *Fortune* Global 500, and number 7 on the *Fortune* "most admired" lists of companies. The company employs approximately 34,400 team members around the globe and has revenues of approximately $32 billion. In addition to several other accolades, Michael Dell has been ranked among *Worth* magazine's Best CEOs of the Year, *Upside* magazine's Elite's 100, *BusinessWeek*'s Top 25 Executives, *Time* magazine's Top 50 Cyber Elite, *Financial World* magazine's CEO of the Year, *Inc.* magazine's Entrepreneur of the Year, and *PC* magazine's Man of the Year.

Deutsche Post World Net
Klaus Zumwinkel, Chairman of the Board of Management

Deutsche Post World Net (DPWN) is a leading provider of mail communication, parcels and express delivery, and logistics and financial services in Europe and an expanding network of global markets. With more than three hundred thousand employees, DPWN is one of the largest high-performing logistics companies in the world. With four flagship brands, Deutsche Post, DHL, Postbank, and Danzas, the company offers integrated solutions over a broad range of logistic and financial services sectors.

FedEx Corporation
Frederick W. Smith, Founder, Chairman, and Chief Executive Officer

Federal Express, the world's number one express delivery company, is the flagship business of the Memphis-based FedEx Corporation, a holding company organized to offer a growing customer base a single source for a variety of delivery services. It has 56,000 drop-off locations, 640 aircraft, and nearly 54,000 vehicles delivering more than three million packages to 210 companies and territories during a working day. Under the leadership of Smith, FedEx continues to innovate and build new opportunities for growth through strategic alliances complementing the core business. These include a strategic contract with the U.S. Postal Service and other FedEx operating companies: FedEx Ground, FedEx Freight, FedEx Custom Critical, and FedEx Trade Networks. Smith is a director of the Business Roundtable, the Cato Institute, and numerous other industry, civic, and business organizations. He also serves as Chairman of the U.S.-China Business Council.

Goldman Sachs
Steven Kerr, Chief Learning Officer

In the highly competitive arena of investment banking and brokerage, The Goldman Sachs Group is an unquestioned leader, both in terms of the number of initial public offerings produced in the United States and Europe and in terms of public image. It is ranked fifteenth in *Fortune*'s Best Companies to Work For listing and thirteenth in *Fortune*'s Global Most Admired Companies. Before joining Goldman Sachs as chief learning officer and managing director, Kerr was CLO and vice president of leadership development at General Electric, where he was responsible for its leadership education center at Crotonville. Prior to joining GE, he was on the faculty of the University of Michigan, and before that he was dean of the faculty of the University of Southern California business school.

Heidrick & Struggles International
Gerard R. Roche, Senior Chairman
John T. Thompson, Vice Chairman

Roche was named "Recruiter of the Century" by his peers in an industrywide poll in late 1999. Since 1990, he has been recognized as the number one general management recruiter in all three editions of HarperCollins' *Career Makers*. Thompson has also been recognized in *Career Makers* as one of America's most respected executive search consultants, and internationally as one of the top 200 best recruiters in the United States, Europe, Asia, and Latin America by *The Global 200 Executive Recruiters Guide*. Roche and Thompson are widely recognized as two of the leading CEO recruiters in the United States. In their 50-plus collective years of executive search, they have conducted hundreds of senior-level search assignments for start-ups, midcap companies, and multinational organizations across a broad spectrum of industries. Together with John T. Gardner and other vice chairmen of Heidrick & Struggles, they lead the firm's office of the chairman (OOC), which is charted with providing the highest-quality search execution at the board and chief executive level for clients worldwide.

Human Genome Sciences (HGS)
William A. Haseltine, Chairman and Chief Executive Officer

Human Genome Sciences is a pioneer in the use of genomics—the study of human genes—and the development of new pharmaceutical products. The HGS mission of is to develop new means to prevent and cure disease through understanding human genes. The company's goal is to become a global pharmaceutical company that discovers, develops, manufactures, and sells its own genomics-based drugs. Haseltine founded the company in 1992. He holds a doctorate in biophysics from Harvard University and was a professor at Harvard Medical School and the Harvard School of Public Health from 1976 to 1993. He has a distinguished record of academic achievement in both cancer and AIDS research, for which he has received numerous awards and honors. He is the author of more than 250 published scientific manuscripts. He is currently the editor-in-chief of the online journal *E-Biomed: The Journal of Regenerative Medicine* and is former editor-in-chief of the *Journal of AIDS*. Haseltine is president of the William A. Haseltine Foundation for Medical Sciences and the Arts, chairman of the board of trustees of the National Health Museum of Washington, D.C., a member of the executive committee of the Brookings Institution board of trustees, and a member of the Trilateral Commission and the French-American Business Council.

IBM Corporation
Linda Sanford, Senior Vice President and Group Executive,
Storage Systems Group

IBM, the world's largest computer company, makes software, personal computers, mainframe and server systems, notebooks, microprocessors, and peripherals and also offers the world's largest, and still growing, service business for computer products. The giant known as "Big Blue" continues to move its software operations away from an operating focus toward database, messaging, and server software, while reorganizing its hardware business by merging the desktop and laptop operations and concentrating on its leading enterprise server and storage products. Continuing its long history of technological innovation, the company is at the forefront of today's leading-edge technologies such as the Linux operating system, Bluetooth wireless networking, and biotechnology. Sanford has been named one of the Top Ten Innovators in the Technology Industry by *Information Week*, one of *Working Woman* magazine's Ten Most Influential Women in Technology, and one of *Fortune*'s 50 Most Influential Women in Business.

Kleiner Perkins Caufield & Byers
Ray Lane, General Partner

Lane is the former president and chief operating officer of Oracle Corporation, where he led what some have described as "the transformation of the century." Under his eight years of leadership, Oracle grew into an e-business and consulting powerhouse, seeing a tenfold increase in revenues and an increase of more than 9,600 percent in market capitalization. Today, Oracle is the second-largest software company in the world; consulting and related services account for more than half of the company's $10 billion business. Previously, Lane held a variety of management or consultancy roles with Booz-Allen, Electronic Data Systems, and IBM Corporation.

Lehman Brothers
J. Stuart Francis, Managing Director and
Head of Global Technology Investment Banking

Lehman Brothers, an innovator in global finance, serves the financial needs of corporations, governments and municipalities, institutional clients, and high-net-worth individuals worldwide. Founded in 1850, Lehman Brothers maintains leadership positions in equity and fixed income sales, trading and research, investment banking, private equity, and private client services. The firm is headquartered in New York, London, and Tokyo and operates in a network of offices around the world. Francis is head of global technology investment banking and a member of Lehman Brothers' operating committee. During his 25-year career as a technology investment banker, he has been the senior client banker on hundreds of financing and M & A transactions for technology clients. Lehman Brothers' global technology investment banking group includes technology bankers in nine countries across the globe.

Manugistics Group
Gregory J. Owens, Chairman and Chief Executive Officer

Manugistics Group is a premier provider of Enterprise Profit Optimization (EPO) solutions—the powerful combination of supply-chain management and pricing and revenue optimization initiatives—for enterprises and marketplaces. Its supply-chain management software directs the flow of products from the raw-material stage through manufacturing, distribution, and delivery. Its Web-based NetWORKS suite provides tools for capacity management, demand forecasting, and inventory replenishment. Through acquisitions, the firm has moved beyond these core areas of expertise into the rapidly expanding arena of applications in revenue optimization. The Maryland-based firm has offices in Australia, Belgium, Brazil, Canada, France, Germany, Italy, Japan, Mexico, New Zealand, Singapore, Spain, Sweden, Taiwan, and the United Kingdom, as well as the United States. Before joining Manugistics in April 1999, Owens was global managing partner for Accenture's Supply Chain Management Practice.

Pearl Meyer & Partners
Pearl Meyer, Founder and Chief Executive Officer

Pearl Meyer & Partners is a leading executive compensation consulting firm specializing in the creation of innovative compensation programs to attract, retain, motivate, and reward key executives and board members. Meyer, who founded the consultancy in 1989, is a nationally known expert on corporate governance issues and a regular speaker at events of the National Association of Corporate Directors, WorldatWork, American Management Association, and the Conference Board. The firm is a Clark/Bardes consulting practice.

JPMorgan Partners
Dana Beth Ardi, Human Capital Partner

JPMorgan Partners (JPMP), formerly Chase Capital Partners, is a global partnership with over $25 billion under management. It is a leading provider of private equity and has closed over 1,800 individual transactions since its inception in 1984. JPMP has more than 160 investment professionals in eleven offices throughout the world. The company's primary limited partner is J. P. Morgan Chase & Company, one of the largest financial institutions in the United States.

National Association of Corporate Directors
B. Kenneth West, Chairman

Founded in 1977, the National Association of Corporate Directors (NACD) is the premier educational, publishing, and consulting organization in board leadership and the only membership association for boards, directors, director-candidates, and board advisors. The NACD, representing three thousand total members, is an authoritative voice and vital forum on matters related to board and governance policy and practice. West is also senior consultant for corporate governance for Teachers Insurance & Annuity Association–College Retirement Equities Fund (TIAA-CREF). (See TIAA-CREF hereafter for a full description of its business.)

Onex Corporation
Gerald Schwartz, Founder, Chairman, and Chief Executive Officer

Onex Corporation is the Toronto-based holding company and investment umbrella for Celestica, ClientLogic Corporation, Lantic Sugar, Dura Automotive Systems, J. L French Automotive Castings, MAGNATRAX Corporation, InsLogic Corporation, Performance Logistics Group, Radian Communication Services Corporation, and Galaxy Entertainment. It was founded in 1983 by Schwartz, whose dynamic style of leadership drives its continuing expansion into new business sectors. The third-largest company in Canada, Onex had consolidated annual revenues of $24.5 billion in 2000. With consolidated assets approaching $20 billion, the firm has 97,000-plus employees engaged in building industry-leading companies to continually enhance value for its shareholders. Before establishing Onex in 1983, Schwartz was the cofounder and president of CanWest Capital, now CanWest Global Communications. Prior to that, he worked at a major Wall Street investment banking firm where he specialized in mergers and acquisitions.

Orbitz
Jeffrey Katz, Chairman, President, and Chief Executive Officer

Orbitz is a full-service online travel agency offering consumers the widest selection of low airfares, as well as deals on lodging, car rentals, cruises, vacation packages, and other travel. Orbitz's state-of the-art flight search engine searches 450 airlines—up to two billion flight and fare options—offering the most unbiased and comprehensive list of airfares and schedules. According to Nielson Net Ratings, the Orbitz launch in June 2001 was one of the biggest e-commerce launches since 1999. Founded by the world's leading airlines—American, Continental, Delta, Northwest, and United airlines—Orbitz also has the Internet's biggest collection of low-cost, Web-only fares—from a wide array of airlines. Katz is a 20-year veteran in the airline industry and an expert in electronic reservations systems technology.

PBS Corporation
Pat Mitchell, President and Chief Executive Officer

The Public Broadcasting Service is the nation's largest and only noncommercial broadcasting system, comprised of nearly 350 member stations reaching more than 99 percent of U.S. television households and an increasing number of digital multimedia households. A private, nonprofit media enterprise, PBS uses the power of noncommercial television, the Internet, and other media to enrich the lives of Americans, reaching nearly one hundred million people each week with quality programs and education services. Mitchell began at PBS in March 2000, after a distinguished career in television. She has worked for all three broadcast networks, as well as cable with Turner Broadcasting, and founded her own production company. She has served as a news reporter, anchor, talk show host, producer, and executive. Documentaries produced under Mitchell's direction have won more than one hundred major awards, including 41 Emmys, seven Peabodys, and 35 CableACEs.

PeopleSoft
Craig Conway, President and Chief Executive Officer

PeopleSoft is the world's leading provider of software for enterprise collaboration. Its industry leading applications include customer relationship management, enterprise service automation, supply chain management, human resources management, financial management, and enterprise performance management. More than 4,700 organizations in 107 countries run on PeopleSoft software. PeopleSoft is ranked number 33 on *BusinessWeek*'s InfoTech 100. Conway joined the company in 1999. In March 2001, a study by McKinsey & Company called PeopleSoft's turnaround "an excellent example of how a company can improve financial returns by strengthening its performance environment."

PepsiCo
Steve Reinemund, Chairman and Chief Executive Officer
Lucien Alziari, Vice President, Staffing and Executive Development

PepsiCo has diversified beyond its soft drink business anchored by the world's number two soft drink brand, Pepsi-Cola, into related and faster-growing segments of the beverage and food industries, with such recent initiatives as Aquafina, a bottled-water category leader, and SoBe, the noncarbonated beverage brand of South Beach Beverage Company, in which PepsiCo holds a majority stake. With the acquisition of the Quaker Oats Company in 2001, the company landed the dominant sports drink brand, Gatorade, as well as a number of leading food brands to complement its market-leading salty snacks brands managed by its Frito-Lay division. The firm's diversification away from lower-margin soft drink bottling operations into niche foods and beverages, accommodating growing demand for nutritionally fortified and health-enhancing products, has enabled it to continue building brand leadership as well as profitability on a global basis. Reinemund started his career at PepsiCo in 1984.

Pfizer
Hank McKinnell, Chairman and Chief Executive Officer

Pfizer, following its 2000 acquisition of Warner-Lambert, is the world's most valuable pharmaceutical company. Its products include category-leading Lipitor, a cholesterol-lowering drug; Viagra, to treat erectile dysfunction; and Norvasc, a treatment for hypertension. Pfizer also markets leading consumer brands such as Benadryl, Neosporin, Schick and Wilkinson Sword shaving products, Halls, and Visine. Pfizer has the world's largest privately funded biomedical research effort and markets its products in more than 150 nations. The company is also entering new fields such as a joint-venture software initiative to automate clinical procedures in physicians' offices. McKinnell, with Pfizer since 1992, served as the 2001 chairman of the Pharmaceutical Research and Manufacturers Association. He is a director of the Business Roundtable and is vice chairman of the Committee for Economic Development.

Procter & Gamble Company
A. G. Lafley, President and Chief Executive Officer

Procter & Gamble, with more than 250 household product brands available in over 140 countries, is a corporate institution in the global marketplace and a leader in innovative product development, sales, and marketing. The Cincinnati-based giant, with $40 billion in annual revenues and nearly 106,000 employees, is responsible for some of the world's best-loved and longest-lived brands, including Pampers, Tide, Always, Actonel, Pantene, Bounty, Pringles, Folgers, Charmin, Downy, Iams, Olay, Crest, and Vicks. The company has steadily enhanced its lineup both through R & D and strategic acquisition, including its 2001 acquisition of

Clairol, the largest deal in the company's history. Under the leadership of Lafley, who began his P & G career as a brand assistant and moved up through the ranks, the company is focused on building its biggest brands globally and increasing its leadership in faster-growing, higher-margin, more asset-efficient businesses such as health care and beauty care.

Research in Motion
Donald H. Morrison, Chief Operating Officer

Research in Motion (RIM) is a leading designer, manufacturer, and marketer of innovative wireless solutions for the mobile communications market. Through development and integration of hardware, software, and services, RIM provides solutions for seamless access to time-sensitive information, including email, messaging, and Internet- and intranet-based applications. In addition, RIM technology enables a broad array of third-party developers and manufacturers around the world to enhance their products and services with wireless connectivity. The company's portfolio of award-winning products includes the RIM Wireless Handheld product line, the BlackBerry wireless email solution, wireless PC card adapters, embedded radio modems, and software development tools. Based in Waterloo, Ontario, Canada, RIM was founded in 1984 and has offices in Canada, the United States, and Great Britain. Prior to joining RIM, Morrison held a series of successively responsible positions at A T & T Canada, ACC TelEnterprises, and Bell Canada.

The Charles Schwab Corporation
David S. Pottruck, President and Co–Chief Executive Officer

The Charles Schwab Corporation is one of the nation's largest financial services firms, serving 7.8 million active accounts with $790.1 billion in client assets. The San Francisco–based company offers access to its brokerage services, investment advice, and a full range of financial and investment products through a mix of the Internet, 24-hour telephone service centers, 430 nationwide branch offices, and approximately six thousand independent fee-based investment managers. The company is listed in *Fortune*'s Best Companies to Work For and Global Most Admired Companies rankings, as well as the *Fortune* e-50 Stock Index and Hoover's 500. During his tenure as co–chief executive officer, Pottruck has been recognized as a Chief of the Year by *InformationWeek*, and he has been ranked as a CEO of the Year by both *Worth* magazine and Morningstar. He serves on the board of governors of the Nasdaq Stock Market.

Sempra Energy
Stephen L. Baum, Chairman, President, and Chief Executive Officer

Sempra Energy, based in San Diego, is a *Fortune* 500 energy services holding company with annual revenues of approximately $9 billion. Through its eight principal subsidiaries—Southern California Gas Company, San Diego Gas & Electric, Sempra Energy Solutions, Sempra Energy Trading, Sempra Energy International, Sempra Energy Resources, Sempra Communications, and Sempra Energy Financial—the Sempra Energy companies' 12,000 employees serve more than nine million customers in the United States, Europe, Canada, Mexico, South America, and Asia. Baum has been with Sempra since 1998 and in his current post since September 2000. Previously, Baum served as chairman, chief executive officer, and member of the board of directors of Enova Corporation, the former parent company of San Diego Gas & Electric. Prior to that, he held legal positions with New York Power Authority and Orange & Rockland Utilities.

Siemens AG
Heinrich von Pierer, Chief Executive Officer

Siemens is a world leader in electronics and electrical engineering, operating in the energy, industry, information and communications, health-care, transportation and lighting sectors. With annual revenues in excess of $78 billion, Siemens operates in more than 190 countries and has over 450,000 employees. Pierer serves on the board of directors of several German companies, including Bayer and Volkswagen. He joined Siemens in its legal department in 1969 and has been the company's chief executive officer since 1992.

Teachers Insurance & Annuity Association–College Retirement Equities Fund (TIAA-CREF)
John H. Biggs, Chairman, President, and Chief Executive Officer

For 80 years, TIAA-CREF has provided pensions and life insurance to educators and researchers. As a major institutional investor in corporations both in the United States and abroad, TIAA-CREF maintains an active interest in corporate governance and has taken positions on a number of stockholder issues that range from executive compensation to board diversity and antitakeover initiatives. As an actuary and economist, Biggs has long been involved in corporate and public finance and in the move for global accounting and auditing standards. He serves on the boards of the Boeing Company, the J. Paul Getty Trust, the National Bureau of Economic Research, and Washington University in St. Louis and is a member of the Business Roundtable. He is past chairman of the United Way of New York City.

Unisys Corporation
Lawrence A. Weinbach, Chairman, President, and Chief Executive Officer

Unisys is a major provider of consulting, network integration, project management, systems support, and other high-tech services, focusing on the financial services, communications, transportation, publishing, commercial, and public market sectors. The company has moved away from low-margin hardware and redirected its technology focus toward high-end servers through co-branding alliances with other manufacturers and toward high-growth technology markets such as customer relationship management, e-commerce, and mobile commerce. Weinbach, formerly managing partner–chief executive of Andersen Worldwide, led Andersen to global market leadership in its field during his tenure there and has moved rapidly toward an innovative and dynamic repositioning of Unisys since being named its CEO in 1997.

WWF International
Claude Martin, Director General

WWF, the conservation organization, is dedicated to the protection of the world's wild plants and animals through the conservation of forests, oceans, and freshwater ecosystems and through countering climate change and toxic pollution. Its ultimate goal is to build a future in which humans can live in harmony with nature. For this work, WWF receives funding from foundations, corporations, governments, and individuals. Since becoming director general of WWF International in 1993, Martin has initiated several new approaches in conservation. He is a member of the China Council for International Cooperation on Environment and Development, a board member of the Ghana Heritage Conservation Trust, and a member of the advisory board of the Swiss Federal Institute for Environmental Science and Technology. His career with the conservation organization began in the early seventies.

Academic and Other Leadership Experts
Jim Collins
Leadership Expert and Author

Collins describes himself as a student and teacher of enduring great companies—how they grow, how they attain superior performance, and how they sustain greatness over time. In more than a decade of research on the subject, he has coauthored four books, including the classic *Built to Last*, which remained on *BusinessWeek*'s best seller list for more than five years, generating over 70 printings and translation into 17 languages. His work has been featured in a wide variety of publications ranging from *USA Today* to the *Harvard Business Review*. His latest book is *Good to Great: Why Some Companies Make the Leap . . . and Others Don't*. A *New York Times* bestseller, the book is based on five years of research into the question of what distinguishes a good company from a great one. From his management research laboratory in Boulder, Colorado, Collins teaches and consults for both corporate and nonprofit organizations. Formerly a faculty member of the Stanford Graduate School of Business, Collins is a recipient of its Distinguished Teaching Award.

Jay Conger
Professor of Organizational Behavior, London Business School, and Senior Research Scientist at the Center for Effective Organizations, University of Southern California, Los Angeles

Formerly the executive director of the Leadership Institute at the University of Southern California, Conger is one of the world's experts on leadership. An author of over 80 articles and 10 books, he researches leadership, innovation, boards of directors, organizational change, and the training and development of leaders and managers. He has been selected by *BusinessWeek* as the best business school professor to teach to executives. In 2001, he was chosen by *BusinessWeek* as number five out of the Top Ten management gurus in the world.

John Hagel
Business Consultant and Author

Hagel is a business consultant and the bestselling author of *Net Gain: Expanding Markets through Virtual Communities* and *Net Worth: Shaping Markets When Customers Make the Rules*. In October 2002, Harvard Business School Press will release his latest book, entitled *Out of the Box: Strategies for Achieving Profits Today and Growth Tomorrow through Web Services*. Hagel spent 16 years at McKinsey & Company, where he was a leader of the strategy practice and founder and global leader of the e-commerce practice. He also served as chief strategy officer of 12 Entrepreneuring, a new form of operating company focused on building and operating businesses to deploy Web services technology. Hagel brings distinctive expertise on the role of information technology in shaping business strategy, organization, and opportunities for economic value creation.

John P. Kotter
Retired Konosuke Matsushita Professor of Leadership,
Harvard Business School

Kotter is one of the world's most highly regarded speakers on the topics of leadership and change. Kotter made history at Harvard when he was given tenure of a full professorship at the Business School in 1980 at the age of 33—one of the youngest faculty members in the history of the university to be so honored. His *Harvard Business Review* articles over the past 25 years have sold over a million and a half reprints. He is the author of a number of pathbreaking books, including *What Leaders Really Do, Matsushita Leadership, Leading Change, Corporate Culture and Performance,* and *A Force for Change.* His latest book is on the subject of navigating change. His many honors include the Exxon Award for Innovation in Graduate Business School Curriculum Design and the Johnson, Smith & Knisely Award for New Perspectives in Business Leadership. *Matsushita Leadership* won first place in the *Financial Times*/Booz Allen Global Business Book Competition. His works have been printed in more than 70 foreign languages editions, with total sales approaching two million copies.

Henry Mintzberg
Professor of Management, McGill University

Mintzberg joined the Montreal-based McGill University's Faculty of Management in 1968 and has earned a worldwide reputation as a global scholar on the topic of management. The first Fellow to be elected to the Royal Society of Canada from the field of management, Mintzberg is also a past president and founding member of the Strategic Management Society, which is an association of 1,800 academicians and practitioners from 44 countries. He holds honorary doctorates from 12 universities and has been a visiting professor at Carnegie Mellon, the London Business School, the Ecole des Haute Etudes Commerciales in Montreal, INSEAD, and the University of Aix-Marseilles in France. His many publications include *The Rise and Fall of Strategic Planning,* which was named best book of 1995 by the Academy of Management.

Elspeth Murray and Peter Richardson
Professors of Strategic Management,
School of Business, Queen's University

Murray researches and teaches in the area of strategic management, with a special interest in innovation and the management of new ventures. Her prior corporate experience includes stints at IBM and Accenture and as an owner-operator of a series of Canadian Tire retail stores. In addition to her teaching and research activities, Murray also consults to corporations on strategic management and new venture management. Some of her clients include Microsoft Canada, Bombardier, Roche Canada, GlaxoSmithKline, Working Ventures, Bell Canada, Med-Eng Systems, and MDS Capital. Richardson is an authority on leading strategy implementation and change, focusing on innovation as it relates to business performance. He has developed a novel, strategic approach to cost management and margin improvement that has been adopted by public and private sector organizations around the world. His books include the groundbreaking *Cost Containment: The Ultimate Advantage* and a coauthored book with Murray, *Fast Forward: Implementing Rapid Organizational Change*. Richardson's clients include Inco, GlaxoSmithKline, Acklands-Grainger, the Supreme Court of Canada, and Falconbridge.

Jeffrey Pfeffer
Thomas Dee II Professor of Organizational Behavior,
Graduate School of Business, Stanford University

Pfeffer has authored or coauthored numerous articles and 10 books on organizational design and development, including *The Human Equation: Building Profits by Putting People First* and *Competitive Advantage through People: Unleashing the Power of the Work Force*. Many of his publications have been translated into other languages. He serves on several corporate boards as well as the Academy of Management. Formerly director of executive education at Stanford, he teaches executive seminars for companies all over the globe and lectures and consults for many organizations in the private and public sectors. His many accolades include the Richard D. Irwin Award for Scholarly Contributions to Management.

Mohanbir Sawhney
McCormick Tribune Professor of Electronic Commerce and Technology, Kellogg School of Management at Northwestern University

Sawhney is also the director of the Center for Research in Technology Innovation and E-Commerce at Northwestern University's Kellogg School of Management. He has created three new MBA courses at Kellogg—technology marketing, TechVenture, and technology and global resource arbitrage—as well as a popular executive course, *Winning Strategies for e-Business*. He has coauthored two recent books, *The Seven Steps to Nirvana: Strategic Insights into eBusiness Transformation* and *Techventure: New Rules for Value and Profit from Silicon Valley*, and authored many articles in leading business publications, including the *Financial Times*, *CIO* magazine, and *Business 2.0*. His many awards and accolades include *BusinessWeek*'s list of the 25 Most Influential People in e-Business and Outstanding Business Professor of the Year at Kellogg.

Index